Penguin Handbooks
The Penguin Book of Sewing

Renée and Julian Robinson are fashion designers, authors
and lecturers with an international reputation. They first
achieved fame in the early 1960s with their own fashion
collections, which were sold in many leading shops and
stores in Britain and abroad. In 1965 they wrote the first
of their new-style sewing books, *Streamlined Dressmaking*,
followed by *Streamlined Curtains and Covers*, *Streamlined
Sewing for Fun* and *Streamlined Decorative Sewing*.
Seven years ago they were asked to reorganize the Fashion
Course at Hornsey College of Art, Julian being made
Director of Fashion Studies and Renée teaching Fashion
Design, and in the process have achieved international
recognition, with their students winning many national and
international awards. Their latest book is *Instant
Dressmaking* published by the Bodley Head.

The Penguin Book of Sewing

Julian Robinson

with illustrations by

Renée Robinson

Penguin Books

Penguin Books Ltd, Harmondsworth,
Middlesex, England
Penguin Books Inc., 7110 Ambassador Road,
Baltimore, Maryland 21207, U.S.A.
Penguin Books Australia Ltd, Ringwood,
Victoria, Australia

Published by Penguin Books 1974

Made and printed in Great Britain by
C. Nicholls & Company Ltd
Set in Monotype Times

Contents

Acknowledgements

We would like to thank the following people and organizations for their help and encouragement in the production of this book:

Barney Blackley
Julia Vellacott
J. & P. Coats Sewing Group
Jones/Brother Sewing Machines
Waddington Toys
Simplicity & Style Paper Patterns
McCalls Toy Patterns
The Bodley Head Ltd
Hornsey College of Art
A T V Birmingham

Preface　　　The Purpose of this Book

This book tries to show that sewing can be easy and fun: being an exciting challenge rather than an exacting task. It is based on the completely new streamlined methods we have developed during the past few years, which aim at simplicity and easy adaptability, and not only show ways of short-cutting traditional methods but also by-pass the usual inhibiting rules and complicated mumbo-jumbo of old-fashioned techniques.

To see just how easy sewing really is, we believe it is best to take the plunge without delay and start making something simple, hence the first chapter describes how to make soft toys and children's garments. These are not only fun to make but provide sufficient sewing experience for a beginner to tackle curtains and bedspreads, a summer dress or a tailored coat.

This book is divided into four main sections, all of which are intended to be interrelated so that the ideas and designs in each can be applied generally. One of the main points we have stressed throughout is that it is not necessary to be a great designer to be able to make attractive things, but you do have to enjoy using fabrics in interesting and unusual ways – textures and colours should mean something to you. It helps enormously to keep a scrapbook of new designs – magazines and newspapers provide a continual stream of new ideas on fabrics and trimmings, decorative techniques and styles. Whenever you see something you like, make a note of it in your scrapbook, pasting in fabric cuttings, photographs and diagrams, so that when you are about to make something new you can leaf through it and remind yourself of what caught your fancy. Have the courage of your convictions so that you develop a sixth sense about your work. Your ideas will then have a touch of alchemy which turns ordinary sewing into original and exciting work, whether for your family, your friends, or yourself.

Julian and Renée Robinson

Part One   General Sewing

The following four chapters deal with the basic techniques of
general sewing. Chapter 1 on Starting to Sew provides a brief
introduction by explaining how to make some simple things.
Chapters 2 and 3 then move on to basic information, such as
equipment, fabrics and sewing methods. Chapter 4 is devoted
to toys and presents. Our techniques may seem slightly
unorthodox: intentionally the emphasis is on ease and enjoyment,
unfortunately so often lost when following traditional methods.

1. Starting to Sew

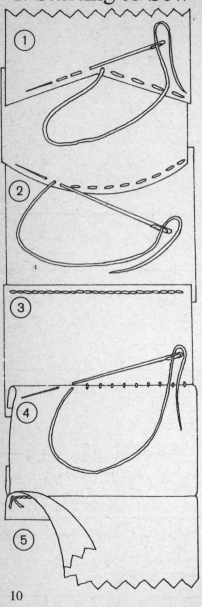

Basic Stitching

On these two pages are shown a few basic stitches to help you start to sew. Once you understand them, start making some of the simpler things shown in this chapter, adding a few more stitches from Chapter 3 as the need arises.

Running Stitch is the simplest stitch to use for joining two pieces of fabric together. It is worked from right to left with the needle passing over and then through the two layers of fabric, picking up the same amount of material each time. Several stitches can be made at one time, as shown in diagram 1.

Back Stitch is much stronger than running stitch and should be used when extra strength is required. It is worked from right to left, starting each stitch halfway back over the preceding one (diagram 2).

Machine Stitch is a continuous stitch (diagram 3) made by a sewing machine for joining two or more sections of fabric together or for holding edges flat. If you are uncertain about how to use a sewing machine turn to page 59 or follow the instructions given in the sewing-machine manual.

Side Stitch (diagram 4) is made over a folded edge of fabric on to a single layer, and is particularly useful when running or back stitch are unsuitable. It can also be used over the raw unfolded edges of felt and suede.

Flat Seam (diagram 5) is made by placing the pieces of fabric right sides face to face and raw edges level. Stitch through both layers of fabric, keeping the stitches an even $\frac{1}{2}''$ from the edges, then press the seam open. The raw edges can be neatened by hand or by machine.

Tacking Stitch (diagram 6) is a long even handworked stitch used either on single fabrics for marking

are pulled apart and the threads cut, an identical tufted marking stitch is left on each side (diagram 7).

Edge Neatening, illustrated in diagram 8, is a simple over-casting stitch which is used on raw edges to prevent them from fraying. This is one of the many types of neatening methods which, together with

fitting lines, or through several layers ready for machine stitching or fitting. The stitches, $\frac{3}{8}''$ to $\frac{1}{2}''$ long, pass over and then through the fabric layer or layers at regular intervals.

Spot Tacking is a largish double stitch made with double thread through double material, leaving a loop so that when the fabric layers

various types of seams and general making instructions, are explained in Chapter 3.

Remember that it is of major importance that you should work cleanly and quickly, never short-cutting or glossing over an important detail. Odd though it may seem, the correct way of doing any sewing is the easiest in the end. By this we don't mean fussing endlessly over it, hand-stitching everything as if the sewing machine had never been invented, but we do mean working out a particular problem correctly before you begin and then sewing with speed.

When you are starting to learn

Felt Animals

Many different animals, birds, fishes or insects can be made quite easily. All you need is a few scraps of coloured felt, stitching thread, and some old stockings, kapok or other inexpensive stuffing.

There are no hard and fast rules

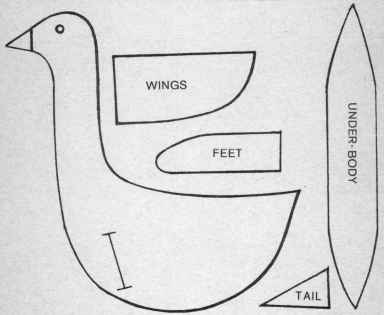

to sew it is best to tackle something which is both fun to do and quick to make. Simple toys are an ideal choice. You can either buy a small toy-making kit such as those sold by Waddingtons or use a paper pattern as published by a well-known paper pattern manufacturer. Here are a few starting ideas.

to worry about in making a simple felt toy. The shapes and colours can be chosen according to your own whim: if it looks amusing to you and your children like it, it is a good toy, whereas a beautifully stitched one that nobody likes and the children won't play with is undoubtedly a complete failure.

In general the basic method for making each toy is exactly the same, whether it is a cat, pig, duck, snail or even a monster. Your first step should be to buy a paper pattern such as McCall's Stuffed Animals 2183 or Winnie-the-Pooh 8087, or make a simple pattern, the easiest of these consisting of just two or three body pieces. Cut out your coloured felt to the shape of the pattern, and stitch the pieces together with a running stitch $\frac{1}{8}''$ from the edge, leaving a $1\frac{1}{2}''$ opening along the tummy line for stuffing. Use cut-up pieces of stocking or kapok for this, and then sew up the opening. You can then complete your animal by adding buttons for eyes, embroidery stitches for a mouth, rug wool for a tail, pipe cleaners for antennae, etc.

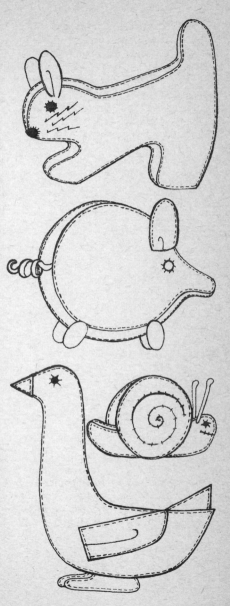

Fabric Animals

These can be made by following the same design and sewing instructions but the shapes should be much larger. Alternatively they can be made inside out, just like the normal cushion, explained on the following page, with a 3″ opening left unstitched for turning through. Do avoid using any small trimmings which are easily detachable, as these can be dangerous to very young children. Generally speaking it is better to concentrate on large, bold areas in striking or unusual colour combinations, rather than intricately sewn details.

Another idea is to leave an 8″ gap in the tummy and sew in a zip instead of filling the 'creature'

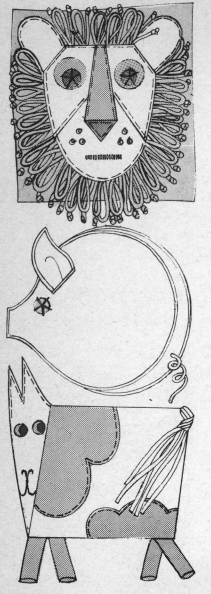

with kapok, so that it can be used as a nightie case, as illustrated on the opposite page.

Cushions

There are about as many ways of making cushions as there are people sewing; they can be all shapes and sizes, covered in all sorts of fabrics, decorated with all kinds of different surface treatments. The only guiding principle is that the cushion should look right and be either useful or decorative. A beautifully made cushion which is ugly or uncomfortable is far better forgotten by making another to replace it.

Simple Cushion

To make a simple 15″-square cushion cut two identical squares of fabric 16″ by 16″ and place them together face to face with their edges exactly matching. Stitch all round $\frac{1}{2}$″ in, leaving a turning-through opening 6″ long in the middle of one side. Next turn the cushion cover through this gap so that the fabric is right side out and then fill with kapok, foam cuttings or similar inexpensive filling before hand stitching together the gap edges.

Shaped Cushion

Shaped cushions or cushions with a side gusset are best made to fit an existing inner cushion or a polythene foam or latex shape which can be bought from most stores or sewing shops.

First cut two pieces of fabric $\frac{1}{2}$″ larger all round than the inner cushion, and then a gusset section

14

1" wider than the depth required and long enough to go right round, plus 1" extra for the side seam allowance. Next measure the exact perimeter of the inner shape and join the gusset section together to fit this size. Pin the gusset to the base section, face to face and edge to edge, snipping the gusset at $\frac{1}{2}"$ intervals around the corners as shown on page 235. Stitch $\frac{1}{2}"$ in from the pinned edges and then attach the top section in the same way, but leaving one end open for inserting the inner shape before finally hand stitching the gap together.

Toy Cushions

Toy, animal or nursery cushions are generally made out of two pieces of strong decorative material cut to a rectangular shape, and made as explained. The success of the actual design and method of decorating them depends as much on the inventiveness of the maker as on sewing skill. The design possibilities are unlimited, and you can have great fun using your own ideas, or copying those you have seen in magazines, books, newspapers or shop windows.

One of the simplest toy cushions to make is the lion design shown opposite. It is made from two pieces of sand-coloured corduroy 16" square, placed with right sides of the fabric together exactly edge to edge and stitched $\frac{1}{2}"$ in, leaving a turning-through opening 6" long in the middle of one side. Turn the cushion through this gap and stuff

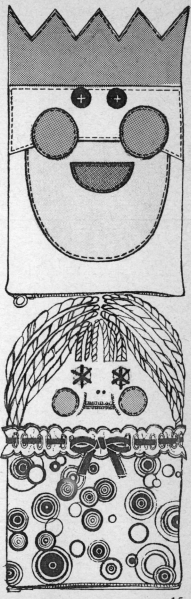

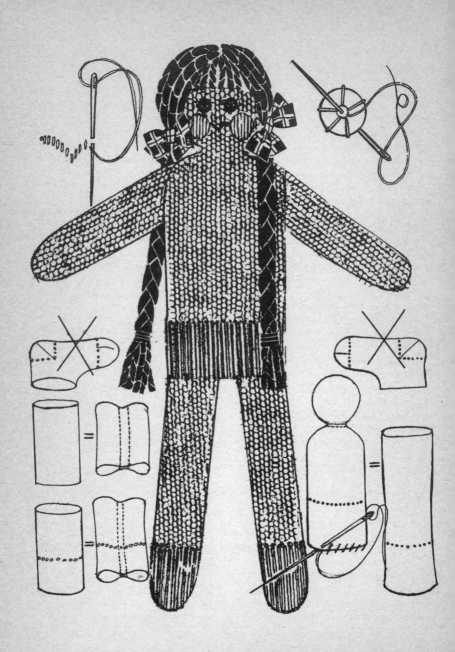

with foam or similar inexpensive filling before stitching the gap edges together. Finally Evo-Stik and stitch sections of coloured felt for the face, looped and knotted rug wool for the mane, adding embroidery stitches for the eyes, nose, mouth, etc.

Stocking Dolls

One of the simplest dolls to make is this stocking doll, based on the traditional rag doll, and usually made from a pair of patterned socks, together with oddments of raffia, lace, ribbons, colourful felt, buttons, beads, etc.

Requirements. A pair of knee-length socks or patterned stockings – old ones will do as the foot sections will be discarded – small circles of brightly-coloured felt for the eyes and cheeks, some rug wool for the hair, scarlet embroidery silk for the mouth, and sock-coloured thread for sewing. The filling can be kapok, cut-up stockings, pieces of polythene foam or similar lightweight stuffing.

1. Cut off and discard both foot sections. To make the arms and legs, first turn one sock inside out and machine stitch two lines, $\frac{1}{2}''$ apart, right down the centre from top to bottom. Then cut in half across the leg, as shown, before cutting between the stitched lines.

Next run a hand gathering stitch $\frac{1}{2}''$ in from the cut edge, and pull tightly, oversewing at seam junction for extra strength. Turn through and fill with pieces of lightweight stuffing. When firm enough turn in

$\frac{1}{2}''$ at top and oversew edges together.

2. To make the body section turn the other sock inside out and run a gathering stitch round the ankle edge $\frac{1}{2}$ in. Pull this tight and oversew several times for strength. Turn to right side and pack in sufficient stuffing to form the head. When this is large enough – 2″ to 3″ from the closed end – run a gathering stitch around the neck and draw in tightly, hand stitching through the neck several times for extra strength. Put more stuffing into the rest of the sock to form the body, and when firm enough oversew edges together.

3. Place oversewn ends of arms on to curved end of shoulders, and stitch into position. Similarly attach the oversewn ends of the legs to the base of the body.

4. Cut two button-sized pieces of green or blue felt for the eyes and sew into position, as shown top right opposite. Cut two larger-sized pieces of red felt for the cheeks, run-stitching these into position. Embroider a small mouth and nose, as shown top left.

5. Cut a number of 6″ lengths of rug wool, or raffia, to make the doll's fringe, and a much larger quantity of 30″ lengths for the plaits. Place the fringe $\frac{1}{2}''$ above the eyes, bringing over and down the back of the head, and stitch across the crown with matching wool. Trim lengths even above the eyes.

6. Make the plaits by first folding the 30″ strands in half, so that loops and not cut ends can be attached to the head. Divide each bunch into

17

three equal sections and plait these together, starting 2″ from the loop, and introducing coloured ribbon into the plaiting if required. Fix ends with a few stitches, an elastic band and a gay ribbon.

Hand stitch loops on to the centre of the head to cover the fringe seam, and stitch around curve for extra strength with matching wool.

Dolls' Clothes

To make a simple dress for the doll you have made, or any similar soft doll, start by placing it onto the centre of a piece of brown paper.

1. Draw a simple dress shape around one side of the doll, as shown on the right, marking the centre line between the legs and middle of the neck.

2. Remove the doll and fold the paper in half along the centre line of your pattern. Pin through both layers of paper just above the hem, at sleeve end, and just below the shoulder marks before cutting through the double layer to get a full-sized pattern. Check this against the doll.

3. For a simple felt dress cut out two identically shaped pieces of coloured felt, using your pattern as a guide, but adding ¼″ seam allowance all round. Place both pieces together, right sides out, and machine or hand stitch ¼″ in along both side seams and across shoulders, leaving a 2″ or 3″ gap for the neck opening.

4. Cut 3″ down top centre back and make several buttoned loops

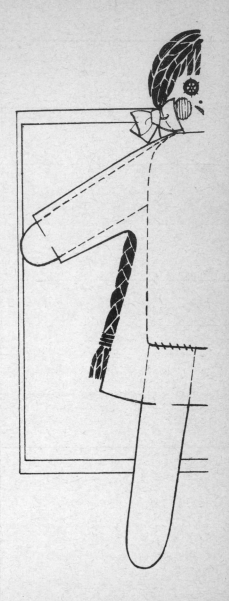

18

for dressing and undressing, or stitch in a zip.

5. Decorate the dress with stuck-on cut-outs of pretty coloured felt pieces, beads, ribbons, or embroidered stitches, as for the nursery cushions. As felt does not need hemming the dress is now complete, though you could, of course, stick or stitch some lace around the hem.

6. For a fabric dress an extra ½″ turning allowance should be added for side and shoulder seams, and an extra 1″ for the hem. The pieces should be stitched inside out and the ½″ seams oversewn or pinked to prevent fraying. The hem should also be neatened, either by turning under and stitching flat, as in normal dressmaking, or by double turning and then machining ¼″ from edge and trimming with narrow cotton lace or similar edging.

7. To finish the doll's feet make a pair of flat shoes out of 1″ × 1½″ oblongs of coloured felt, and use a piece of coloured ribbon crisscrossed around the ankle, and tied into a bow.

As you can see, making a doll and simple dolls' clothes is easy, but you may want to be more adventurous and add some decoration so we have listed a few ideas below.

Inset Edge can be incorporated into a design by using the method shown on the next page. You simply tack the trimming to the edge, cover with a second piece of fabric, right sides inside, and stitch through all thicknesses before turning right way out (see diagram 1 on page 20).

19

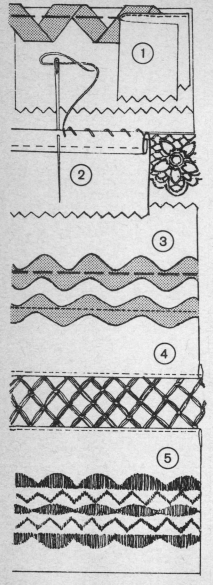

Lace Edging. To attach lace by hand place the right side of the lace against the right side of the fabric with edges together and hand stitch as shown in diagram 2. You can also attach by top stitching as shown on page 76, diagram 5.

Set-ons. Many braids, cords and ribbons can be set on top of fabric by first tacking and then top stitching into position as shown in diagram 3.

Insets. Mark accurately and then cut along the line where the inset is required. Crease under $\frac{1}{4}''$ of fabric each side and place over a decorative strip, stitching through $\frac{1}{8}''$ from creased edges as shown in diagram 4.

Machine Embroidery. A wide range of easy stitches can usually be made on most automatic swing-needle machines, which can be used in many new and exciting ways. Just set your machine and experiment a little on some spare fabric, trying out colour and pattern variations before stitching the actual design into place. Diagram 5 shows one such idea.

Satin Stitch. Make even diagonal stitches in a thickish embroidery thread closely together across the shape to be filled as shown by diagram 6, taking care to form a neat even edge.

Flower Stitches can be made in many different ways as can be seen by the two illustrated in diagrams 7 and 8. The simplest is worked by making stitches from a central point

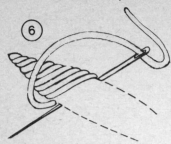

around a marked circle the size of a jacket button. Turn to page 316 for actual working instructions; in this section you will find alternative embroidery stitches, and on page 312 working instructions for the chain-stitch flower of diagram 8.

Fishbone Stitch is used for filling small shapes such as leaves or petals. First bring the needle through at the left-hand corner of the shape to be worked and make a small straight stitch along the centre. Next bring the thread through again at a point just below the first one and make a diagonal stitch as shown on page 317.

Child's Beach Tunic

Materials required: ¾ yard of 36″ wide cotton or synthetic fabric and matching sewing thread. For the pattern you will need a largish sheet

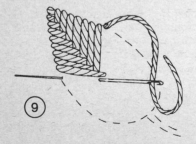

of plain wrapping paper, a sheet of tracing or greaseproof paper, a sharp pencil and a ruler.

1. Working from the top left corner A of the paper measure down 2¼″ and continue measuring for length required plus 1½″ for allowances, i.e. 16½″ for a 15″ finished length, and mark spot B. From here measure 8″ across the paper for spot C as shown on page 23.

2. Measure 6″ down from A and then 6½″ across the paper for spot D.

Draw lines connecting A to B, B to C, and C to D. Next measure across top of paper 3⅛″ and then down ¾″ marking X for press-stud position.

3. Using tracing or greaseproof paper mark out front neck shown on page 23 by the double dashed line, and copy on to your pattern; similarly for the front armhole. Mark A to B FRONT FOLD as shown on page 23.

4. Working from top right corner A of the paper measure down $1\frac{3}{4}''$, and continue measuring to point B as for the front pattern, and across paper $8\frac{1}{2}''$ for point C.

5. Measure $6''$ down from point A and then $6\frac{1}{2}''$ across the paper for point D. Draw straight pencil lines connecting A to B, B to C, and C to D. Next measure across top of paper $3\frac{1}{8}''$ and then down $\frac{3}{4}''$ marking X for press-stud position.

6. Trace back neck and back armhole shapes as for front pattern.

Making. This pattern has a $\frac{1}{4}''$ turning allowance on neck and armhole, $\frac{1}{2}''$ on side seams and $1\frac{1}{2}''$ for hem.

1. To cut out first press the material to eliminate creases and fold lines, then fold in both selvedges to meet in the centre, thus making two folded edges on which to place the pattern pieces.

2. Place front pattern section on left fold and back one on right fold, so that lines A to B are exactly level with folded edges and hems level with raw edges. Pin pattern to fabric at $6''$ to $8''$ intervals.

3. Re-check that fabric pattern is right way up and then cut out accurately. Next cut neck and armhole facings using the upper part of the paper pattern to a depth of $7''$ or $8''$ so that you cut a double bodice. Alternatively cut separate crossways strips or buy bias binding and use as explained on page 73.

4. Join side seams by the simple flat fell method explained on page 61. Next join neck and armhole facing seams with an ordinary flat open seam.

5. Place front facing on to front of dress, right sides together, and pin on to the shoulders, front and side, and repeat for the back facing. Stitch together $\frac{1}{4}''$ in from the edge all round the neck, armholes and shoulder curve.

6. Turn facing through to inside and press flat. Next check the length, turn up the hem and neaten. Finally press the facing edges and stitch into position first by hand on to the side seam junctions and then by top edge stitching $\frac{3}{8}''$ to $\frac{1}{2}''$ in from folded edges if required, as explained on page 63, before adding a shoulder press-stud or buttoned fastening.

Design Adapting

If you have made one beach tunic which fits reasonably well and would like to make another, you will find it very easy to adapt the same paper pattern to a design of your own choosing, provided you follow a few basic rules.

1. If you want to add a patch pocket or a collar, try out various shapes in paper or calico first before cutting the actual material to be used; or use a previously made collar or pocket as a guide. When the shape is correct, mark the exact position onto the dress and then make the design detail in fabric, remembering to add on a turning allowance before cutting out.

2. To achieve a change in surface decoration, such as embroidery stitches, appliqué sections, novelty cut-outs or ready-made trimmings,

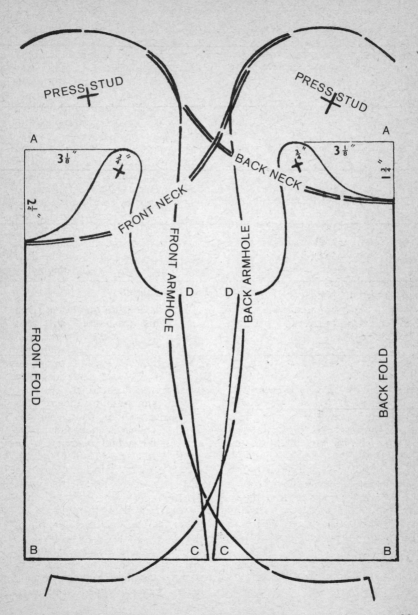

PRESS STUD

PRESS STUD

A

$3\frac{1}{8}$"

$4\frac{1}{2}$"

$2\frac{1}{4}$"

A

$3\frac{1}{8}$"

$1\frac{3}{4}$"

$\frac{3}{4}$"

BACK NECK

FRONT NECK

FRONT ARMHOLE

D

D

BACK ARMHOLE

FRONT FOLD

BACK FOLD

B

C

C

B

first spend a little time experimenting before actually starting to stitch as quite often your first idea can be improved with a little practice.

3. If you wish to add special edgings, insets or frills make sure that you know how to attach these correctly, by practising the making methods explained in Chapter 3.

4. Keep a scrapbook of design and decorative ideas, press-cuttings, photographs and how-to-do-it notes, so that whenever you feel in the mood for making another dress you can refer to your scrapbook for ideas in much the same way as you refer to a cookery book when you feel like experimenting with a new recipe.

Play Aprons

Make these in a similar way by using the front section only, replacing the back with ribbon ties as in a traditional butcher's apron, using P V C or a plastic-coated fabric.

They can be gaily decorated with various coloured felt shapes, stuck or stitched into position. Add embroidery details, raffia work, beads, bits and bobs or any other novelty which takes your fancy so that they are not only fun to make but also fun to wear.

Party Dresses

Once you have gained sufficient skill and confidence from successfully making several simple garments and toys you can try your hand at making a party dress for a little girl or a tucked satin shirt

and velvet trousers for a boy, or you might like to make something equally attractive for yourself. Obviously it is impossible to show you how to make all those garments on these few pages, but you can turn to Part Two on dressmaking and try your skill at making something for your children to wear at their next Christmas or birthday party. However, here are some hints and ideas so that you will feel confident enough to try making something more adventurous.

Many pretty things can be made for a children's party, from dresses trimmed with lace edging, decorative insets, tucks and gathers, smocking and embroidery to frilly knickers, petticoats, and, of course, many fancy-dress clothes. To start with, however, the simplest party dress can be based on the beach tunic shown on page 23, and made in a pretty fabric with a lace insertion down the front between groups of narrow pin tucks – see page 79 – or maybe a *broderie anglaise* hem or some colourful slotted ribbon work with bows, possibly even adding a lace-trimmed collar and button stand together with some decorative buttons or bead-work embroidery.

Pretty Petticoats

Make in much the same way as the beach tunic except that you will only require ½ yard of fabric as the neck and armholes do not need turning through with a double bodice. Instead they are either turned under and machined flat or bound with a bias strip. They are also shorter and do not require as much hem allowance and are better

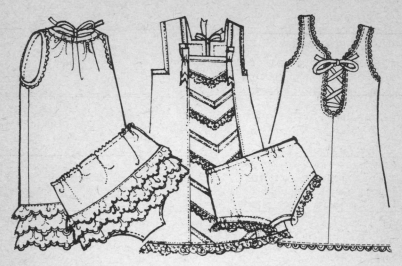

finished with a strip of *broderie anglaise* or lace, attached as shown on page 20. All sorts of other trimmings can be used and pretty knickers trimmed to match.

Boys' Designs

These, ranging from a satin shirt with velvet trousers to all sorts of fancy-dress ideas (see pages 98 and 99), can also be made for most party occasions. Now that the restrictive conventionalism of male dress has been broken by the new wave of young designers, boys' clothes can be decorated with tucks and pleats, jewelled buttons and cuff-links, embroidered waistcoats, crochet ties and fancy belts. So if you are planning to design something for your son to wear at his next party make him something special, something which will be a joy to sew and which he will be proud to say his mum made especially for him.

Here are a few hints on decorative techniques used on boys' designs.

Pin Tucks. Many twin-needle machines make automatic pin tucks which can also be raised and corded, or they can be made on most other sewing machines by accurately top stitching $\frac{1}{8}''$ away from a folded edge of fabric. Accuracy when marking is essential as each tuck must be on the exact grain, creasing along this mark before stitching close to the folded edge as shown on page 184.

Insets. Mark the position on the fabric with coloured tackings, keeping the edges on the exact grain line. Cut a strip of the decorative inset to the length required and then cut the fabric exactly between the coloured tacking lines. Fold under the surplus material, edge stitching the fold on to the inset strip. See page 20, diagram 4.

Faggoting, drawn threadwork, cording, couching and many other forms of surface decoration can be used. Turn to chapter 7, page 172; chapter 11, page 286, etc. for ideas and sewing instructions.

Decorative Buttons. These can be bought in a wide variety of sizes and interesting designs, ranging from shaped metal, coloured cording, moulded glass and plastic, to jewelled and sequinned buttons. Decorative buckles are also available, or button and belt sets can easily be made by following the instructions on pages 338–9.

Carry-cot

This is a useful and easy present to make for a very young baby. The materials needed are: a strong rush shopping basket such as the one illustrated on page 28; a medium-sized travelling rug for lining and making the covering blanket, or 1–1¼ yards of a checked woollen fabric; 3 yards of upholstery webbing; a ball of string, and some strong linen carpet thread.

1. First strengthen the basket with webbing. Start by tacking the webbing around the handle and then diagonally down one side, across the base, and up the other side, taking care to lay the webbing tightly but evenly. Continue tacking

the webbing, wrapping it round the other handle and diagonally down the other side, across the base and back to the beginning, leaving a 2″ overlap around the handle with the webbing firmly back-stitched together. Bind the handles with string to secure the webbing and give a strong grip. Along each side of the webbing hand stitch at $\frac{1}{4}″-\frac{1}{2}″$ intervals right through the rush basket, using linen carpet thread and a darning needle, carrying the stitching across the base and down both sides, and double stitching at the base of both handles for extra strength.

2. A reasonably accurate paper pattern is needed to line the basket. Use a sheet of cheap brown paper to trace around the outside of the bottom shape and then cut to size.

Lay this shape into the basket and tuck the edges into the corners, marking and trimming to the exact size. Then place the basket on its side and draw half its outside shape onto the paper by tilting it on to each end whilst continuing the outline. Cut a duplicate side pattern and mark one left and one right. Remember to check each piece on the inside of the basket, re-marking and trimming to exact inside dimensions. Also cut a paper pattern for the blanket size required, allowing for plenty of tuck-under allowance. Place these four patterns on the travelling rug or woollen fabric, add $\frac{1}{2}″$ to 1″ turning allowance, and cut out.

3. First join the end seams and then stitch in the base section. Insert the lining into the basket and

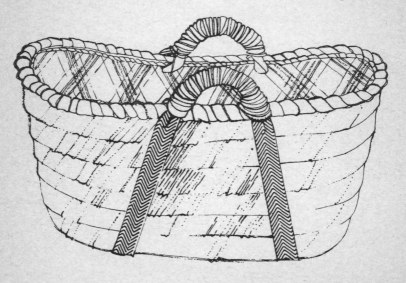

tuck firmly into corners. Check that the end seams are correctly centralized and then back-stitch along the bottom seam through the blanket and the basket weaving between the gaps in the rush to conceal the stitches from the outside. Hand stitch at regular ½″ intervals in this way right round the base. Tack round the top 2″ below the edge and then turn in about ½″ so that the lining lies just below the top thickness. Stitch at ½″ intervals around the top edge of the basket and lining, concealing the stitches as much as possible.

4. The final piece to make is the matching blanket, which can either be bound with a simple blanket stitch, a self-fringed edge, an applied wool trimming or a crochet edging as described in chapters 11 and 12.

Decorative Cradle

The same methods can be used to make a decorative baby's cradle. The one shown overleaf has a deep border of *broderie anglaise* with some draped cradle curtains.

1. First cover the top edge of the cradle with some crossway strips of fabric. Cut sufficient crossway strips 3″ wide to cover the top circumference – see page 73 – joining the sections together neatly. Lay this strip over the top edge and stitch through the cradle ½″ down from the top, leaving the raw edges hanging down unfinished and overlapping one end by 1″, ½″ of which is folded under.

2. To line the inside follow the instructions for lining a carry-cot, making an accurate paper pattern as described in paragraph 2 opposite.

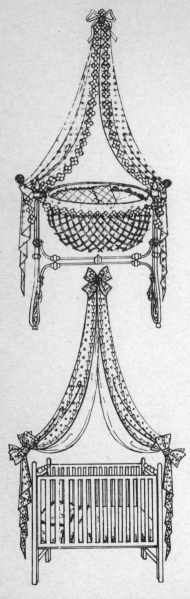

3. To cover the outside first cut a strip of fabric – or join several sections together – long enough to encircle the top plus 12″. The depth of this strip should be the cradle side depth plus 3″ for finishing allowances. Join all the side seams together so that you have a circular strip and then crease over ½″ top and bottom. Next fold over 1″ on both of these edges and stitch ⅛″ from both crease and fold to form a top and bottom casing. Slot in several yards of ribbon or two yards of ¼″ elastic, unpicking ¼″ of folded-over side seam to enable the bodkin to pass through. Place the side cover into position and draw the top tape or elastic tight and secure with a few stitches, adding a few other stiches to secure the top edge to the binding. Next draw up and fasten off the bottom tape or elastic.

4. The frill is made by cutting a length of *broderie anglaise* 12″ longer than required and slotting in a decorative ribbon through its ready-made ribbon slots – or you can make a top casing and slot through an elastic which is then fixed with a few stitches to the binding in the same way as the outside covering. A separate lace edging can also be added around the top if required, hand stitching this into position.

5. The cradle drapes are generally fixed to a special pole and loop which can be purchased with the cradle, or to the wall with a curtain loop or decorative bracket. With the pole or loop in position measure the drop required and add 2″ for the top hem. Cut a full width of fabric the length required and crease over $\frac{1}{2}$″ along the top. Fold down $1\frac{1}{2}$″ from the crease and stitch $\frac{1}{4}$″ in from both fold and crease line to give a self-neatening casing which is to be drawn up to fit over the decorative bracket. A double length of fabric can also be used as can swags and festoons similar to those shown on pages 273–5.

6. Measure the front edges of the cradle drapes and across the hem for the *broderie anglaise* or edging required and join this in as simple a self-neatening way as possible, the method depending on the type of trimming used. The top fixing is then passed through the casing, or a ribbon is slotted through, to fix the drapes into position.

7. Finish off with decorative braiding or some other style of trimming selected from Part Four.

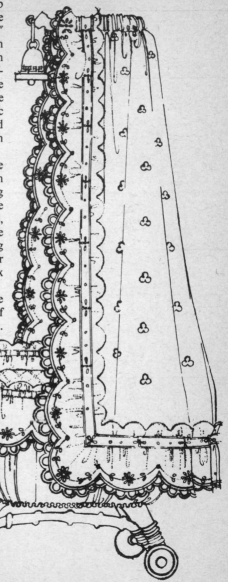

2. General Sewing Information

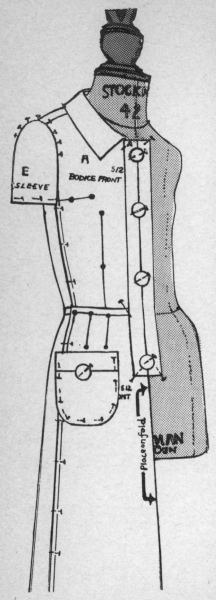

For sewing to be enjoyable and successful a certain amount of thought has to be given to your equipment. The most important requirement is a sewing machine. It need not be an automatic super-special one: an ordinary straight-forward upright straight-stitch – not necessarily new but preferably at least reconditioned – is quite adequate. A work table is very important, as most families do not take kindly to scraps of fabric and pin marks all over the dining-room table. A hardboard top made to fit over this, which can be lifted away, makes an excellent working surface. Then follows an iron and an ironing board, the normal household ones being ideal. Small items like scissors, tape measures, thimble, pins and needles – always clean and never rusty – chalk and a perspex ruler should all be kept in a box together with your sewing threads, sample buttons, odd zips and other bits and pieces. Another useful item is a dress stand, but if you only sew occasionally and are fairly average in size this is not essential. For those who do dressmaking a great deal, most stores stock ready-made fabric-covered or wire stands and some will make a special one to fit your figure for very little extra cost.

Essential Equipment

The following items are listed as a guide for beginners, for, as anybody who sews knows, good tools encourage good work and are essen-

Stitching foot　　　　　　　Hemming foot

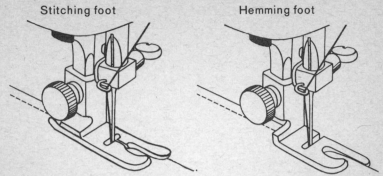

tial for a professional-looking finish. Choose your equipment with care and understanding, look after it properly, and it will give you good and continuous service.

Dressmaking Shears, which generally measure 6″ or more in length, have one small ring handle for the thumb and a larger handle for two or three fingers to give control and leverage.

Sewing Scissors. These are used for general cutting, trimming and clipping. A smaller pair with very sharp points are also useful for fine trimming, needlework and embroidery.

Pinking Shears. Not as essential as the shears and scissors mentioned above but very useful if you sew a lot. They give a regular zig-zag cut edge finish to seams and hems to stop fraying. Also useful for decorative finish on felt, vinyl, suede, leather, etc.

Plastic Ruler. This should be made of clear plastic to mark straight lines, cut bias strips and adjust patterns. The advantage of clear plastic is that pattern lines and fabrics are visible through the ruler to aid accuracy.

Sewing Gadgets such as the Wendy

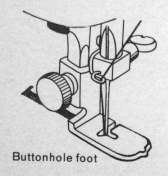

Buttonhole foot

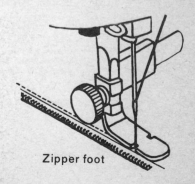

Zipper foot

Flower Winder, Twilley Flower Loom, Notched Measuring Guides, Patchwork Templates, Tufting Shapes (see pages 59, 291 and 302) are very helpful for decorative work, but do avoid having too many gadgets as they tend to make sewing complicated.

worn on the middle finger of the sewing hand and should fit securely.

Bodkin. A large-eyed blunt-ended needle which makes it easy to slot elastic or tape through a casing, and to turn through bias strips, button loops and belts. It is also useful for

| Type of Material | Needles | | Type of Thread |
	Hand	Machine	
Sheer: Net, lace, organdie, voile, chiffon, etc.	9 or 10	9 or 11	Mercerized No. 60/100 cotton, or Gütermann/Perivale No. 100 for most man-made fabrics.
Lightweight: Crêpe, gingham, taffeta, foulard, lawn, etc.	8 or 9	9 or 11	Mercerized No. 60/100 cotton or Gütermann/Perivale No. 100 for most man-made fabrics.
Medium weight: Poplin, flannel, piqué, chintz, dress wools, etc.	7 or 8	11 or 14	Mercerized No. 40 cotton or Gütermann No. 100 for most man-made fabrics.
Medium heavy: Denim, corduroy, velveteen, sailcloth, suitings, etc.	6 or 7	14 or 16	Mercerized No. 36/40 cotton, or Gütermann/Perivale No. 40 for most man-made fabrics.
Heavyweight: Coatings, fur fabrics, canvas, curtainings, leathers, upholstery fabrics, etc.	5 or 6	16 or 18	Heavy-duty mercerized cotton, six cord No. 36, or Gütermann/Perivale No 30 or 40.

Tape Measure. The most practical and accurate are metal-tipped reversible, stretch- and shrink-proof with English and metric markings.

Thimble. Always wear a thimble when hand sewing. It should be

threading lacings through eyelets and in decorative ribbon work.

Electric Iron. The most useful type is a combination steam-and-dry iron provided you follow the instructions carefully for filling and steaming. See pages 40–41.

Ironing Board. This should be well padded. The most convenient is a board that can be adjusted to different heights for different jobs.

Sewing Needles. Always keep a supply of needles in various sizes – fine, medium and coarse – ready for different weights of fabric and various sewing purposes. Large numbers indicate fine needles, small numbers coarser ones. Sharps are usually used for ordinary sewing, while Crewel, Chenille, Tapestry or Darners are useful for special types of sewing (see chart opposite).

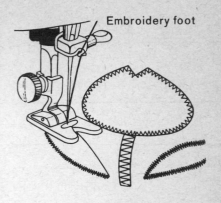

Embroidery foot

Steel Pins. These are used for all pinning jobs, such as pinning patterns to fabrics and holding edges together. It pays to have good sharp steel dressmaker pins as they are less likely to leave marks in the fabric, whilst 'silk pins' should be used for very fine fabrics.

Pin Cushion. It is convenient to have one attached to your sewing machine and another as a wrist pin cushion when pinning patterns, fitting darts, etc.

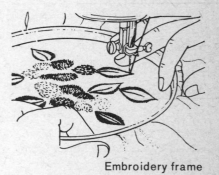

Embroidery frame

Transfer Paper or dressmaker's tracing paper is a specially coated paper for transferring pattern markings onto your fabric. Apply to the wrong side of your fabric with the aid of a tracing wheel.

Tracing Wheels are used with dressmaker's tracing paper to mark important details when sewing, such as pleats, tucks, darts, buttonholes, etc. Several types are available, but those with a serrated edge are the most versatile.

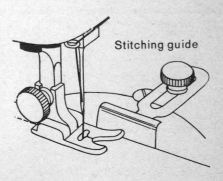

Stitching guide

35

1. Bobbin Winder Tension
2. Upper Thread Guide, Front
3. Pressure Adjusting Darner
4. Thread Take-up Lever
5. Thread Guard
6. Thread Take-up Spring
7. Upper Thread Tension Dial
8. Upper Thread Tension Knob
9. Thread Cutter
10. Needle Bar Thread Guide
11. Presser Foot Thumb Screw
12. Needle Clamp Screw
13. Presser Foot
14. Slide Plate

Tailor's Chalk. Used to mark construction lines, hems and fitting alterations. Use only white or pale colours when working on most fabrics: the wax variety can be used on heavy wools. Edges should be kept thin and sharp for accuracy.

Dressmakers' Stands. In most dressmaking shops you will find three

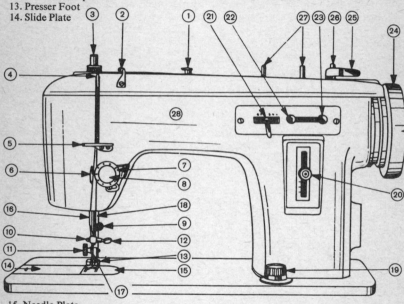

15. Needle Plate
16. Needle Bar
17. Needle
18. Presser Bar
19. Drop Feed Knob
20. Stitch Length Regulator
21. Zigzag Width Lever
22. Zigzag Width Stopper
23. Zigzag Width Stopper
24. Balance Wheel
25. Bobbin Winder Finger
26. Bobbin Winder Stud
27. Spool Pin
28. Jones/Brother Sewing Machine 1681

basic types to choose from, together with a range of sizes. The ideal type to buy is a shaped stand of a size similar to your own, covered in fabric, which is sold complete with a detachable tripod base. Or you could have one of these stands made to your own shape for an additional charge. Flexible wire and clip-together cardboard stands are also available, but although they are cheaper they are only suitable for occasional use.

Sewing Machines

A sewing machine is the most expensive piece of equipment you will require, so spend a little time looking around and studying all the available makes and models. When model, the type of mechanism, and whether time-saving attachments can be added at a later date. Study all the available information before purchasing your machine and do not hesitate to complain if it isn't as good as the manufacturer claims.

Because of the great variety of sewing machine models and variations available it is impossible to

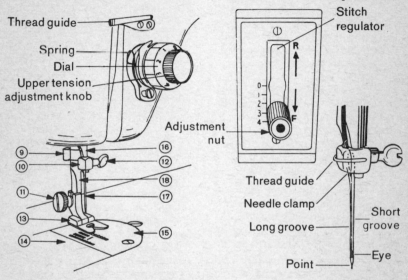

making your choice consider that an expensive model with many attachments may be a good investment and a time-saver if you use it often, but if the machine is seldom used a cheaper model will be more economical and just as satisfactory. Other factors may also influence your choice, such as the availability of servicing and spare parts, whether it is a portable or cabinet give actual threading-up and working instructions. However we have chosen one moderately priced model – a Jones/Brother 1681 – to illustrate the basic principles which in general are the same on all machines. Before starting to use your machine spend a little time reading the sewing manual provided and experimenting on scraps of fabric. You might also benefit from a

37

demonstration and a free lesson. This service is generally included in the purchase price and can prove invaluable in getting to know what can be done, or for that matter what cannot be done, with your machine.

Attachments. Most machines are supplied with a range of pressure feet for different sewing jobs – zipper foot, blind-stitch foot, darning foot, tacking foot, zig-zag foot, buttonhole foot, etc., together with other extras such as stitching guides, embroidery hoops, eyelet attachments, automatic gatherers, etc. Check through them to see that you have all those that are needed for the sewing you wish to carry out, and make sure that you can use them in the way illustrated in your manual. As there are so many makes and models on the market we have only given you a general guide, so read your manual carefully.

Machine Stitching. First practise using your sewing machine by trying out normal machine-stitched seams, experimenting with corners and varying fabric thicknesses.

Machine Tension. One of the commonest faults when using a sewing machine is stitching too loosely or too tightly. In most cases this can be rectified by adjusting the top thread tension, which is done by altering the tension dial. If the top tension is too tight, the stitching will lie on the top and probably pucker the fabric. Adjust the tension dial to a lower number by turning anti-clockwise. If the tension is too loose, allowing the under-stitching

to lie on the underside, sometimes forming little loops, then the tension dial number should be increased by turning the dial clockwise. Ideally the threads should interlock in the middle of the fabric so that the stitches look the same from both sides. This can be seen in the little diagrams under the sewing machine illustrated on page 58, the middle one being correct, the left one too tight, and the right one too loose. Always try to rectify this fault by adjusting the top tension; the bobbin tension should be adjusted only as a last resort. Always check the tension by testing out on a spare cutting of the fabric to be used as it will vary slightly on different fabrics.

Stitching Faults. Opposite there is a machine adjustment chart: there should be a similar one in your sewing-machine manual. If you use these charts wisely you can save a lot of time, trouble and money by simple adjustments which you can easily do for yourself. Our experience has shown that nearly 90 per cent of what appear to be service faults are in fact simple adjustments that most people can easily carry out for themselves. Moreover, once these simple adjustments are understood, it becomes much easier to use your machine and problems do not arise. As a guide to help you avoid stitching faults we have listed below six points.

1. Unless otherwise specified always use the same kind of thread for both top and bobbin stitches.

Machine Adjustment Chart

Trouble	Probable Cause	Remedy
Machine binding, locking, or noisy	A: Bobbin case inserted incorrectly.	Refit bobbin as shown in instruction book
	B: Feed or darning indicator wrongly set	Set these as described in your book
	C: Thread or lint caught in bobbin race	Turn to the section of your instruction manual which tells you how to remove and clean the bobbin race. Follow the directions carefully
Upper thread breaking	A: Machine wrongly threaded	Refer to threading instructions in your instruction book
	B: Tension too tight	Turn tension knob left to loosen upper tension
	C: Needle wrongly fitted	Your instruction book will tell you how to fit needle properly
	D: Bent or damaged needle	Replace with new needle
Lower thread breaking	A: Bobbin wound unevenly	Remove thread and rewind evenly
	B: Too much thread on bobbin	Remove excess thread
	C: Bobbin case wrongly threaded	Refer to threading diagram in instruction book
Needle breaking	A: Bent or damaged needle	Fit new needle
	B: Material being pulled while sewing	Never pull material when sewing – just guide it
	C: Machine set to zig-zag when using straight stitch foot and needle plate	Ensure swing lever set for straight sewing
	D: Needle not pushed up to stop screw in needle bar	Loosen needle clamp, push needle up to stop
Missing or irregular stitches	A: Needle wrongly fitted	Fit correctly. See instruction book
	B: Top tension slack	Increase tension
	C: Machine wrongly threaded	Thread correctly. See instruction book
	D: Bobbin wound unevenly	Rewind bobbin

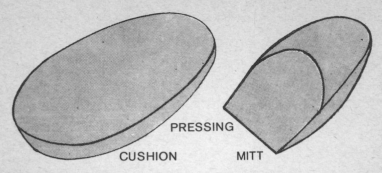

PRESSING CUSHION

PRESSING MITT

2. Make sure that the correct threading sequence is followed as illustrated in your sewing-machine instruction manual.

3. Never overwind the bobbin as this prevents it from revolving easily inside the bobbin case. Also make sure that it is fitted correctly into the machine.

4. Always use the correct needle size for a particular fabric, as well as using the correct type of thread.

5. Oil your machine occasionally as instructed, taking care to clean any surplus away before re-using.

6. Finally, use the sewing manual supplied with your machine to check and regulate your machine in use.

Pressing and Ironing

As already mentioned on page 34 an electric iron and an ironing board are essential for general sewing. A number of other items are also helpful, if you do a lot of sewing.

Pressing Cloths, together with a bowl of clean water, should always be to hand when pressing to protect your sewing from shine and scorching. Use washed lawn or thin cotton for general pressing on cottons, linens and blends; and washed holland or a linen tea towel for most woollen and heavy fabrics. Canvas cloths can be bought which are specially treated

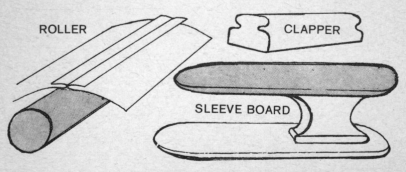

ROLLER

CLAPPER

SLEEVE BOARD

SLEEVE

SKIRT

with silicone to prevent sticking and to help the iron glide freely.

Sleeve Board. A small sleeve board can generally be bought as an extra with most ironing boards. Alternatively a separate sleeve board similar to the one illustrated below may be preferred. This is helpful for pressing sleeve seams and small hard-to-reach areas, and, like your ironing board, should be well padded.

Tailors' Cushions are used for pressing areas that need shaping, such as curved seams, darts, sleeve crowns, suit collars, lapels, etc. They can be bought in a range of sizes – 8″ by 12″ is a good average

size – or you can easily make one out of two 10″ × 14″ ovals of sturdy drill or heavy cotton fabric as you would a cushion – explained on page 14 – using small clippings of woollen fabric or sawdust as the filling. Pack tightly and carefully join the turning-through gap so the cushion does not leak. One side can have an extra layer of wool added for use when pressing wool. Simply cut a piece of melton or similar woollen fabric from the oval pattern used and hand sew it securely over the side seam onto the drill cover.

Pressing Mitt. This is really a small tailors' cushion which fits over the hand for rounded and small hard-

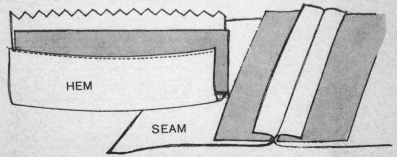

HEM

SEAM

Pressing and Ironing Chart

Fabric	Iron Temperature	Method
Cotton	Medium Hot	Most cotton materials can be either sprinkled with water and rolled so that there is an even dampness, or can be pressed with a steam iron. Alternatively, a damp pressing cloth can be used with a hot iron.
Linen	Medium Hot	As for cotton fabrics. Linen types made from man-made fibres should be treated as such.
Lace	Medium	Lace fabrics are best ironed or pressed face downwards on a thick piece of towelling.
Man-made Fibres	Warm to Medium	Rayon fabrics should be ironed on the wrong side of the fabric, possibly using a slightly damp cloth. Other synthetic fabrics are best ironed completely dry as for silk.
Silk	Warm	Iron on the wrong side using a warmish iron. Avoid dampness if possible as this water-marks if applied unevenly.
Velvet	Warm to Medium	Iron on the wrong side only with the fabric face down on a velvet board or thick strip of towelling. Alternatively pass the material to and fro close to the spout of a fast boiling kettle and then dry in front of a fire – not too close or it will scorch – before dry brushing in one direction.
Wool	Medium	Iron from the wrong side using a medium warm iron. A damp pressing cloth can be used on pre-shrunk or shrink-resistant wools, but if you are uncertain first test for shrinkage on a spare piece at the temperature required for their fibre type.

to-reach areas. It allows movement of the hand inside the padding to reach into pockets, sleeves etc.

Tailors' Clapper or wooden pounding block is used to flatten seams after they have been steam-pressed open. When the iron is removed the clapper is held down on the seam for several seconds to give a crisp finish to hard-to-press wools, tailored details and enclosed seams.

Seam Roller which is shown in the diagram at the bottom of page 40, is used to prevent marks on the outside of a garment when seams are pressed open. This roll can be easily made by covering an old wooden rolling pin with a firm woollen fabric.

Velvet Board. This is a professional device for pressing velvet, velveteen or other high pile fabrics. It is a bed of needles angled carefully so that the fabric pile falls between them to prevent matting and bruising. An alternative method is to use a terry towelling cover on your board and to place the fabric being pressed face downwards.

Fabric Strips of melton or similar firmly woven woollen fabrics are useful to protect a garment from the imprint of hem or seam turnings when pressing. These should be placed under the turnings before pressing as illustrated on page 41. Brown paper or thin card serves a similar purpose.

Pressing Methods

There are three basic methods of pressing: dry, steam, damp, as detailed below. Which method to use on a particular fabric depends partly on your previous experience and partly on experiment. However, never experiment on an important section of your fabric; instead test out the heat of your iron on a snipping of the actual material being used, or if this is not possible on an inconspicuous turning. In this way you will find out which fabrics scorch easily or shrink with steam, and which fabrics harden, shrivel, or even melt if the iron is too hot.

Dry Ironing uses no moisture. The ironing is done on the inside or outside depending on the material being used and the finish required.

Steam Pressing. This can be done with either a steam iron or an ordinary iron and a damp cloth. Generally steam pressing is done on the inside of a garment with a warm to hot iron.

Damp Pressing. For this method the garment to be pressed should be lightly sprinkled with clean water and rolled up to obtain an even dampness. The actual pressing is then done with a dry iron.

Over-pressing should be avoided as this gives sewing a cheap laboured look instead of the desired freshness.

Never use steam on a material which has not been pre-shrunk or on a material which was not steam shrunk before making up.

Test all materials to decide whether wet or dry pressing is best.

Always remove thread markings, tailor's tacks, odd strands of cotton, pins, fabric scraps and other such things before pressing so that they do not bruise the fabric.

Remember to press at each stage during the construction of an article as well as on its completion – darts must be thoroughly pressed before the side seams are joined, and side seams must be pressed before finishing the hem, etc.

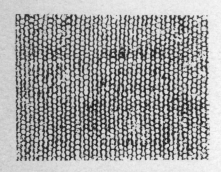

If during making a few press marks or fabric bruises dc show then remove these by steaming with a boiling kettle, or with an upturned iron covered with a damp cloth. Alternatively cover the marks with a damp cloth and hold a very hot iron half an inch above this until steam begins to rise, then lightly brush the surface with a soft brush.

When you are giving a garment its final press cover the floor around the ironing board with paper or an old sheet to prevent it picking up dust and odd scraps of cotton or fabric as these will spoil the finished look if they are pressed into the fabric.

Fabrics and Fibres

Understanding fabrics is as important as understanding your sewing equipment or methods of construction. On the following pages we are going to explain what fabrics are, where they come from and how to select and use them. First we need to define the term fabric: in general usage it means a man-made material which is produced from fibres that are twisted, looped, interlaced, bonded, compressed or joined together in a way that allows the natural strength, flexibility, elasticity and other innate characteristics of the fibres to be used to best advantage. Many types of commercial fabrics are produced from fibres coming from many sources – animal, vegetable, mineral and chemical, but they generally fall into two main categories: those produced from natural fibres – Cotton, Linen, Silk and Wool – and the man-made chemically produced fibres – Rayon, Orlon, Terylene, Nylon, etc. The properties of these fibres vary enormously but with the widely differing end uses for fabrics in the modern world, even the most adaptable cannot be considered entirely suitable for all purposes. This is why, although natural fibres are extremely versatile and possess many excellent qualities, man-made fibres have been introduced. The fabric manufacturer thus has a wider choice of fibre, and the consumer a wider choice of fabric. In some respects the borderline between natural and man-made fibres is becoming less clearly defined, since many finishes are now applied to fabrics made from natural fibres, which increases their versatility. Resin treatment, for example, can give crease resistant properties to cotton fabrics, or shrink resistance to wool. In general it should be remembered that man-made fibres do not replace natural fibres: they complement them.

Fabric Terms

These are the generally accepted meanings though not necessarily the scientific definitions.

Alpaca. A very fine but costly fabric with a highly lustrous smooth surface.

Bedford Cord. A woollen or woollen-type fabric which incorporates a rounded rib or cord.

Bias. A term used when cutting fabric diagonally between the true straight- and cross-grains.

Bonded. Two fabrics that are sealed together back to back with a bonding agent. This term is also used for non-woven fabrics pressed together with a special bonding substance to hold the fibres in place.

Bouclé. A fabric which has looped or knotted yarns to give a curly look to the surface.

Braid. A narrow tape or woven strip used for binding or ornamenting fabrics.

Broadcloth. Smooth, soft-finished closely-woven fabric with a nap.

Brocade. A Jacquard woven fabric which has a richly figured pronounced design on a satin ground.

Broderie Anglaise. A traditional embroidered cotton fabric with regular openwork as the feature of the design.

Brushed. Fabric with a suede-like finish with the surface fibres brushed in one direction.

Buckram. A coarse open-weave interlining which has been stiffened with glue sizing.

Calico. A plain woven unfinished cotton fabric which is coarser than muslin.

Cambric. A fine fabric, either linen or cotton, with a glazed finish.

Canvas. A coarse, firm cotton or linen material used for stiffening tailored garments. The term canvas is also used for a heavy weave fabric used for tents, sails, mail bags, etc.

Cavalry Twill. A woollen or woollen-type fabric with a pronounced double diagonal twill weave.

Cheesecloth. Thin lightweight fabric used as an interlining or for mock-ups when draping.

Chenille. A velvet-like fabric woven from chenille yarns giving a novelty ribbed appearance.

Chiffon. A plain sheer delicate fabric with a soft floating quality.

Chintz. A fine cotton fabric, brightly printed with flowers, birds, and other traditional designs and usually with a glazed finish.

Ciré. A shiny wet-look fabric which has been treated with wax or resin to give the surface a high lustre.

Coarse. Fabrics in this group are generally made of very thick uneven yarns giving a home-spun unfinished appearance.

Colourfast. A special feature of fabric in which colours do not noticeably change during the life of the fabric. The colours should not rub off and should resist fading in laundering or dry cleaning, sunlight, high temperature or pressing and ironing, etc.

Cord. This fabric has a raised cord or ribbing on the surface, formed by a heavier thread running through it.

Corduroy. A tough fabric which has a cut pile in narrow or wide ribs on a plain backing.

Cotton. A name for a vegetable fibre produced from the cotton plant seed pod which is used for many fabrics.

Crease Resistant. A finish that minimizes the tendency to crease and helps the fabric to shed wrinkles.

Crêpe. A fabric with a crinkled or grainy surface formed by weaving various combinations of highly twisted yarns together. The surface textures range from a fine flat grain to a pebbly or bark-like appearance.

Crêpe de Chine. A lightweight satiny very luxurious crêpe.

Crinkled. Fabric with a wrinkled or puckered effect obtained chemically or with heat setting.

Crinoline. An open-weave interlining filled with sizing. Used for stiffening.

Crochet. A handmade lace-like fabric made with a special hook and a single thread.

Cross-grain. This is the true diagonal between the warp and the weft threads in a woven fabric.

Denim. A twilled fabric usually made from cotton which is very tough and washable.

Doeskin. A closely woven woollen fabric with a smooth short nap.

Double-faced. Dual-personality fabric with two face sides made to be interchangeable. The sides may contrast in weave, texture or colour, or they may be two layers of the same fabric.

Drip-dry. A phrase used to describe fabrics which, after washing and without wringing, are hung on a hanger to drip dry. Garments dried in this way should have a minimum of wrinkles and require little or no ironing.

Duck. A heavy cotton fabric with a slightly ribbed weave which is very tough and washable.

Embroidered. Any fabric which has decorative needlework designs applied by hand or machine.

Felt. A non-woven fabric that is made of fibres of wool and fur, held together by a combination of heat, moisture and pressure.

Flameproof. A special finish which is marketed under several names such as flare-free, anti-flame, or glow-proof. It is a highly desirable treatment for children's clothes. Although the fabrics treated by these processes will burn slowly when in direct contact with a naked flame they will not flare up or smoulder when they are removed from the flame. Laundering instructions are generally attached and should be followed to preserve the finish.

Flannel. A slightly napped woollen fabric with a plain or twill weave.

Flannelette. A cotton fabric with a slight napped surface. Also made with man-made fibres.

Flocked. A printed fabric using stuck-on coloured fibres instead of pigment to give a raised flocked design.

Foulard. A light soft silk or rayon fabric with a twill weave.

Fur Fabric. A deep pile fabric made to imitate fur.

Gaberdine. A tightly woven woollen or cotton fabric with a distinctive diagonal twill weave.

Gauffred. From a French term for embossed velvets, ribbons and trimmings. A plain material is passed between heated engraved rollers which emboss the pattern into the surface of the fabric. The pattern is not permanent and wetting will remove it.

Georgette. A fine crêpe-like fabric made of silk, wool or man-made fibres.

Gingham. A cotton fabric in colourful stripes, plaids or checks.

Glazed. A surface sheen achieved with a special finish, such as in durable glazed chintz or polished cotton.

Grain. The term used to denote the warp and the weft threads in a woven fabric.

blended together in a fabric to give subtle combinations in a range of tones originally reminiscent of Scottish heather.

Herringbone. A distinctive tweed fabric with a chevroned weave.

Hessian. A fabric of strong coarse hemp or jute yarns generally used as a packing material.

Grosgrain. A fabric with a pronounced horizontal rib which can be made from silk or man-made fibres.

Guipure. A heavy open-worked cotton lace.

Heather. Vari-coloured yarns are

Holland. A plain-woven glazed linen or cotton fabric used for blinds.

Hopsack. A firmly woven woollen fabric with an evenly textured finish.

Horsehair. An interlining fabric which includes horsehair or similar stiff springy fibres. Used in tailoring, inside curtain headings and hems, around cushion gussets, or in valances, etc.

Houndstooth. A traditional tweed fabric with a distinctive tooth-like woven design.

Interlinings. Any fabric used in between the main fabric and the

Jap silk. A fine plain weave silk fabric.

Jersey. Fabrics made by interlocking loops of one or more yarns. The main types are jersey and tricots in single or double knits.

Lace. A general term applied to a hand- or machine-made open-work fabric consisting of a web of threads intricately worked into a design.

facing to give a crisper finish to an article.

Jacquard. Fabrics with woven patterns that produce a raised design. Damask patterns stand out from the ground with contrasting lustre; brocade has a heavy raised design on a contrasting surface.

Lamé. A metallic thread which is incorporated into many types of fabric to give it a gold or silver sparkle and glitter.

Laminated. A term usually associated with fabrics that are joined to a backing or when the surface is covered with clear P V C.

Lawn. A fine lightweight cotton or man-made fabric.

Linen. A fabric woven from the fibres of flax. Fabrics described as 'linen-types' are generally man-made.

Macramé. A knotted lace-like fabric generally used as an edging or for belts and trimmings.

Madras. A fine multi-coloured cotton fabric with a striped, plaid or check weave.

Matelassé. A material having a raised design similar to Italian quilting.

Melton. A thick heavy woollen material used in traditional tailoring.

Mohair. A glossy fabric made from the natural fibres of the angora goat.

Moiré. A horizontally ribbed fabric which has a special heat and pressure finish to give it a wavy water-marked look.

Mothproof. Fabrics such as Nylon or Terylene are inherently moth-proof because moth larvae haven't the right digestive system to attack them. Others are mothproofed, generally for life provided the instructions regarding laundering or dry cleaning are followed, by treatment against attack by moth larvae.

Muslin. A soft-finish cotton fabric of loose weave.

Nap. This is a term used by paper pattern manufacturers to indicate a one-way fabric.

Napped. Fabric with a suede-like finish. Some of the fibres are brought to the surface and are brushed to give a napped effect.

Needlecord. A thinnish corduroy with narrow cording.

Net. An open-mesh fabric available in various weights.

Nuns' Veiling. A traditional plainly woven fine fabric generally made of wool.

Organdie. A crisply finished very fine plainly woven cotton fabric.

Organza. A semi-sheer very fine plainly woven fabric made from silk or nylon.

Ottoman. A heavy silky-looking fabric with a pronounced horizontal rib.

Paisley. An Indian inspired pattern of a pine figure used on many fabrics. Originally denoted fabrics woven at Paisley to imitate Cashmere shawls.

Pile. A fabric which has been woven with an extra set of looped yarns raised on the surface and clipped to stand up and form a rich texture, such as velvet or corduroy.

Piqué. True piqués are woven with lengthwise or crossway ribs, or both, whilst waffle piqué has a pronounced honeycomb weave. Some fabrics with embossed surface are also commonly called piqué, as are some sculptural cottons with novelty patterns.

Plaids. Patterns of coloured stripes or bars crossing each other at right angles. They can be printed or woven in any fabric.

Plush. A rich velvet fabric much used for Victorian curtains.

Polished. A glazed fabric which has been put through a hot finishing roller to polish the surface.

Poplin. A plain woven cotton fabric of medium weight.

Pre-shrunk. Fabrics which have been specially treated to prevent shrinking when laundering.

Print. A general term for any fabric that has a printed pattern or design applied after the fabric is made.

P V C. A material made from expanded plastic which can be used by itself or laminated on to a wide variety of fabric backings.

Quilted. Two layers of fabric stitched together with a padding between. The stitching may be done by hand or machine.

Raw Silk. A rough uneven woven silk fabric heavier than wild silk.

Rayon. A man-made fibre from the cellulose group which is used in the manufacture of many fabrics.

Rep. A very firm material woven with a heavier weft than warp which gives it a ribbed effect.

Sailcloth. A very strong plain fabric available in several weights.

Sanforized. A trade name denoting a pre-shrunk cotton fabric.

Satin. A smooth shiny fabric with a silky look. Can be made from silk or man-made fibres.

Seersucker. A light-weight fabric in plain weave with an irregular crinkled surface.

Selvedge. The outside edges of a length of cloth. Selvedges are generally made from yarns different from that of the body cloth.

Serge. A plain woollen fabric used in traditional tailoring.

Shantung. A plainly woven silk fabric with slight irregularities in the yarn giving a slubbed effect.

Sheer. A general term applied to very fine thin transparent fabrics.

Silk. A fine glossy natural fibre obtained from the cocoons of the silk worm, used to produce many different fabrics.

Slubbed. Fabric distinguished by a roughness or unevenness in the weave, which may be due to natural thick and thin slubs in the yarn or can be artificially introduced to give a natural-looking unevenness.

Spot Resistant. The terms spot- and stain-resistant were commonly used for home furnishing fabrics, but are now often applied to fashion fabrics which repel water and oily substances and resist their absorption, so that stains do not penetrate the fibres and may be wiped off.

Stayflex. This is a brand name for an iron-on interlining which is made in several weights.

Stretch. A specially constructed texturized yarn which is woven into fabric to allow it to stretch when pulled and then bounce back into shape.

Surah. Soft pliable silk fabric without dressing added.

Synthetic. A man-made fibre or fabric.

Taffeta. A fine smooth glossy fabric made from silk or man-made fibres.

Tartan. Originally a Scottish twilled woollen plaid fabric with a distinctive design for each clan.

Terry. A fabric with a looped pile formed by extra warp yarns, which may cover the whole fabric or only parts of it to form a pattern.

Thread. A thin cord of two or more yarns twisted together and used in the construction of a garment.

Ticking. Firm, twilled cotton fabric in stripes and herringbone patterns.

Towelling. A cotton fabric with closely woven loops on one or both sides.

Tricot. See Jersey on page 49.

Tulle. A very fine net made from silk or nylon.

Tussore. A plainly woven slubbed silk fabric.

Tweed. A traditionally woven roughly surfaced woollen fabric with varying distinctive patterns or colourings.

Twills. There are several types of twill weave. The basic twill runs from right to left in a diagonal line, whilst variations include herringbone and chevrons.

Velour. A woollen fabric with a short thick pile brushed in one direction.

Velvet. A fabric with a short thick pile giving a rich luxurious finish. Velvet can be plain or figured.

Velveteen. A cotton fabric similar to velvet.

Vilene. A trade name for a synthetic, non-woven interlining.

Vinyl. An expanded plastic which may be used by itself or fused to a fabric backing. Patent vinyl has a shiny finish or it can be embossed to simulate reptile skins and leather. A vinyl-coated fabric has a thin layer of clear vinyl applied over a normal fabric.

Viyella. A trade name for a cotton and wool fabric with a slight nap.

Voile. A plain semi-sheer open-textured fabric.

Warp. The lengthways thread in woven fabric.

Washable. A term describing fabrics which will not noticeably fade or shrink when washed. This description is usually accompanied by directions as to hand or machine washing and correct water temperature. Special processes on some all-wool fabrics are now making them completely machine washable and dryable.

Watered. A method of finishing fabric which produces a moiré effect. A warp ribbed fabric is passed through a calender machine which uses heat, moisture and pressure to flatten some of the ribs producing the characteristic moiré or watered effect.

Waterproof. A process for making cloth completely waterproof so that no moisture or air can penetrate. Usually a coating of rubber, resin or plastic is applied to close the spaces between the yarns.

Water Resistant. Different from waterproofing in that it resists penetration by water but does not close the spaces between the yarns, thus allowing the fabric to 'breathe'.

Weave. This is a method of constructing a fabric on a loom with a weft yarn passed over and under the warp yarns with the aid of a shuttle.

Weft. The widthways thread in woven fabric.

Wild Silk. A plainly woven slubbed silk fabric of an uneven texture. Also referred to as Tussore.

Wool. A natural fibre obtained from sheep. It is used in the manufacture of many fabrics.

Worsted. Wool yarn of superior quality and appearance spun in a special way from the better qualities of wool.

Choosing Fabrics

Fabrics are becoming increasingly available in different designs, weights, textures and special finishes, but to begin with those made from natural fibres – possibly with a percentage of man-made fibres that will add to the durability but not detract from the original handle of the fabric – are ideal for most jobs, particularly when you are an

inexperienced worker. Man-made fibres wear and launder well but they are much more difficult to sew and probably take twice as long to make up satisfactorily. Fabrics made from natural fibres which have been specially treated do not have these disadvantages, and in the field of uncrushable, showerproof and shrink-resistant fabrics the choice is unlimited. The same is true of non-inflammable fabrics which are so essential for children's wear. So shop around, visiting several stores to compare fabrics and prices and study snippets, before making a decision. Do not get browbeaten by an over-eager salesman into selecting something that you do not really like. It is your money and it will be your time, possibly many hours of it, that will be spent in sewing. Be patient and decide on the right fabric for your particular needs. You must also be certain that you have the necessary skill to handle the fabric chosen, particularly if you are an ambitious beginner. If you are unsure of a particular fabric buy a quarter of a yard first to test your sewing skill. If it has a predominant pattern that requires matching then buy extra yardage or ask the salesman to reserve a length until you have cut and matched all the pieces required.

Preparing Fabric

1. Generally speaking most fabric is at its best if cut on the true grain, which involves straightening the ends of the fabric. To do this, first

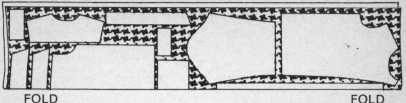

FOLD   FOLD

cut along one thread if the weave is bold enough, or clip the selvedge and pull a single thread which will pucker along its length. Cut along this puckering for about six inches before pulling a little more and cutting again. See diagram 1 opposite.

2. If after trimming the ends on the grain the fabric does not look square, pull it diagonally across the bias grain to straighten it, and continue doing this along the entire length of the fabric before giving it a final press to set the grain correctly.

3. If the selvedge is holding the fabric in, causing it to pucker along the edge, then simply snip every 2″ or so.

4. If you notice a little coloured tag or knotted string on the selvedge of a fabric (diagram 3), inspect across the grain for a fault in the weave so that you can avoid this when cutting out.

5. Next fold the fabric in half widthwise so that both selvedges are together and pin along both the fold and the selvedge checking that the ends are square and matching, right side of fabric inside.

6. When cutting out make sure that all seams match across the printed or woven design – as shown by the middle diagrams opposite – and that any predominant pattern is centralized. Also check to see that each piece is cut with the pattern or pile facing the way required.

7. Finally lay out your pattern pieces as instructed on the pattern envelope, marking out the shapes as required, cutting out each piece

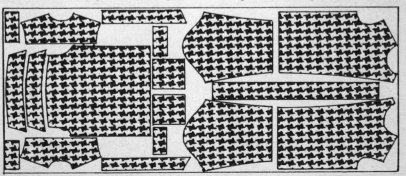

on the indicated lines, avoiding over-cuts and general wastage.

8. After cutting out check that nothing has been forgotten such as bias strips for facings or pipings. Before starting to make up spend a little time testing off-cuts of fabric for pressing temperature or for machine stitching so that when you start making up you know how the fabric will handle.

Fabric Stains

In spite of every care taken during making up stains are unavoidable. They should always be treated quickly before they have a chance to dry, and, if you don't know the cause or are uncertain how the fabric will react, do a little experimenting with an off-cut to avoid damaging the fibres. Alternatively experiment on an inside turning or hem allowance. In treating dry stains it is wise to proceed slowly, trying a mild simple treatment first and then if the stain won't budge trying a stronger one.

Cleaning Methods

Water. Certain stains such as egg or blood can be easily removed by soaking in cold or tepid water and then washing in warm soapy water. Never use hot water as this often sets the stain.

Chemical Solvent. Proprietary solvents, surgical spirit, methylated spirits, turpentine, etc. are amongst many others in this category which will deal adequately with a large number of stains. However, always test on a scrap of the fabric or an inconspicuous turning first. To remove the stain first place a folded piece of clean rag on top of it and apply from the back of the fabric with a clean cloth dipped in the solvent. The top rag will absorb the surplus cleaner. To remove final traces of the stain place another piece of folded rag under the stain and using a clean piece of cloth dipped in the solvent dab an uneven circular shape around the stain from the top gradually working towards the centre until completely removed. This will prevent a ring forming around the edge.

Blotting Paper. Many oil stains can be partially removed by pressing the stain between two pieces of clean blotting paper, pressing the wrong side with a warm iron through the blotting paper before removing the final traces with a chemical solvent.

French Chalk is very useful for drawing out an oily or greasy stain from fine fabrics. Cover the area with French chalk and leave overnight or hold over a warm upturned iron to melt the stain which the chalk will then absorb.

Biological Powders such as Radiant and Ariel remove many stains – blood, chocolate, biro, lipstick, etc. – overnight, if the stained fabric is soaked in a lukewarm solution for a few hours as directed on the packet. On some fabrics, however, the biological action has a tendency to change or remove the colour, so it is advisable to test for this first.

Treatment of Stains

Stain	Cleaning Method
Biro	Use surgical spirit or a proprietary solvent following the method explained opposite, removing the final traces by washing in tepid water.
Blood	If the stain is fresh, wash in tepid water and a little white soap. If set, soak the stain in lukewarm water to which a little salt has been added, then wash with white soap.
Chocolate	Moisten the stain with a little methylated spirit and wash in cool soapy water. Rinse in tepid water which has had a little borax added.
Coffee	Sponge with a tepid solution of borax – 1 tablespoonful dissolved in ½ pint of water – rinse and wash in warm soapy water.
Egg	First sponge with lukewarm water and then wash in warm soapy water.
Grease	Use surgical spirit or a proprietary solvent following the method explained opposite. Alternatively use blotting paper or french chalk as explained opposite.
Ink	If fresh, ink stains can be removed immediately by applying a little tepid milk or cold water. For older stains cover with table salt and then moisten the salt with milk, sponging with clean water after an hour.
Lipstick	Wash in warm soapy water and then remove any final traces with surgical spirit or proprietary solvent as explained opposite.
Milk	First sponge with cold water, then wash in warm soapy water, removing any final traces with surgical spirit or proprietary solvent as explained opposite.
Oil	Use surgical spirit or proprietary solvent as explained opposite.
Paint	Scrape off as much paint as possible and then treat with turpentine as explained for proprietary solvents.
Tea	Rinse immediately in cold water and then wash in warm soapy water.

3. Basic Sewing Methods

In this chapter we are going to explain a few basic processes and simple sewing methods. Alternatives will not be described, as we feel this would lead to confusion. Before starting, a few fundamental details need to be clarified.

First of all it is essential that you work cleanly and quickly, short-cutting as many out-dated methods as possible. Do avoid fussing endlessly over your sewing, hand-stitching everything as if the sewing machine had never been invented, and do avoid getting confused by using laborious traditional techniques which are surrounded by mystical mumbo-jumbo. Instead choose to make things which are enjoyable and exciting, in bold colours and simple patterns that are quick and easy to make.

Secondly, always work with clean equipment, with your sewing on a clean work-table, assembling the things you need for ease of use. Then you won't spend half your time looking for your scissors and the other half rushing between the sewing machine and ironing board.

Finally, always try to make your sewing both interesting and fun. Set yourself a time limit and then put your work away contentedly until the next time. Never sew when you are tired or irritable, as you will not only hate doing it but you are bound to make mistakes which take valuable sewing time to rectify.

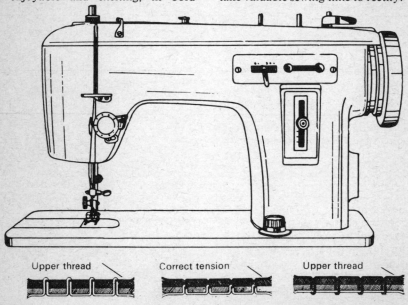

Upper thread   Correct tension   Upper thread

Using your Machine

When learning to sew one of the most important methods to master is the correct use of your sewing machine, as good machine stitching is essential for a well-made article. First of all make sure that you have your sewing machine set at an easy working height, with adequate natural or artificial light, and a reasonable amount of space in which to work comfortably.

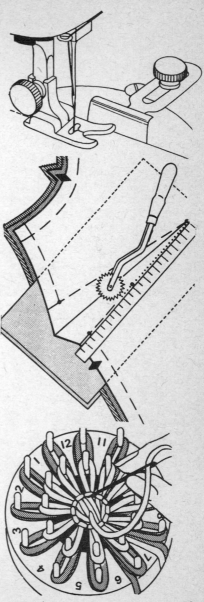

1. When you are preparing to sew always wind the bobbin carefully and then place it correctly into the bobbin case.

2. Raise the pressure foot by lifting the pressure-foot lever and then thread the upper thread following the instructions given in the sewing-machine manual.

3. With your left hand hold the end of the needle thread and turn the balance wheel slowly towards you with the right hand. Turn until the needle moves down and up again to its highest point, thus catching the lower bobbin-thread loop.

4. Pull the needle thread – which you are holding in your left hand – gently and it will bring up the lower bobbin thread. Lay both ends of the thread back under the pressure foot.

5. Place the pieces of material to be joined under the raised pressure foot and needle. Lower the pressure foot lever and start to sew by slowly turning the balance wheel towards you with your right hand. Do not pull the material through as this will bend the needle: merely guide it.

6. To remove your work first stop the machine and then raise the needle to its highest point by slowly turning the balance wheel toward you with your right hand.

7. Lift the pressure foot by lifting the pressure-foot lever, move the material you have just sewn to the

as the axis. Lower the pressure foot and start to sew again.

10. On page 39 there is an adjustment chart: there should also be a similar one in your sewing-machine manual. If you use these charts wisely you can save a lot of time, trouble and money with these

right and cut both threads on the thread cutter.

8. Place both ends of the machining threads once again under the pressure foot and you are then ready to begin sewing again.

9. If you wish to turn a sharp corner the machine should be stopped when the needle is in its downward position in the material you are sewing. Lift the pressure foot and turn the material in the direction you wish with the needle acting

simple adjustments which you can easily do for yourself. Read again the advice given on page 38.

Sewing Methods

Tacking Stitch. Long even hand stitches used for marking or for attaching pieces of fabric together for machine stitching or fitting. See diagram 1 above.

Running Stitch. A small hand stitch

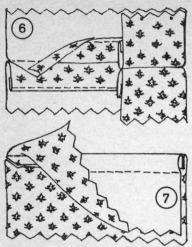

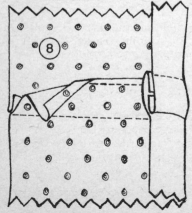

made by passing the needle in and out of the fabric in order to make several stitches at one time, as shown on diagram 2.

Slip Stitch. A stitch which is worked between two layers of fabric in such a way that it is concealed from the front, as in diagram 3.

Catch Stitch. Used to hold inter-

linings into position. Catch alternatively the fitting line and then the interlining as in diagram 4 opposite.

Overcasting. A slanting stitch used on raw edges to prevent them from unravelling, as in diagram 5.

Machine Stitch. A continuous stitch made by a sewing machine for joining fabric sections together or for holding edges flat. Ideally the threads should interlock in the middle of the fabric so that the stitches look the same from both sides (see page 58). If, however, the stitching is loose, or loops form, then turn to page 38 for further information on the adjustments required.

Stay Stitch. A line of machine stitching made around an edge – prior to making up – to prevent the edge from stretching. See page 123.

Flat Seam. Place the two fabric pieces to be joined face to face and edge to edge. Machine stitch along the fitting lines before pressing open as in diagram 6 above.

French Seam. A self-neatening seam used on thinnish fabrics. Lay wrong sides of fabric together and machine stitch $\frac{1}{4}''$ from edge. Press open and trim turnings to $\frac{1}{8}''$. Turn fabric so that the right sides are now facing and machine $\frac{1}{4}''$ away from fold on fitting lines, thus binding in the raw edges, as can be seen in diagram 7.

Flat Fell. This is made by placing the fitting lines to be joined edge to edge with the wrong sides of the fabrics together (diagram 8, page 61). Machine stitch along fitting line, then press seam open. Trim one side to $\frac{1}{4}''$ and the other side to $\frac{5}{8}''$. Fold under $\frac{1}{4}''$ of larger turning over the smaller one and then machine along the folded edge through the garment.

Machined Hem. This is the simplest of all hems to make. Attach the special hemming foot to your machine as explained in your machine manual, and stitch through the fabric from the wrong side as it is being turned in by the hemming foot.

Slip-stitched Hem. This is made with a hand stitch which is worked between the folded machine neatened hem and the garment, catching several threads of each side every $\frac{1}{2}''$, taking care not to show the stitches on the right side.

Automatic Hemming. This is an automatic hemming stitch made with the aid of a hemming foot which can be used on many zig-zag machines.

Stuck-up Hem. For a once-only party skirt a double-sided Sellotaped hem reinforced with a few catch stitches on seam overlaps is often sufficient. Double-sided Sellotape can be bought at most stationery shops and is used by sandwiching 2″ strips under the hem allowance at regular 4″–6″ intervals.

False Hem. This type of finish is used on shaped hems or for very bulky fabrics. First cut a 2″ wide

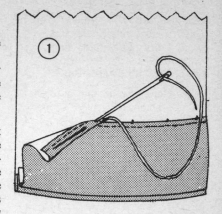

facing strip of self or matching fabric on the true crossway – prepared as shown on page 73 – and join together to the length required. Trim hem turning allowance on the garment to $\frac{1}{2}''$ and then stitch this strip around the hem $\frac{3}{8}''$ in, with the fabric pieces face to face and edge to edge. Press both turnings in the direction of the facing strip and then tack hem up into position. Trim strip to an even depth of $1\frac{1}{4}''$

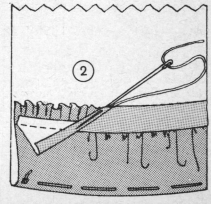

62

and then turn in $\frac{1}{4}''$ and machine neaten before finally slip stitching as for a normal hem, as shown in diagram 1, curving the strip to the hem shape with a warm iron.

Taped Hem. This finish is used on a circular hem when fullness in the hem turning needs to be gathered

round the neck of a dress or an armhole. To illustrate the basic method an armhole facing has been chosen, but this can be adapted for any shaped facing required.

1. Cut a piece of fabric the same shape as the area to be faced, using the paper pattern or outline of the

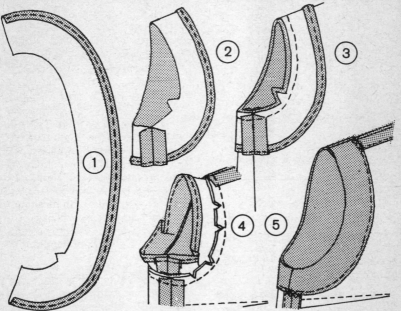

in. First turn hem to an even $1\frac{1}{2}''$ or $2''$ and then run two gathering stitches as explained on page 127, drawing up as described. Steam press to shrink as much of the fullness away as possible and then stitch on some bias strip before slipstitching into position as shown in diagram 2 opposite.

Facings. These are generally used

garment to get the correct shape, making quite sure that the grain on the facing section matches exactly that on the garment. Alternatively, if shape is not too difficult, curve a $2''$ wide strip of true crossway fabric, preparing the strip as explained on page 73, using a medium hot steam iron to set the shape. Turn in $\frac{1}{4}''$ around the outside edge and stitch flat.

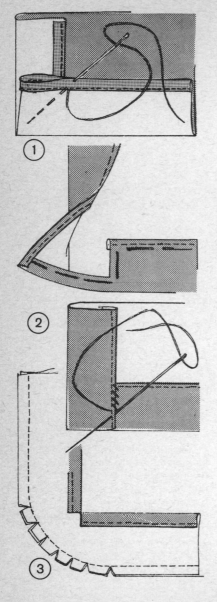

2. Join any seams together in the facing shape so that you have a continuous strip. Check this shape against the part to be faced.

3. Pin the facing to the right side of the garment, with fabrics face to face and edge to edge, and balance marks exactly matching. Tack and then machine stitch right round on the fitting line, neatening the machine ends to avoid unravelling.

4. At regular ½″ intervals clip the turnings so as to release any tightness, thus allowing the turnings to lie flat when the facing is turned through. Turn the facing through onto the wrong side and tack edges flat. Press lightly, remove tacking and then press normally.

5. Fix facing into position at seam junctions with cross-stitches, possibly even slip-stitching around the outside curve if the stitches do not show on the right side. Alternatively top-stitch around the outside ¼″ to ½″ away from the faced edge to hold the edges flat and secure the facing.

Mitred Corner. Turn the hem up onto the right side of the fabric and then turn edge along on to the right side. Even out the corner pleat so that a matching diagonal line runs from corner to edge junctions and crease neatly. Run-stitch along crease line as in diagram 1 before cutting pleat away, leaving ¼″ turnings. Turn corner through so that the hem and side allowances are now in their correct positions before slip-stitching them down.

Lapped Corner. First turn up and

tack hem into position in the normal way. Next fold over the side turning into its correct position, marking with chalk exactly where it laps over the hem. Trim away the overlapped section to within 1″ of chalk line and ½″ from bottom edge before lapping back and hand sewing as shown in diagram 2 opposite.

Round Corners. A separate facing is required when neatening a round or curved corner on curtains, dresses, bedspreads, etc. Pin, tack, and machine stitch the facing into position and then trim turnings to ¼″. Notch the seam edges of the turning around the curve as shown in diagram 3 before turning through and pressing flat.

Faced Opening. This opening has many uses such as for cuff openings, skirts or dresses. It can also be used as a simple pocket opening with bold decorative zips, eyelets, or unusual buttoning.

1. First mark on the garment the length and position of the opening required – e.g. 2″–3″ for cuff or 5″–6″ for a child's gathered skirt – in chalk or with a straight tacking stitch but do not cut the opening. Cut a facing strip of fabric 1″ longer than the marked opening and 2″ wide, machine neaten it along both long sides and across the top as shown in diagram 1. Place this facing strip in position face to face and tack ready for stitching, checking that the centre line of the facing strip is directly over the proposed opening. Machine stitch up from the fabric edge ⅛″ to ¼″ away from

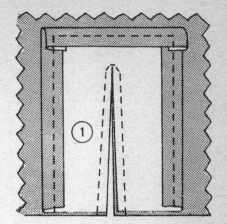

the centre, angling the last few stitches towards the top centre mark, turn the stitching line so that one stitch is across the exact point of the marked opening, and then machine stitch down the other side angling the first few stitches away from the point.

2. Carefully cut from edge to point through the centre of the

fabric and facing, snipping right up to the end stitch as illustrated. Turn the facing through the cut edges and crease the stitched edges flat so that the raw edges and stitching are sandwiched between the fabric and facing.

3. Finally top-stitch around the creased edges (see diagram 2, page 65).

Continuous Opening. This is a strong, neat opening which can be used effectively on children's clothes, shirts and blouses, casual skirts, etc.

1. Mark the position and length of the opening with chalk or tacking stitches, preferably along the exact grain line of the fabric. Cut a bind-

ing strip of crossway fabric $1\frac{1}{2}''$ wide, double the length of the opening plus $\frac{1}{2}''$. Cut along the marked opening line and place the slit – opened out – on the binding with the right sides face to face. Stitch the two fabrics together, $\frac{1}{4}''$ in from the raw edges, but at the centre point of the opening allow the cut point to approach the stitching so that it is just held in, as in diagram 1. This prevents an ugly pleat forming in the finished opening.

2. Press seam towards binding and then crease in $\frac{1}{4}''$ along the outside edge of binding to the wrong side. Fold the binding strip in half along its entire length, so that the crease line is level with the back of

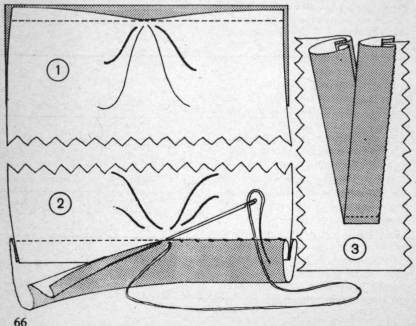

the machine-stitched line, and slip-stitch as in diagram 2 opposite. Press.

3. In order to strengthen the bottom corner of this opening, machine or hand stitch through the binding $\frac{1}{8}''$ up from the centre fold as in diagram 3 opposite.

If a machine-stitched finish is required, the first process described above should be worked with the wrong side of the garment against the right side of the crossway binding strip. The second process is to crease, fold and tack flat onto the right side, so that a second line of machine stitches can be made $\frac{1}{8}''$ from the creased edge instead of slip-stitching into position. The opening is then pressed and completed in the way previously described.

Tab Opening. This is the opening which is generally used on sleeves and at the neck of men's shirts, school blouses, casual dresses, children's nighties, etc. When finished it shows in the form of a tab on the outside of the garment, adding detailed interest to the design.

1. Cut a strip of paper the length of the tab indicated, shaping one end into a round, square or point as detailed in the paper pattern. Lay this pattern into position on the garment and chalk or tack around it accurately, as in diagram 1.

2. Cut the facing and tab fabrics according to the pattern, turning in and tacking flat the seam allowances on the outer edges, and stitching the inner edge to the marked tab line on the underside of the

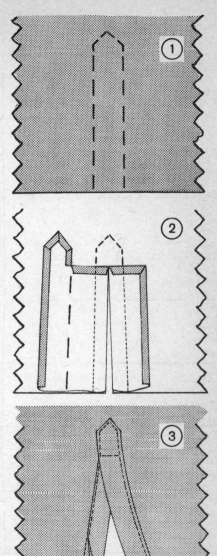

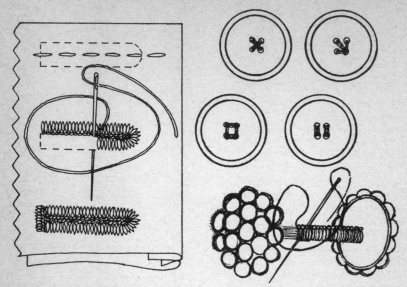

garment. Cut along the centre of marked tab, to within ½″ of the top, as in diagram 2, page 67.

3. Turn facing and tab sections through the cut opening and tack into position before top-stitching ⅛″ in from the folded edges as detailed in the pattern instructions and shown in diagram 3, page 67.

Buttons

These should be sewn on to their exact position, preferably with a shank which allows the button to move freely over the buttonhole without straining. This is done by leaving ⅛″ to ¼″ of slack between the button and the fabric, and twisting the thread around these strands to form the shank.

Worked Buttonholes. These can be made automatically on most modern sewing machines, or they can be

hand stitched as shown above or using a close blanket stitch, which is shown on page 320.

First mark the length of the buttonhole accurately on the exact grain. This should be ⅛″ longer than the button and should generally be about ½″ to ¾″ away from the edge of the garment. Next machine or run-stitch by hand around the buttonhole ⅛″ away from the centre tacking, rounding the front as shown. Cut along the middle and then oversew the raw edges on very frayable materials. Starting at the inside edge, by bringing the needle through the opening, work either a purl edge buttonhole stitch as shown in the diagram, the stitch being worked from right to left, or work from left to right using the blanket stitch shown on page 320, making the stitches ⅛″ deep and

$\frac{1}{16}''$ to $\frac{1}{8}''$ apart, depending on the fabric and the effect required.

To make the round corner, work six small over-stitches to the back of the fabric, finishing the buttonhole with an end bar, worked over several strands of thread, or use a bullion stitch as shown on page 317.

Fabric Buttonholes. These can be made in self or contrasting fabric.

1. Cut a crossway strip 1″ wide and four times the length of the buttonhole. Fold strip in half widthwise with right side outside, and machine stitch $\frac{1}{8}''$ from folded edge. Trim edges $\frac{1}{8}''$ from machining and cut strip in half.

2. Place on buttonhole marks on the outside of the garment with raw edges together and stitch directly over the centre of the strip, matching the exact length of buttonhole as in diagram 2 on the right. Fasten off threads.

3. From the wrong side cut along centre of marks and into machined corners as in diagram 3. Turn strip so that folded edges are facing and press, making sure that the triangular cut end pieces are folded under.

4. Folding garment material back to expose triangular and strip ends, machine or stab-stitch across several times as in diagram 4.

5. Cover back of buttonhole with facing, then put pins straight through each end of buttonhole from the right side of the garment to mark its length on to the facing. Cut facing from pin to pin and turn in the raw edges in an oval shape,

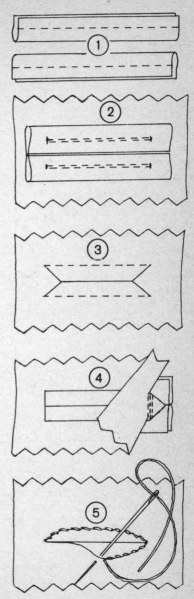

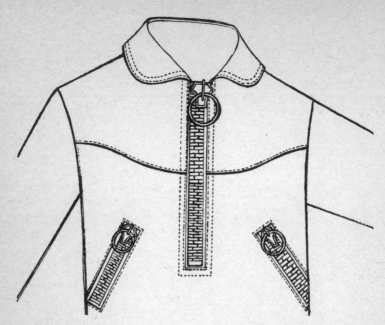

hand sewing securely into place as shown in diagram 5.

Zip Fasteners

Many types, weights and makes of zip fastener can be bought at most haberdashery shops. As with any other trimming great care should be taken when selecting one for a particular job, whether for a cushion cover, baby's sleeping bag, or for a new dress. Always buy the correct weight and type as recommended by the manufacturer, matching the colour to the material used.

Exposed Zip. First mark the exposed zip position, which should be 1″ longer than the zip length. Either face out the proposed opening as explained on page 65 for a faced opening, or cut along the centre line in the exact position where the zip fastener is required. Crease under ¼″ turning along each edge of the cut, snipping diagonally ¼″ into each corner at the bottom. Turn under the snipped end and hold flat with a 1″ strip of Sellotape, folding side turnings flat with tacking. Place zip fastener behind this opening so that the slide starts approximately ½″ away from the outside edge, with the teeth lines in the centre of the opening. Sellotape or tack zip into position and stitch ⅛″ away from the folded edges and across the bottom. Remove Sellotape or tacking and press flat.

Concealed Zip. First tack the opening together along the seam lines and press open in the normal way. Buy a zip fastener approximately ½″ shorter than this opening and Sellotape it behind the tacked opening – or tack stitch into position if preferred – so that the teeth run down the centre with the slide of the fastener facing the fabric turnings. The top of the slide should be ½″ below the top fitting lines. Turn fabric to right side and machine stitch ¼″ away from the centre folds down one side, across the bottom, ½″ below end of opening, and up the other side. In order to do this stitching accurately you should attach a zipper foot to your machine – see diagram on page 33 – as directed in your machine sewing manual. It can be done with an ordinary foot but this is more diffi-

cult, as the narrow side of the foot must be made to run along the side of the zip. Remove Sellotape or tacking and test out the zip.

Decorative Zips. Bold novelty zips made of brass, coloured plastic or even see-through perspex can be used to give an interesting look to a suede jacket, as shown on the left, children's and teenage wear, jeans, or in some cases even to evening casuals. If the design works and the effect looks interesting then use it.

Snap Fasteners. These are put on with a hammer, following the manufacturer's instructions carefully. They are available in a wide range of colours and sizes including large brass and silver ones which are most suitable for casual and

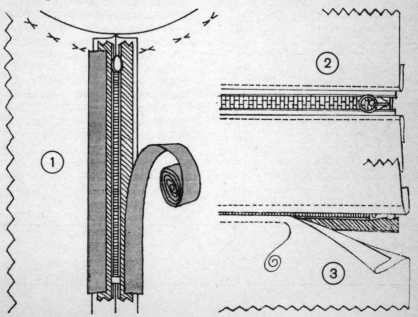

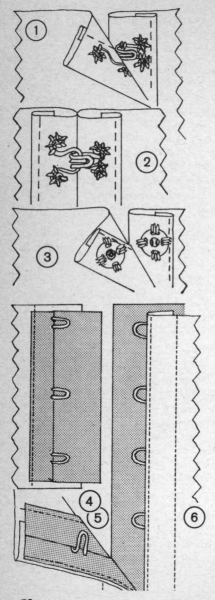

sports clothes as well as many children's and teenage designs.

Metal Eyelets. These are punched in the same way, made of the same materials and used on the same types of garments as snap fasteners. They can also be used with lacing or slotted rouleaux belts, etc. As with decorative zips and snap fasteners if they look interesting and work as part of the design you should use them.

Velcro. This is a fairly new type of strip fastening, which combines some of the characteristics of a zip fastener with those of press studs. Use as directed on the information sheet supplied when purchased.

Hooks and Eyes. Hooks are sewn to the wrap-over side of an opening, both at their base and under the hook with simple over-stitch that does not show on the right side of the garment. The eyes are sewn on to the underlap right through the material at both ends. If the opening is edge to edge with no overlap, sew hook on as indicated, but sew the eye so that it extends over the edge $\frac{1}{8}''$, making sure no stitches show on the right side.

Press-studs. Always make sure that the ball and socket parts are directly opposite each other. Sew the ball part on first, then move the under-wrap into position and press so that the ball makes an impression on which the socket can be placed correctly.

Hook Tape. This is a particularly useful and strong fastening used in much the same way as a zip fastener on cushion or chair covers, evening dresses or foundation garments, etc. Using a zipper foot, stitch the hook section of the tape on to the front fitting line with the hook tape the wrong way round, as in diagram 4. Next, turn the hook tape on to the inside of the garment as if it was part of the fabric turnings and machine stitch a second line ¾″ from the fold as in diagram 5. Fold the back seam allowance under and place this over the eye tape, machine stitching

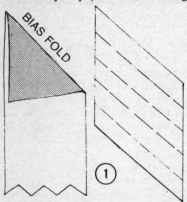

⅛″ from the edge with a second line ⅜″ away as in diagram 6, making sure that the hooks and eyes match across the openings.

Bias Binding

The true crossway or bias grain runs diagonally across the fabric. This line can be found by folding the corner of the fabric over so that the cut end runs parallel to the selvedge edge. Crease along the diagonal fold and then cut along the crease line.

Cutting Bias. Mark by chalking or tack-stitching parallel to the bias cut edge a line which should be three to four times the width of the finished width required. Mark several other lines if more than one length is required, cutting along the final line so that you can make a continuous strip as detailed below.

Continuous Strip. Having marked and cut the bias piece to be joined, fold into a tube so that the ends are placed one mark up as shown in

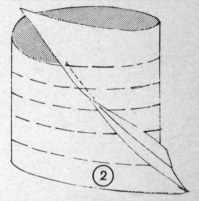

diagram 2, with the marking lines forming a continuous spiral, remembering to place the right side of the fabric inside. Machine stitch the seam together and press open. Cut into a continuous bias strip along the spiralling marked lines.

Single Strips. If the bias binding is being made from several individually cut pieces, then these should be joined along their straight grain, giving a diagonal seam as shown on page 244.

Corded Piping

Cut a length of cord $\frac{1}{2}''$ longer than the length required and place it on to the wrong side of the bias strip. Fold the strip in half so that the raw edges meet and tack stitch through the turnings so that the cord is pushed tightly against the folded edge of the binding. Using a piping foot

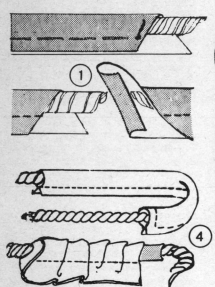
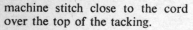

machine stitch close to the cord over the top of the tacking.

Joining Piping. Cut along the exact grain lines of piping pieces to be joined so that they are complementing diagonals. Cut the cord of one end $\frac{3}{4}''$ short and fold under a $\frac{1}{4}''$ turning, leaving the other cord end protruding $\frac{1}{4}''$. Slot in together so that the fold covers the raw

edges and then slip-stitch together.

Piped Seam. Lay the piping on to the seam so that the raw edges are together, and the piping stitch line exactly matches the fitting lines. Tack piping into position before adding the other section which is being joined. If there is a square corner, snip the piping turnings as shown in diagram 2 below.

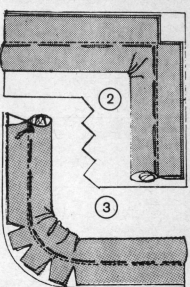

Curved Piping. If a curved seam is to be piped then the turnings of the piping will need to be notched at $\frac{1}{2}''$ intervals, as shown in diagram 3. The piping is then tacked into position, easing the corner slightly, then attached in the normal way.

Corded Rouleaux

To make a corded rouleaux for a belt or buttoning, the fabric should

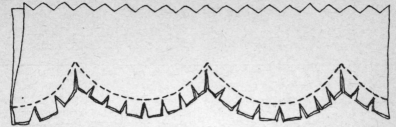

be cut on the cross grain four times wider than the cord which in its turn should be twice the length of the fabric – the extra length being required to make the turning through of the rouleaux easy. Fold the right side of the fabric over the cord and stitch close to the cord using a piping foot. In the middle of the cord where the fabric ends, stitch through all thicknesses so that when the cord is pulled the rouleaux turns right side out as in diagram 4. (also see page 185).

Scalloped Edges

Scalloped edges can be made automatically on most swing-needle machines or alternatively they can be faced out in many different shapes and sizes. This is done by machine stitching a strip of fabric around the required shape and then turning this strip on to the wrong side and stitching flat in the normal way.

1. Cut a strip of stiffish paper the exact length of the scalloped edge required. Divide the length into equal sections by measurement or by folding. Next roughly mark the first shape using a coin, a lid or similar object as a guide. Cut the first shape accurately and then use this to mark the second and third scallop shape, etc.

2. Using the paper pattern as a guide mark the scallop shapes in HB pencil on to the wrong side of the fabric hem. Place a facing strip of fabric on to this edge with the right sides together and tack around the scallop markings.

3. Machine stitch around the tacked markings as shown by the diagram below and trim turnings to $\frac{1}{8}''$ clipping into the corners and notching the curves at regular $\frac{1}{4}''$ intervals.

4. Turn facing to wrong side, easing out the curves by rolling between finger and thumb before

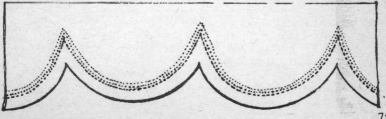

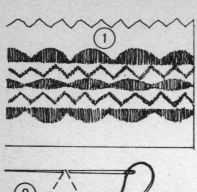

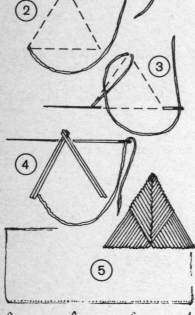

pressing flat. Finish scallops by top stitching $\frac{1}{4}''$ to $\frac{1}{8}''$ from edge as shown on the previous page.

Decorative Methods

No chapter on sewing methods would be complete without a mention of decorative techniques. In the following pages we show just a few of the wide variety of methods which can be used. Many of the actual working instructions and variations have not been fully detailed as they are in Part Four of this book, which deals exclusively with Decorative Sewing Methods, starting on page 286. Broadly speaking this type of sewing can be divided into two main sections: Surface Decoration and Edge Decoration.

Surface Decoration

There are many interesting and decorative types of surface embellishment which can be incorporated into the design of most sewn articles, from babies' christening gowns and evening separates to draped curtains or nursery cushions, and ranging from the traditional forms of beading or embroidery to *avant-garde* shaped cut-outs.

Edge Decoration

This type of decorative treatment is generally the easiest to apply as it involves very little preparation since it is usually made on a completed or almost completed article. In its very simplest form it need be no more than bold edge-stitching – which, incidentally, is an ideal way of keeping edges flat and facings in place – or it can be as adventurous as hand crochet, sequin strips or beaded tassels.

Which type to use on a particular design depends partly on one's own particular taste, partly on the fabric used, partly on the shape and use of the article, and partly on the dictates of the prevailing fashion. The basic idea is to enhance the general look of a design, making it more interesting or adding a touch of originality. In order to do this satisfactorily remember that the decoration should be well made. Experimentation is also very important, as this prevents your sewing from becoming dull or boring, so always be on the look-out for new ideas, making a note of them in your scrapbook, as explained on page 7, as well as using the ideas from our other sewing books.

Machine Embroidery

Used to decorate many garments in the same way as hand embroidery. Usually a wide range of easy-to-make stitches are available on most modern sewing machines, ranging from zig-zag shirring for children's smocks to colourful cord-work for evening skirts.

Arrowheads

These can be used not only as decoration but also to add strength

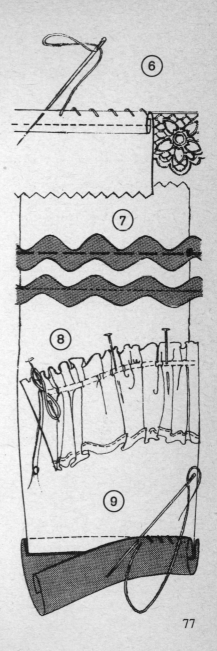

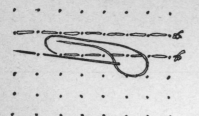

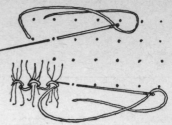

at the top of a pleat or at each end of a pocket. First mark a $\frac{1}{2}''$ to $\frac{3}{4}''$ triangle with chalk or tacking. Make the first stitch from the lower left corner taking the needle up to the top and bringing it through $\frac{1}{16}''$ before the first stitch. Continue in this way, placing each thread inside the previous one and gradually filling the triangle to complete the arrowhead, as shown in diagrams 2 to 4 on page 76.

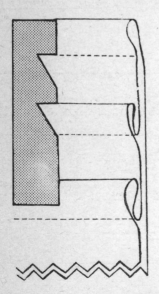

Bound Edge

First of all prepare a $1\frac{1}{4}''$ wide crossway strip in the manner explained on page 73. Lay this strip face to face on the edge to be bound and stitch the two thicknesses together $\frac{1}{4}''$ in from the raw edges.

Turn strip over the raw edges and turn in $\frac{1}{4}''$ of the binding before hand stitching into position along the back of the machine line, as shown in diagram 9 on page 77.

Tucks

Tucks are a very traditional way of decorating a plain surface in dressmaking. Tucking relies not only on interesting groupings and gradations of tucks, but also on the accuracy of spacing and stitching. Each tuck should be made on the exact grain line, creasing along the grain to mark each position accurately before stitching. As it is almost impossible to judge how much extra material is required for a particular tucked area it is best to cut the material much larger than the pattern, tucking as required before trimming accurately to shape.

Tuck guide. Cut a 4" by 1" strip of stiff cardboard, squaring the corners accurately. Measure $\frac{1}{2}''$, or the

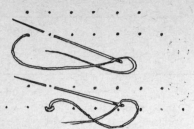
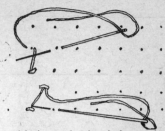

width of the tuck required, down from the top and make a $\frac{1}{4}''$ cut parallel to the top, making a second cut diagonally from below the first to form a triangular notch, as shown on the left. Make a second straight cut 1" away from the first, or the distance required between tuck and stitching, again cutting out a diagonal notch.

Pin Tucks

Pin tucks are very narrow tucks which can be made automatically on many of the modern twin needled sewing machines, or they can be made on most other sewing machines by accurately top stitching $\frac{1}{8}''$ away from a folded edge of fabric. Accuracy of marking is essential, as each tuck must be on the exact grain. Crease each tuck position separately along the grain of the fabric to mark neatly before stitching close to the creased edge, using a notched guide to space each tuck.

Shirring

Machine shirring is usually made with a special elasticated shirring thread wound on to the machine spool. The stitch length and tension should be adjusted as detailed on the shirring elastic information sheet, and then tested on odd lengths before stitching the actual area required. Elasticated shirring can be used on children's wear, swimming costumes, lingerie, casual summer dresses, etc.

Gauging

Decorative gathering may be made either by hand or by machine, and is used to gather in fullness

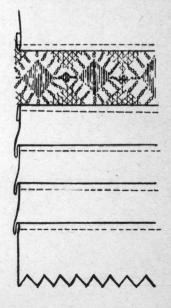

evenly. In order to ensure even spacing for the gathering stitches, measure the gaps with a notched guide as for pin tucks.

For hand gathering in small areas of gauging, make an even running stitch along the marked lines, leaving a reasonable length of thread at each end for pulling up, adjusting the fullness evenly before fastening the threads securely. Embroidery stitches are often worked on top of small gauged areas to give an extra decorative finish.

Smocking

This is an attractive way of decorating gathered fullness. It consists of working various ornamental stitches into geometric groups on top of the small tucks formed by even gathering. The use of smocking varies with the changing moods of fashion, but as a general rule wherever fullness is shown smocking can be applied, particularly on children's clothes, lingerie or casual and holiday wear.

First cut a section of fabric allowing three times the required width. Cut a section of smocking transfer dots – these can be bought at most sewing shops – the depth required and three times the finished width. Iron on to the material and then gather to size as explained on pages 286–7.

Finally, work the smocking stitches to make a decorative pattern – using cable, zig-zag or similar stitches – before removing the gathering threads.

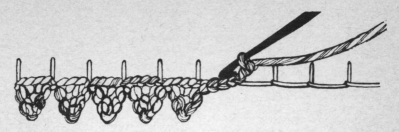

Crochet

This interesting method of making lacy fabrics by the simple use of a crochet hook and thread has come back into fashion recently. At first glance it may seem a little complicated, but the stitches are surprisingly simple to work. First of all buy the correct crochet hook for the chosen thread – here a Coats Milward needlework stockist will be able to advise you. The threads can vary from those readily obtainable in a wide range of colours to dyed string, braid, raffia, ribbons, coloured wools, or other novelty threads.

Working instructions can be found on page 298, whilst many crochet instruction pamphlets can be bought from most needlework shops in much the same way as knitting patterns, or a book on crochet work together with patterns can be obtained from the Coats Sewing Group, 50 Bothwell Street, Glasgow, G25 PA.

Embroidery

A wide range of easy embroidery stitches can be made on most automatic or swing-needle machines, whilst many more stitches and traditional motifs can be hand worked by those who have the time and patience, using string, braids, leather, raffia, plastic, beads, sequins, ribbons and many other novelties. In most needlework shops there is always a large selection of embroidery designs to choose from as well as embroidery pamphlets and books. When you glance through most of them you will see that there

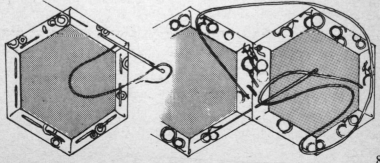

are almost as many methods for transferring a design on to the surface of the fabric being worked as there are materials and workers. Some workers prefer one method, others another, and the many materials available require varying treatments. Many of the most successful designers do not work to a pattern at all, or even from a design drawn on the material, finding that inspiration comes as the work proceeds and as the

needle or a special beading needle. Single beads can be sewn on to outline a design, or groups of beads can be threaded on to the needle and held with a single stitch as shown on page 332. Combine this and other beading methods with your embroidery and ribbon-work so that you have a range of skills to use on your next design.

Patchwork

There are many ways of making

stitches selected dictate. For most beginners, however, a transfer is advisable. This is ironed on to the fabric to give an outline design and is sold, together with an instruction sheet for the stitching details, by most needlework shops. See Chapter 12 for stitching methods.

Beads and Sequins

These can be sewn on with silk or terylene thread using a thin sewing

and using patchwork. First there is the classic geometric style which is made by using accurately shaped lozenge, hexagonal, triangular or square pieces of assorted fabrics. Crazy patchwork is the other extreme, as this uses random shapes overlaid on each other with a design based on the interplay of coloured and decorated fabrics. Appliqué patchwork can also be used. See Chapter 14 for the various making details.

Appliqué

Appliqué also has many uses and design possibilities, and is made in many ways. One method is stuck-on appliqué which is made with boldly cut areas of felt stuck on with a little Uhu glue or Copydex and strengthened with a few hand stitches, another is overlaid appliqué. The first essential here is to become really efficient at using an automatic swing-needle sewing machine, unless, of course, you enjoy many hours of hand sewing.

An alternative method is turned-edge or blind appliqué, which is described in Chapter 14 together with several other methods.

Italian Quilting

Another of the many traditional ways of enriching a fabric. The raised quilted design is achieved by stitching through two layers of fabric, in two parallel lines $\frac{1}{4}''$ apart around a formal design motif. With a darning needle a length of thick wool is slotted between the layers to raise the design, as shown on page 289. Coloured lengths of wool can be used for decorating sheer fabrics to give colour to the quilted design.

Macramé

Macramé or knotted string work has recently come back into fashion as an unusual edge trimming and dress accessory, as have many of the other decorative techniques explained in Part Four of this book.

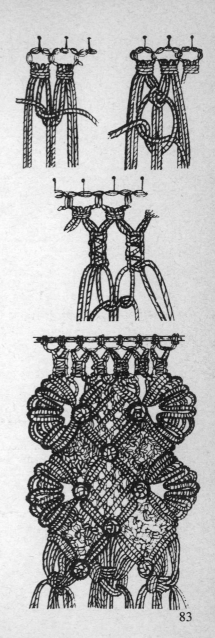

4. Toys and Presents

This chapter is devoted to describing how to make toys and presents and to explaining some of the simplest ways of making party things, from felt masks to fancy-dress ideas. Many of the designs and instructions are only intended to be used as a basis from which to work and develop further designs of your own, and we hope they will encourage you to attempt to make all sorts of things you have never tried before.

Glove Puppets

On a piece of fairly stiff brown paper measure out and mark a rectangle 6″ wide by 10″ deep, extending the top two corners upwards and outwards to form rough arm shapes. Take two

oddments of printed cotton fabric and cut them to the shape of your pattern. Place the pieces face to face and machine round the edges, allowing ½″ for the seam, and leave the bottom 6″ width open for the hand. To neaten this bottom part, simply turn under ½″ and machine or attach a strip of lace edging.

Cut two oval shapes of plain cotton fabric, 2″ × 3″, to form the head. Stitch these together, leaving a 1″ gap for turning through and for stuffing with small pieces of stocking or kapok. Sew gap edges together, and hand stitch head to centre of glove between the arm shapes. Finish head with penny-sized felt eyes, stuck on and then stitched, embroidered nose and mouth, and rug-wool hair. Decorate the body with lace and a jagged-shaped felt collar, brightly coloured buttons, brass bells, etc.

Christmas Stockings

These can be made from bold stocking-shaped pieces of coloured felt stuck and stitched together and then decorated with stuck-on pieces of ribbon, coloured cut-outs, various beads, buttons and novelties, etc.

Hobby Horse

A simple hobby horse can be made out of a large-sized colourful sock, some strips of patterned fabrics, a selection of felt pieces, ribbon, cord or webbing together with a 3-ft long broom handle, kapok or similar filling and small bells, beads, buckles or anything else you choose.

If you haven't a sock you cut two pieces of patterned fabric to a large sock shape, place these face to face and sew up the edges, leaving the top open like a sock. Turn through to right side, and stuff the foot section very tightly with pieces of stocking or kapok to form the head. Push in a brightly painted broom handle and then stuff the neck. Turn the opening in 1″ and with several strands of button thread stitch it together, using very tight stitches around the broom handle, and adding extra stuffing as required. The handle can be even more firmly secured with two metal washers and ¾″ dome-headed screws fixed 1″ from the end.

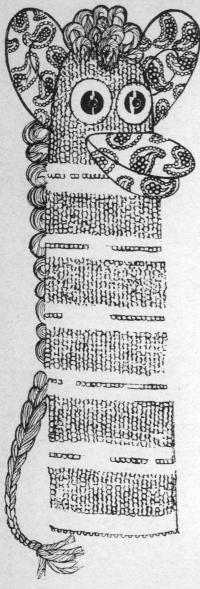

To make the eyes and nostrils, stick on and stitch pieces of coloured felt cut to the size of two-penny and penny pieces. Then make the ears and mouth. Make the bridle from chunky piping cord or colourful braid, and a mane from loops of rug wool. Finally add two brass baby bells and decorative studs.

Arm Puppets

Arm or sock puppets are similar to glove puppets, but instead of being shaped to fit like a glove over the hand they are made stocking-shaped to fit over the hand and arm. To make one similar to the illustration you will require a brightly striped or patterned sock or the sleeve of an old jumper. Form the foot into the face of an animal or make a fabric head as described for the hobby-horse. Add coloured pom-pom eyes, felt ears, embroidery markings and rug-wool hair and mane. In fact, add anything that fits the design which is fun to do and creates an amusing plaything.

Bean-bag Toys

These are fun particularly for young children, provided the fabric cover and stitching are strong enough to prevent the bean stuffing from spilling out or the decoration from coming adrift. Basically, they are made in exactly the same way as the felt animals already described on page 12, but they can also be small versions of simple dolls, as illustrated on the previous page.

The only real difference is that dried beans instead of kapok should be used for the stuffing of the main body section.

Bean-bag toys are decorated in much the same way as we have suggested for some of the other toys in this chapter, but if they are intended for very young children any trimmings which are easily detachable should be avoided. It is better to concentrate on large bold areas with striking colour combinations rather than intricately sewn details.

Party Masks

To make these you will need some pieces of coloured felt measuring 10″ × 8″, rug wool, decorative edge trimmings, ribbons, elastic, beads

or coloured buttons, raffia, and anything else which you think can be used successfully. Start by cutting two or three rough 10″ × 8″ face shapes in brown paper and marking on the various features such as eyes, cheeks, mouth, etc. with coloured felt pens, exaggerating these features but positioning them correctly.

When you have designed one which you like and which will fit most children for size and shape, cut out the sections of felt from the pattern.

Next cut some small holes for the eyes, nose and mouth and decorate around these holes with coloured felt cut-outs and selected trimmings, sticking these into position with Evo-Stik and then adding

a few embroidery stitches to secure neatly. Sew on an 8″ length of elastic to the middle of each side for going around the back of the head, and attach the ears, whiskers, hair or other details required, making a Zooful or a United Nations selection with different designs and colours.

Party Games

Children's party games, similar to those shown here, can easily be made out of odd scraps of coloured felt, an assortment of plain and printed fabrics, odd lengths of ribbon and raffia, pieces of stiffish cardboard and various other bits and pieces.

Racing Animals. For this game you need to make several 4″ to 6″ animals of differing shapes and colours as explained on page 12.

Materials required: Pieces of coloured felt, a ¾″ brass curtain ring for each animal, several lengths of string, pieces of ribbon, pieces of stocking for stuffing, oddments of wool, beads for eyes, some embroidery or sewing thread, various novelties, etc.

1. Cut two identical animal shapes in coloured felt and stitch together ⅛″ from edge, leaving 1½″ open for stuffing. Fill until well padded with cut-up stocking pieces or other lightweight stuffing and then sew gap together.

2. Add felt ears, beaded eyes, rug-wool hair, coloured feet, string tails and embroidered markings as required. Next sew on a ¾″ brass ring across the back so that it stands upright and the hole is facing the front and back.

3. In the same way make a variety of insects, fish and other animals. Cut string into 12-ft lengths, tie one end to a stick or peg fixed to the ground, and pass the other end through the front of the ring. Fix other animals into a line 12″ apart and then mark a finishing line 6″ in front of pegs.

The game is to jerk the string to move the animals forward, but not so strongly as to pull out the peg. To make the game more fun various obstacles can be added as in a steeplechase or the Grand National.

Simple Dolls

Many simple doll shapes can be made by slightly adapting the methods already explained for felt toys and cushions. First of all you need to draw a paper pattern. Using a piece of stiff paper, rough out the pattern required by making a rectangle approximately 9″ × 12″, and shaping this along the lines illustrated on page 90. Add an extra ½″ all round your pattern for turnings. Sometimes it is best to make the head separately, so trace this on to another piece of paper before cutting straight across the neck.

1. Using your paper pattern cut out two body and limb sections in printed, striped, or brightly-coloured cotton fabric, and lay these together, right sides inside. Stitch along the ½″ allowance line, leaving the neck edge open (or an opening down one side if the doll is all-in-one). Next, cut two pieces of plain cotton for the head and for the main features, and various simple embroidery stitches, decorate the face and head as required. Finish off the body section with oddments of lace, ribbon, decorative buttons, beads, pom-poms, etc., as shown opposite or elsewhere in the book, or simply according to your fancy. Also turn to page 17 for stocking doll-making instruc-

stitch these together in the same way, allowing ½″ for the seam and leaving the neck edge open.

2. Turn both body and head sections through neck gaps and stuff with inexpensive filling. Sew head section to the main body by stitching at the neck.

3. Using rug wool for the hair, coin-sized pieces of coloured felt tions, or to page 109 if you would like to make a dressing-up doll.

Useful Dolls

These are dolls which can be used as pencil holders, needle cases, comb or hairbrush holders, etc. All you need do is follow the method explained for making a simple doll, and then add such decorations as wide pockets, a gay felt apron, wide belt, or sew in a zip with a large bold ring for easy opening and closing.

Nightie Cases

Nightie cases, hot-water bottle covers, travelling happy cases, toy tidies and writing cases are all very simple to make. The basic method

2. For an average-sized case you need $\frac{1}{4} - \frac{1}{2}$ yd of towelling, needle-cord, velvet curtaining or something similar, an 8″ or 10″ zip, several pieces of coloured felt, small pieces of lace or crochet edging, embroidery silks, odd lengths of ribbon, etc.

4. Cut pieces of coloured felt to the decorative shapes required,

for each one is the same, and only the size and decoration requires variation according to the design.

1. Cut a paper pattern to the size required, using a doll, folded nightie or a child's hot-water bottle as a guide. Next add 1″ all round the basic shape for turnings and ease. Do not copy the exact shape of the stopper or other intricate details; instead draw a smooth curve.

i.e. two 1p-sized pieces of blue felt for the eyes and two 10p-sized pieces of red for the cheeks – sticking and stitching these into position. Next cut four ovals for ears, joining two together with a little stuffing sandwiched between, and stitch these firmly to the side seams.

5. Make simple legs and arms, stitch on rug-wool hair, lace or crochet edging, pom-poms, coloured ribbon and finally embroider a mouth and any other features.

Pencil Case

Any one of the dozen or so simple dolls or animals illustrated throughout this book can be made into an attractive pencil case, simply by omitting the stuffing and leaving a large enough opening in one of the side seams to insert a zip, which should be firmly stitched into place. Alternatively a slit 8″ deep can be made down the centre front and a bold ring-ended zip surface-stitched over this as shown opposite.

Beach Bags

Many different types of beach, picnic or casual bags can be made out of a variety of fabrics and decorated in all sorts of ways. To make the flapped bag on page 94 you need ½ yard of 36″ wide coloured sailcloth or cotton drill, some chunky wood or bamboo beads, and sewing cotton.

1. Cut a rectangle of fabric 1½″ larger than the finished size required: for a finished size 12½″ deep × 8½″ side you require a rectangle 14″ × 10″. Cut another rectangle 4″ deeper, i.e. 18″ × 10″.

2. On the 14″ × 10″ rectangle of fabric machine neaten one 10″ end by turning under ¼″ and stitching flat, and then turning in another ½″ and again stitching flat, this time with two lines of stitching ⅛″ and ⅜″ from the edge.

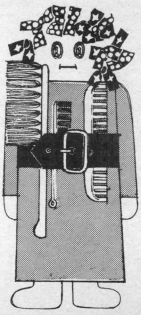

3. Lay the three raw edges of the 14″ × 10″ rectangle of fabric on to the corresponding edges of the 18″ × 10″ section, face to face, and stitch ¾″ from the edge around the three sides, fastening off the thread ends securely. Turn through the top opening, so that the right side is outside, and press flat.

4. To neaten the remaining raw edges, which form the flap, first crease under ¼″ and then fold under another ½″ right round the flap, arranging the corner pleats neatly. Tack these edges flat and then stitch into position with two machining lines ⅛″ and ⅜″ from the edges, continuing either both or only the ⅜″ one around the body section to hold flat.

5. Finally make a bamboo beaded handle and fastening toggle using some strong string.

Children's Handbags

These can be made out of all sorts of colourful scraps of fabric, felt and leather, odd beads, an assortment of trimmings and a few special extras. Cheap ready-made purses and zip-up bags can be decorated in many exciting ways. Try sticking some felt cut-outs or adding a few beads on to a Woolworth purse or embroidering some colourful details and trimmings with ribbon and lace.

Beaded Bag

Materials range from corduroy, cotton rep, velvet or sailcloth to leather, suede and plastic, with added beads and novelty trimmings.

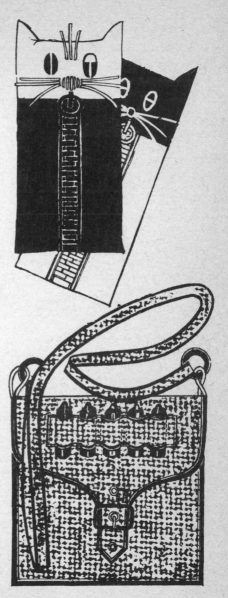

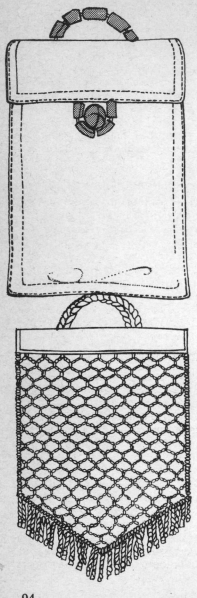

1. To make a round beaded bag, like the one shown on page 96, cut two circles of stiffish fabric using a saucer or plate as a guide.

2. With the normal sewing machine binding foot attachment, stitch on some matching coloured bias binding around each circular piece.

3. Stick and sew on a pattern of beads and sequins, following the general beading instructions given in Chapter 13. Coloured cut-outs of felt or plastic could also be stuck and stitched on as required.

4. Cut two circles of thin felt $\frac{1}{8}''$ smaller than the fabric pieces and with Uhu glue stick these carefully on to the back of the main pieces to cover the stitches, making sure that the edges are firmly attached but not letting the glue get on to the fabric surface.

5. The two circles can now be sewn together around two-thirds of the bag, preferably by hand, stab-stitching right through both circles every $\frac{1}{8}''$ with silk buttonhole twist about $\frac{1}{4}''$ in, adding an extra bead here and there while stitching. The top one third of the circles are left unstitched to form the opening.

6. Sew in a 4″ to 6″ zip and then add a beaded handle, or a handle made from a decorative cord or braid.

Many other play bags can be made in all sorts of shapes and sizes, using this method.

Decorative Belts

Many different belts can be made by plaiting coloured ribbons to-

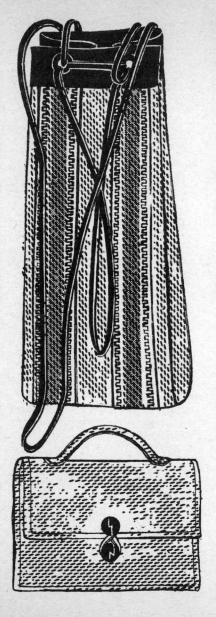

gether, knotting string, and adding beads, or by couching, cording and appliqué-ing, or by decorating a ready-made webbing belt with a pattern of odd buttons, brass curtain rings, metal loops and other decorative oddments as shown. Collect together as many beads, old metal, bone or pearl buttons as you can find, arranging and stitching them on as explained in Chapter 13, page 339.

Decorative Buckles and Buttons

These can be made by twisting, looping, twirling, plaiting or knotting cord, raffia, rouleaux, dyed string, pipe cleaners, or even electrical wire covering, around plain metal buckles or shanked buttons incorporating beads, sequins, motifs, dried seeds, plastic pieces, old trinkets, etc. Try several out and if they are successful make some more.

Winter Gloves

Children's gloves, socks, woolly stockings and many other ready-made garments can be made very attractive with the addition of some colourful wool embroidery. Try adding some embroidered roses in coloured wools, or lazy daisies as shown on pages 312 and 316. Team these with gloves, berets, scarves or even a rose-embroidered sweater and cardigan. Some of the stitches used for this type of embroidery are explained in Chapter 12. Many more can be found in pamphlets and transfer designs on sale at most sewing shops.

neaten one of the triangles on all three sides. Cut two 2½″ wide crossway strips from the other triangle, using the maximum length possible. Fold each of these in half – right sides inside – along the entire length so that they are 1¼″ wide and stitch ¼″ in from the cut edges. Turn through to make 1″ wide ribbon ties and attach these to the diagonal ends as shown. Attach trimming and extra decoration as required.

Head Scarf

There are many ways of making decorative head scarves, such as the attractive one shown on the right. To make this you need an 18″ square of printed softish cotton or silky fabric, 1 yard of decorative edging and sewing cotton.

First fold the 18″ square diagonally across and cut along the fold into two equal triangles. Machine

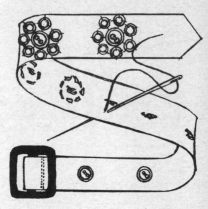

Neckties

These, in a variety of fabrics or in crochet and knitting, can be great fun to do, as well as making ideal birthday and Christmas presents. The easiest way to start making a normal fabric necktie is to first unpick an old one to see how it is cut and made. Note the fabric shape and sort of interlining used, and especially the cross-grain cutting, half-way inset sections, end finishing and hand-stitched back seaming.

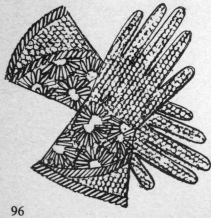

Simply copy it in the fabric of your choice.

For people who crochet making a necktie is an easy task; those who have never done any need only a little practice to discover how easy crochet is – simply a matter of looping threads together with the aid of a hook. To start crocheting first buy a simple pattern, crochet hook and thread – once you have got going you will find you can make up your own designs as you

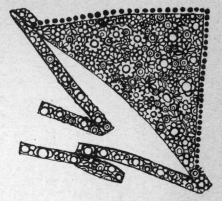

go along. An introduction to crochet can be found on page 298.

Fancy Dress Ideas

Be adventurous and colourful, using big details, unusual trimmings and interesting extras, forgetting as much as possible the intricate details of fine sewing. The designs shown next are only intended to illustrate the range of costumes which can be made for both boys and girls. Other ideas, which can

range from traditional peasant costumes to space-age cosmonauts' outfits, can easily be followed up by those who like to experiment.

Jester's Outfit

This is made from $\frac{1}{2}$ yard of yellow and $\frac{1}{2}$ yard of black felt or fabric, a dozen baby bells, plus three extra bells for the hat and another two for trimming the shoes.

To make the basic Jester pattern

first mark out the simple tunic pattern shown on page 23, but instead of drawing a straight hem mark an evenly jagged hem as shown here, and draw a line across the pattern just above the waist.

Next cut out four 9″ squares of yellow felt or fabric and four of black. Stitch two yellow and two black squares together to form a 17½″ × 17½″ checkerboard square, and then join the other four in a similar way. Now simply continue making the dress in the easiest possible way, marking out the shape with the waist pattern line and centre lines placed on the yellow–black seamings.

If you are using felt the hem can be cut to shape without finishing, but if the tunic is made of fabric

then face back ¼″ with bias binding, applying this as explained on page 78. Similarly for the jagged collar, which can be cut to any size and shape you like.

To make the hat, first measure round the child's head and then experiment with brown paper, using the head measurement as a guide for size. When you have discovered the most successful shape, use your brown paper pattern to cut out the felt, remembering to add on ½″ all round for turnings.

Finally sew on the bells to each jagged corner and a bow and bell on each shoe.

Cowboys and Indians

First trim a pair of ordinary denim jeans with a 2½″ wide strip of

coloured felt which has been
snipped every ¼″ to make a deep
fringe. Evo-Stik this felt fringed
strip on to the side seams and then
hand stitch for extra strength. Next
make a hobby horse as explained
on page 85.

Make the Indian head-dress out
of a 2″ wide strip of felt sewn to
fit on to the head and then trimmed
with real feathers which you can
colour or feathers made from 8″ ×
1½″ felt feather shapes slotted with
pipe cleaners, adding two feathered
ribbons at the back for a Warrior
Chief.

Fairy Dresses

These can vary from the Sugar-
Plum Fairy design shown on page

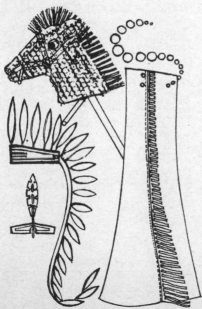

100 to the more elaborate long
Fairy Godmother's dress shown
below it. Remember that in either
case the dress itself is only half
the design – the head-dress, shoes
and magic wand are just as important.

To make the little Sugar-Plum
Fairy design you will find it easiest
to adapt a simple ballet leotard or
dyed cotton vest and knickers,
adding circular cut frills of net
around the hip line.

For the more elaborate Fairy
Godmother's dress a paper pattern
will be needed, cut on the lines of
that shown on page 23, but of a
more flared shape extended to
reach the floor. First of all measure
from the child's front neck to the

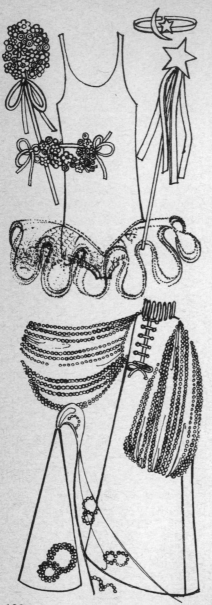

floor and then back neck to floor, extending the line A to B on your pattern to those measurements plus 2″ extra for hem and seam allowance. Next continue drawing down the side seam D to C flaring out so that the new floor length hem line measures 14″ or 16″ or even more if required instead of 8½″.

Using this extended paper pattern in the usual way, make a simple dress, introducing bold details such as neck lacing, frilled collar and gathered sleeves if you like, but remembering to dispense with as much intricate sewing as possible, Sellotaping rather than stitching the hem, etc.

Before going to a lot of trouble to make the head-dress, shoes and magic wand, spend a little time experimenting with coloured paper, tinsel, beads, ribbons and Uhu glue or Durofix to see what is best; you can also stick some extras on to the dress if you like.

Peasant Costumes

Many of these can be made out of prettily patterned fabrics combined with brightly coloured felts, decorated with bold embroideries or smocking, and using big design details, unusual trimming and interesting extras. As there is such a variety to choose from only a brief explanation will be given here, as the garments can be made as explained earlier.

For instance the felt waistcoat is stuck and stitched together, but the front, hem, and armhole edges left raw and then decorated with bold embroidery as shown in Chapter 12, beading and braiding as shown in Chapter 13, and couching as explained in Chapter 11. Similarly the circular skirt, smocked blouse or *broderie anglaise* cap and apron should be made by the quickest and simplest method.

As with all children's fancy dress, novelty, bold colours and interesting design are much more important than beautiful sewing, so provided the dress doesn't fall to pieces, stick rather than stitch as much as possible.

Kite Making

Materials required: Three very thin garden canes 2′ 9″ long, preferably less than ¼″ thick, 1 yard of thin but strong fabric, pieces of coloured felt, Evo-Stik, coloured tissue paper for the tail, a large ball of fishing line or kite twine, a simple ¾″ metal ring and some decorative trimmings, provided they are not too heavy, as the kite must be as light as possible when finished.

1. Cut one cane to 2′ 3″ long and mark into equal 9″ sections. Mark 11″ from one end of each of the other two canes. Lay the shorter cane across the other two so that the 9″ marks on the short cane are on top of the 11″ marks of the two longer canes, forming an H shape, and bind firmly together with twine. Take the two long ends and place together and bind securely for 1″ as in top diagram.

2. Carefully cut ⅛″ notches into the end of each stick. Now stretch

101

twine around the outside, to form outer edge shape of kite and then take the twine round a second time for firmness.

3. Lay the kite frame on to the fabric and mark $1\frac{1}{2}''$ larger all round before cutting out. Now lay frame on wrong side of fabric and fold seam allowances over the twine, pulling fairly taut and stitching turning into place.

4. Decorate the front shape with cut-outs of brightly coloured felt pieces, sticking and stitching them into position, adding other light-weight decorative ideas with the aid of coloured felt-tipped pens, etc. Also decorate a 5-ft length of twine with coloured bows of tissue paper and felt pieces to form a gay tail, then attach firmly to kite.

5. Cut two 2-ft lengths of twine and attach one at each end of the 2' 3" crossway stick, and then attach a 2' 9" length to the tail end of kite. To attach these firmly, simply thread the twine through the fabric with a darning needle, $\frac{3}{4}''$ in from the edge and pull tightly against the side of the support sticks, then back over the other side of the stick before knotting firmly. Bring all three loose ends together and knot on to a $\frac{3}{4}''$ metal curtain ring to form the flying guide strings.

6. Wind remaining kite twine round a fishing line winder, an old fishing reel or a 12" length of thickish stick. Tie the free end on to the metal ring. Now try out the kite.

When flying it, first of all test to see if the flying guide strings and

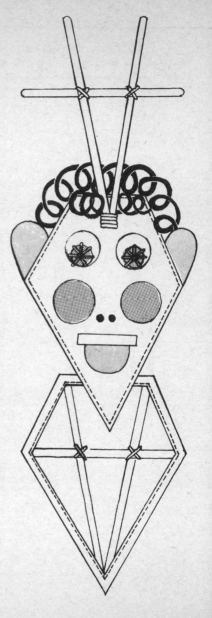

tail are hanging correctly. For instance, if the kite won't lift then the tail is probably too long and heavy. If it twists and spins then the flying guide strings need adjusting. Finally, if the kite moves violently from one side to the other the guide strings need to be shortened. Simply test out and adjust until it flies really well.

Having made one kite, try adapting the instructions to make a kite of a different shape and size, decorating it in a different way by liberally interpreting the various techniques explained elsewhere in this book.

Play Tent

Materials required: 2½ yards of 48″ or 54″ wide calico or cheap unbleached sheeting, 6 yards of 1″ webbing or tape, two 1″ metal curtain rings, a ball of strong string, stitching thread, a selection of different coloured felt-tipped pens, 6 small wooden tent pegs or chunky meat skewers, and some oddments of coloured felt.

1. Crease over ¼″ on the two cut edges of your material and then fold over another ¾″, stitching flat ⅛″ from inside crease and again along the outer edge. These edges form the tent ends. Turn in both selvedge edges 1″ and stitch to form the ground edges.

2. Mark on window shapes as shown, two of which are 12″ by 12″, 20″ up from the hem and 8″ in from the sides, and the third 24″ by 12″, again 20″ up from the hem but 12″ in from each side.

3. Cut away the centre fabric from each of the windows, leaving a $\frac{1}{2}''$ seam allowance around all edges. Snip into each corner and turn allowance on to wrong side and stitch flat, strengthening each snip with a few over-stitches.

4. Cut webbing window bars 2″ longer than the window opening and then stitch to the inside of each window at both ends and at each crossing. Cut six 5″ pieces of webbing and fold them in half to form loops for slotting in pegs. Stitch one on to each corner and another in the centre of each ground edge.

5. Cut a 5-ft length of webbing and double edge-stitch this into the centre of the tent along its entire length and exactly in between the windows, as shown at point 5. Leave an equal amount of webbing out at each end and slot on to them the 1″ metal curtain rings. Fold over the excess webbing and stitch flat to inside of tent.

6. Decorate outside of tent with giant brightly coloured flowers using a variety of felt-tipped pens, adding various felt cut-out shapes and other extras as required.

7. Tie a length of strong cord to each of the metal rings and then fasten the other ends to a post, tree or wall, before finally pegging the loops into the ground, adjusting the height and length of the strings as needed.

Finally make some dressing-up or play outfits as explained for fancy dress clothes on pages 97–101.

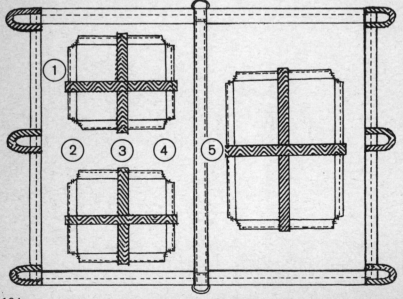

Wigwam

Materials required: 3½ yards of 48″
or 54″ wide calico or cheap sheeting,
four bamboo garden stakes 5′ 6″
long and about ¾″ thick, coloured
bias binding, some strong stitching
cotton, 12″ of 1″ wide webbing or
tape, coloured felt shapes or several
coloured felt-tipped pens, and some
pieces of string.

1. First make the wigwam frame.
Notch each stick 6″ from the top
and then bind all four sticks together with string over the top of the
notches. The notches will prevent
the string from slipping when the
frame is in position.

2. Cut the calico into two equal
pieces, each 5′ 3″ long, and lay
on top of each other so that the
selvedge edges meet. Stitch together
½″ from each edge and then fasten
off securely.

3. Draw a straight line from the
two bottom corners diagonally up
the length to the middle of top
edge, and then cut along these two
lines to give four triangular sections: two attached together with
centre seams and two without.

4. In the centre of one of the
unseamed sections mark a circular
or oval doorway big enough for a
child to crawl through, using a
large meat plate or bucket lid as a
guide for shaping. Cut out this
section and bind the raw edges with
coloured bias binding.

5. On all four sections turn down
top point 3″ on to inside and
stitch ½″ from the fold before
trimming neatly. Along hem first
crease under ¼″ and then fold on to

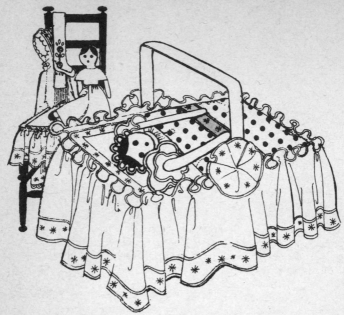

wrong side another 1″ before stitching $\frac{1}{8}$″ from both edges.

6. Starting from the hem of each triangular section and with right sides facing each other, stitch the right-hand diagonal side of one piece to the left-hand diagonal side of the next, which is then seamed to the third and so on until they form a large cone shape. On to the inside corner of each hem edge sew on 3″ of 1″ webbing, doubled over to form a little bag into which the frame sticks can be slotted.

7. Turn cone right sides out and place over wigwam frame to see how it fits, remembering to slot the bamboo ends into the webbing bags.

Using the felt-tipped pens, draw on giant stylized cacti, desert beetles, colourful butterflies and other bright decorations. Or cut out some interesting felt shapes and stick or stitch them into place.

Finish by making a Red Indian head-dress out of a coloured felt headband and some gay feathers, together with fringed trousers – as shown on page 99 – and possibly a special hobby horse as explained on page 85.

Doll's Carry-cot

A cane shopping basket, egg basket, or rush Moses basket when lined makes an ideal doll's carry-cot, particularly if some matching sheets and a simple mattress are made to complete the bed. Brightly checked gingham or traditional floral-printed cotton is the best fabric to use.

1. To line the basket a reasonably accurate paper pattern is needed, using a sheet of cheap brown paper on which to trace round the outside of the bottom shape, which is then cut to size. Lay this shape into the basket and tuck the edges into the corners all round, marking the exact size, and re-trim as necessary, remembering to add a ½″ seam allowance.

2. For the side pattern lay the basket on the paper, tilting it on to each end while continuing to mark the shape. Cut this rough pattern to the middle curve of each end and fit again on the inside as for the base.

3. Making sure you have left sufficient seam allowance, cut out each piece of fabric.

4. For the inside cover cut two side sections, one for the left curve and one for the right, and seam the two ends together. Join your base piece to this by first tacking and then stitching it to the bottom of the side sections along the ½″ allowance marks, easing on slightly.

5. Drop the shape into the basket and attach by tacking 1″ down from the top. Spread the bottom out evenly, and using a long darning needle stab-stitch along the side crevice to hold the fabric permanently to the cane, concealing the stitches as much as possible.

6. To finish the top either turn in ½″ all round and permanently stab-stitch through the gaps between the canework, concealing the stitches as much as possible, or cut cross-

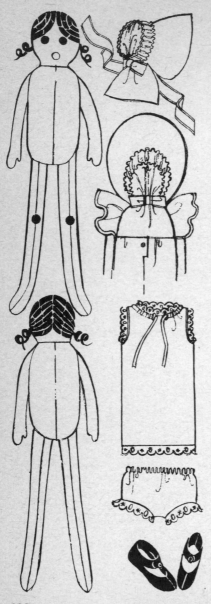

way strips of 4″ wide matching or contrasting fabric and use these to bind the top edge, turning under and stitching flat along all raw edges.

7. All sorts of frills and flounces can now be added around the top. Simply gather these to size and stitch on as required. The outside of the basket can also be covered by exactly the same method described for the inside.

Dolls' Bedding

Dolls' sheets can be made for the carry-cot by cutting out largish rectangles of patterned or coloured fabric and neatening the edges by rolling and stitching. Pillows, a soft mattress and bed covers can also be made to give the carry-cot a complete finish.

Designing Dolls

When you are thinking of starting a new doll, don't just remake the same version again and again simply because it has proved successful. Spend a little time looking at soft dolls in your local store or toyshop; also look at animated puppets to get some different ideas, and in particular note how the arms and legs can be made so that they move about quite freely. Look at dolls' clothes for design ideas and quick ways of making them. Spend a little time browsing through the shop's fabric remnants for new or different sorts of trimmings. Buy a small selection of those you specially like, not for any doll in particular but simply to have on

hand for when you feel like making
something new.

A Dressing-up Doll

This is a more complicated doll to
make than those described on pages
89–90, as it involves twelve basic
fabric pieces and special trimmings,
clothes, underclothes, shoes, socks,
bonnet, etc. However, it is great fun
to make and should not be too
difficult if you have already successfully made several of the simpler
toys. It is well worth the extra time
and effort as small girls love to act
as mother by dressing and undressing a doll, taking her for
walks, pretending to feed her, etc.

1. First you need to buy or make
the paper pattern required for each
section. To make the body, mark
out a rectangular shape 8″ × 5″,
rounding off the corners with the
aid of a cocoa tin. For the arms
mark out a rectangle 2″ × 6″,
shaping out a rough thumb shape
which curves into a hand. For the
leg pattern mark out a rectangle
2½″ × 8″, shaping out at one end
into a rough chunky foot shape.
Finally for the head mark out a
circle 3½″ in diameter but extending
the bottom edge into a neck 1½″
wide by 1″ long.

2. Cut out pattern pieces to be
used as a template for cutting the
fabric, remembering however that
no turning allowances have been
made. Using a fairly hard pencil
trace around each pattern piece
on to the back of cotton body
fabric, repeating the body and head
twice, and the arms and legs twice

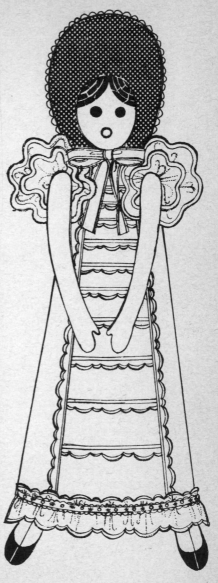

one way and twice reversing the pattern, so that you have left and right sections.

• 3. Cut out the cotton fabric, allowing $\frac{1}{2}''$ turning on body and head but only $\frac{1}{4}''$ for arms and legs. Place right sides of matching pieces face to face and stitch along pencil lines, leaving body and head sections open at neck edge, and arm and leg sections open at straight ends.

4. Turn each section through gap so right side is outside. Stuff with kapok or other inexpensive lightweight stuffing. When arms and legs have sufficient filling turn in raw ends and oversew edges together. Turn in raw edges of body gap, but do not oversew.

5. At the neck end of head insert a 6″ length of $\frac{1}{2}''$ wooden dowelling, or something similar, so that 3″ of it goes up into the head. Next, place neck inside the body gap so bottom of wood goes 3″ into chest and then sew neck edge of the body to neck edge of the head, adding a little extra stuffing if required. The wood acts as a neck support. Sew arms and legs into position just clear of rounded corners.

6. For the face and hair either follow the instructions on page 90, or buy a ready-made fabric face at your local hobby shop or the notions counter of a large store.

7. Make several dresses to fit your doll as explained on page 18, and some simple underclothes, tights, socks, and even felt or leather shoes, etc., as shown on page 108.

Puppet Theatre

If there are several children to make for, see if you can get them interested in producing a puppet show. Many children love taking part in play acting and delight in bringing their toys to life, so try making a selection of glove puppets – explained on page 84 – using the illustrations in this book as a guide. You could design your puppets around some favourite book illustrations so that you will be reasonably accurate, for example, with Alice, the White Rabbit, the Queen, the Mad Hatter and the Caterpillar. If you then read the story while the children act it with their puppets, or if you have a long-playing record with both the story and music, endless hours will be happily spent playing with the things you have made. You can also make character doll puppets in much the same way.

As you can see, there is no limit to the variety of things you can design and make. Choose gaily patterned fabrics and brightly coloured felts. Draw out your shapes on some stiff paper before cutting out your fabric, and use the simplest stitching methods to sew them. Ring the changes in design and decoration, exploiting the many ways you can use buttons and beads, pieces of ribbon and lace, coloured felt cut-outs, embroidery silk, string, rug-wool, etc. Be as creative as you like, trying out new shapes to your own ideas, and if these please you and your children then they are obviously successful.

110

111

Part Two   Making Clothes

During the past fifteen years there has been a great revolution in
fashion. Traditionally accepted ideas of good taste in clothes
have been swept away by a flood of new ideas and original
designs. This revolution has been accompanied by an
enormously increased press coverage of women's and men's
fashions, which has fostered in all women, regardless of age, the
urge to be excitingly and fashionably dressed.

At the same time there has been a great increase in the
variety of fabrics, sewing machines, paper patterns and
original trimmings. This combination of new fashion awareness
and greatly improved aids for home dressmakers, has
opened the way to a great do-it-yourself era. This section on
Making Clothes shows you how to take advantage of this new
fashion feeling; how to progress by easy stages from making
your first simple dress to more elaborate tailored
clothes. It also gives you some hints on fitting and designing,
thus enabling those who enjoy experimenting with their
dressmaking to express their own individual fashion flair.

5. Dressmaking Methods

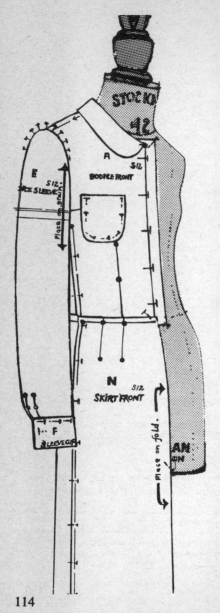

Paper Patterns

Paper patterns of different makes can be bought at most sewing shops and department stores in an ever-changing range of designs. Spend a little time looking around to compare designs and sizes, fabric requirements and trimmings before choosing, and then check that your size and shape correspond with those on the pattern as explained below. Here honesty is the best policy. Be absolutely frank with yourself about your measurements – there is no need to let your friends into the secret.

Body Measurements

When taking measurements, accuracy is of the utmost importance, for there is little value in badly taken or inaccurate ones which only result in many hours of extra fittings and alterations. Also be sure to use a good tape measure, as one which has stretched or has turned ends can lead to sorrow.

Body measurements are the actual measurements of your body taken whilst wearing your usual undergarments such as a bra and girdle. When these measurements are taken you should be wearing a slip, your undergarments, and a pair of normal shoes to give you a normal posture.

Bust. Measure snugly around the fullest part of the bust and straight across the back with the tape high under the arms.

Waist. Measure comfortably at natural waistline.

Hips. Measure at fullest part which is usually 7″ to 9″ below the waistline.

Figure Types

Most paper patterns are made to fit seven different body builds, known as figure types. These figure types are not descriptive of age but are based on height, body proportions and the contours of the figure. These are: Misses, Women's, Half-Size, and Junior Petite for well-developed figures; Girl's, Chubbie, and Young Junior or Teen's for growing figures. Ready-to-Wear fashions are similarly grouped so the figure type you normally wear in ready-made clothes should be right for your paper pattern. Your figure type is based on two measurements: your height and your back neck to waist length. Some teenagers for example will find that a Half-Size pattern fits them best; and there are adults whose measurements and figure proportions are best fitted by a Young Junior pattern. Analyse your own body proportions and shape and compare your figure with the descriptions and illustrations of the figure types in the pattern catalogues. Decide which type you are most like before you choose a pattern size and check with the sales girl if you are unsure.

Body Measurements	
Your Size	How to Measure
Bust	This should be taken over the largest part of the bust, with the tape raised a little higher at the back to go over the middle of the shoulder blades.
Waist	Put the tape straight round the narrowest part of your waistline and then slacken slightly so that it dips at the back to follow the natural curve.
Hips	The hip measurement is taken around the largest part of the hips which is generally 7″ to 9″ below the natural waistline.
Back neck to waist	Measure from the prominent bone on the centre back of the neck to the slightly dropped natural waistline.
Skirt length	This measurement is taken from the centre front of the natural waistline to the length required.
Sleeve length	Measure from the normal armhole seam position down the back of the arm over a slightly bent elbow to the wrist.

Your Pattern Size

Having decided on your figure type your bust measurement becomes the key to your pattern size for dresses, suits and coats. If your measurements fall between two sizes select either one depending on whether you prefer looser- or snugger-fitting clothes. For skirts, pants and shorts your waist measurement is used, unless your hips are larger than the hip measurements on the size chart. If this is the case buy a pattern size to fit the hips as it is easier to adjust the waistline.

When you are buying a coat or jacket pattern choose one which is marked the same size as for a dress or blouse. You will find that the pattern includes the extra amount of ease needed in a jacket or coat. Do remember however that every paper pattern has ease or tolerance – which means that it is larger than your measurements – to allow you to move comfortably in the garment after it is made. If your measurements are only fractionally larger than those listed, this tolerance will often take care of the difference.

Using a Pattern

To get the most out of your paper pattern, you should do more than simply lay the pieces on the fabric and cut them out. The envelope contains valuable information.

1. *Always* check your body measurements with those listed on your pattern to see if the pattern needs some slight alteration, which is best done before you cut out to avoid wasting valuable time and energy when fitting. Ways of making these alterations are explained on the following pages.

2. *Study* the pattern envelope carefully for it contains essential information: for instance it tells you how much fabric to buy and what sort of trimmings are needed, so that you can buy all that you need at one and the same time.

3. *Check* the pattern pieces for these give important constructional information such as width of seam allowance, where to ease, which dots and notches to match when making, and where to fix a pocket.

4. *Instruction sheets* of course give detailed instructions for making your garment. They also show how to lay the pattern on to the fabric for cutting. Be careful to select the right cutting diagram for your chosen style, your size, the width of the fabric being used, and for fabric with or without nap. This is a technical term used by paper pattern manufacturers indicating a one-way fabric, that is a fabric which must be cut in one direction only, i.e., a printed fabric which must not be cut upside down, or a special brushed surface finish known as nap, which shades if cut the wrong way up. Mark the diagram for identification and then pin all the pattern pieces on to the fabric as indicated before starting to cut out.

5. *Trying* to use a pattern which is not the best size for you is an expensive experiment, as many have

found to their sorrow. Once the fabric is cut you've crossed the line of no return. If the garment proves too small, you will have wasted the cost of the fabric, if it is too large you will have to spend valuable time and energy on re-marking and re-cutting completely. Be careful when you choose and be honest with yourself about your figure type and body measurements.

Combining Patterns

When you are looking for a dress pattern and you find one with a bodice you like and another with a skirt you prefer, then provided you select wisely you can combine them into one dress. This also applies if your measurements indicate that you are one size above the waist and a different size below. One warning: the following combinations are easy to make, but they only apply when combining two patterns of the same make. Patterns from different manufacturers are more difficult to combine as they all have a different system for sizing, make different ease-allowances and use different methods of construction.

To combine a bodice and skirt of the same size but different design. Check that the waistlines and side seams match: if they do not they will have to be adjusted as explained on the following pages. But do not be deterred, for the process is relatively easy.

To combine a bodice and skirt of different sizes. If your measurements indicate that you are one size above the waistline, and another below, you can easily combine the two sizes. First decide whether you want to use the waist measurement of the bodice or the skirt. Then alter the pattern as explained below.

Pattern Alterations

Commercial patterns such as those described in Chapter 6 together with those of other manufacturers such as McCalls, Vogue and Butterick are made in accordance with certain standards of body measurements set up by the Measurements Standards Committee of the entire pattern industry. But there are always some figures that do not conform to these measurements in every detail. It saves try-on and fitting time if any necessary adjustments are made in the pattern before it is placed on the fabric for cutting. And some adjustments, such as enlarging or lengthening, cannot be made after the fabric is cut. If you have compared your measurements with the pattern measurements you will know whether your pattern needs adjustment. If it does, follow the directions given on this and succeeding pages. One important point: do be careful when altering a pattern to ensure that all grain lines are kept as marked on the original pattern, or are straightened after altering.

If you are a beginner select a simple pattern with few, easily constructed seams, avoiding complicated or intricately matching pieces, and adjust your pattern as necessary. When you have made these alterations and noted any further fitting adjustments needed whilst making, you can use it as a basic block, keeping it for future reference and re-using it for your own design adaptations.

To Increase the waist and hip size, without altering the bust size, first slash through the back and front skirt patterns, as shown on the right, from waist to hem, positioning the slash $2\frac{1}{2}''$ away from the side seam. Open the pattern to the required amount – i.e. if your waist is $2''$ larger than that stated for the pattern size open the pattern $\frac{1}{2}''$ (that is one quarter of the difference), if only $1''$ larger then open out $\frac{1}{4}''$ – on both front and back sections and pin and then stick a section of paper behind the slash.

To increase the waist size of the bodice section, slash through as shown on the right from waist to lower armhole, opening out the pattern to correspond with the skirt. Pin and then stick a section of paper as required, taking care not to alter the size and shape of the armhole.

To Decrease the waist and hip size, without altering the bust size, first slash through the back and front bodice patterns as explained above but instead of inserting a strip of paper behind each slash simply lap the two waist edges over each other as much as needed – i.e. $\frac{1}{2}''$ for a $2''$ reduction or $\frac{1}{4}''$ for a $1''$ reduction – and first pin and

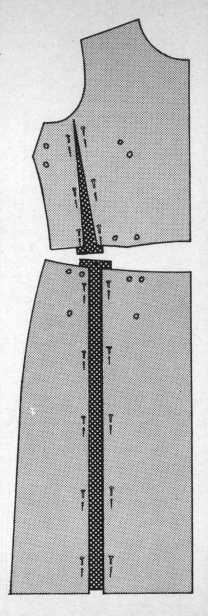

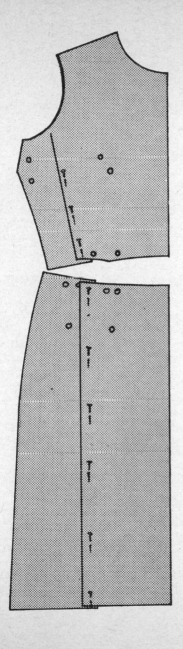

then stick the overlap together as shown on the left. Next slash through the back and front skirt patterns, from waist to hem, positioning the slash $2\frac{1}{2}''$ away from the side seam. Lap the pattern sections over each other as much as needed on both front and back skirt sections and proceed as for the bodice.

To Shorten the bodice pattern length if you have a shorter back-neck-to-waist measurement than that stated on the pattern envelope simply measure up from the printed shortening line the exact amount to be shortened. Draw a straight line across the pattern and then fold to bring these lines together. If you want to shorten the skirt length, mark and fold in the same way.

To Lengthen the bodice pattern first cut the pattern apart on the printed lengthening line. Place a strip of paper under the two pieces with a gap between for the extra length required and first pin and then stick the pieces together, as in diagram 2, page 120. Always remember to keep the grain lines straight. To lengthen the skirt cut and join together in the same way.

Sleeve Lengths can be adjusted in the same way, as shown by diagram 3 overleaf. Do avoid any changes at crown or cuff ends of the sleeve pattern unless you follow the instructions given below for changes in sleeve width.

Sleeve Widths. If you need to adjust widths avoid altering the crown size or the sleeve will not

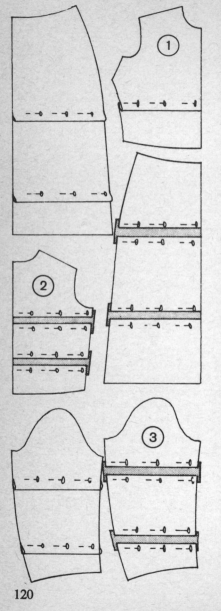

fit into the armhole correctly. Slash as shown in diagram 6 but take care to finish the cuts $\frac{1}{4}''$ below the edge of the top of the sleeve. The pattern can be lapped or opened out as required, pinning or sticking to hold secure.

Bust Adjustments. Usually it is wise to avoid bustline alterations by selecting your paper pattern according to your bust size. If, however, you have to adjust the bodice width during fitting it is important to retain the armhole, neck and shoulder shape.

If you have reduced your bust size, cut the paper pattern along the bottom line of the underarm bust dart to bust point, and then diagonally to point of shoulder, moving this section to lap over bodice pattern, as in diagram 4, and pin in place, tapering side seam from dart to waist.

If your bust is larger, prepare as above but move the pattern outwards, securely pinning a piece of paper behind the gaps and adding a sliver down the side as shown in diagram 5. Bust dart positions can also be changed as illustrated by the two diagrams 7 and explained on page 199.

Pattern Adapting

Having explained how to alter your pattern so that it is the correct size and shape, it follows that it can also be altered to reflect changes in style, with different design features and seam placements. To show how this is done we have written a section on pattern adapting and design at the end of Chapter 7, which deals with Fashion Detailing – pockets, collars, seam lines, trimmings, decorative fastenings, surface decoration, etc. If you are a beginner it is best to limit your experiments to small changes such as varying pocket shapes, but if you are an experienced dressmaker you can have lots of fun, free from the limitations of commercially-produced paper patterns.

Cutting Out

1. Before pinning on your paper pattern pieces inspect your length of fabric for any faults. If you notice a little coloured tag or knotted string on the selvedge, inspect across the grain for a fault in the weave so that you can avoid this when cutting out, also noting any printing smudges or marks so that these can also be avoided.

2. If the selvedge is holding in the fabric causing it to pucker along the edge, then simply snip approximately every 2″ (see page 134).

3. Generally speaking most fabric is at its best if cut on the true grain. To straighten fabric ends simply cut along one thread if the weave is bold enough to show, or if not, clip the selvedge and pull a single thread which will pucker along its length. Cut along this for 6″ or 8″ before pulling a little more, again cutting for 6″ to 8″, repeating right across the fabric at both ends.

4. If after cutting both ends on the grain the fabric does not look square pull it diagonally across the

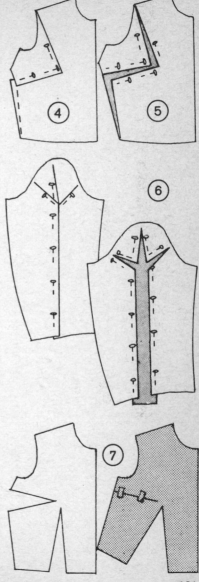

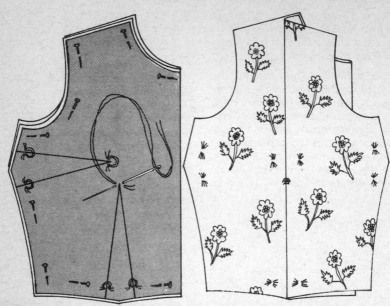

bias grain, pulling and moving along the entire length before pressing to set the fabric. Finally fold the fabric right side inside – in half widthwise so that selvedges are together and stripes or design match, and pin along both the fold and selvedge checking that ends are square and matching.

5. Lay out as instructed on the pattern envelope, cutting out each piece on the indicated pattern lines, avoiding overcuts. See that all the major seams match exactly and that any predominant pattern is centralized. Also make sure that each piece is cut with the pattern or pile facing the way required.

6. After cutting and before marking, spend a little time testing an off-cut of fabric, so that when you

start to make up the dress you know how the fabric will handle.

Marking Up

There are several methods used for marking the essential fitting and detail positions on to your garment after cutting out. Three of the easier methods are explained below.

Spot Tacking. This is a double stitch made in double tacking cotton through double material with a loop left so that when the fabric is pulled apart the threads can be snipped between the layers leaving an identical tufted marking on each piece, as shown on page 11.

Marking Carbon. This is a special dressmakers' marking paper which has a thin layer of chalk on the surface. The chalked side is placed against the fabric and essential details such as darts and corners are trace-wheeled on.

Tailor's Chalk. This method is generally used in tailoring or for difficult forms of dressmaking. You will require a piece of white or very pale tailor's chalk. After cutting out, cut away all the paper-pattern turnings including darts, and accurately chalk seam lines, darts, design details, etc.

Unit Dressmaking

The simplest method of dressmaking which we are going to explain in the following pages has become known as the Unit System. This is a slightly unorthodox method, much frowned upon by the traditional sewing schools, but it is easily understood and achieves quick results.

The system is to divide the garment into easy-to-handle units – such as the bodice, sleeves, skirt, etc. – and to make these in a set sequence. Once you know the method and the sequence you always know which unit of your garment to make first and which sections follow easily.

Bodice Making

Mark each piece as directed on your pattern, taking extra care when marking corners, darts, notches, etc., to be absolutely accurate. Marking should be made either with spot tacks, or using a special

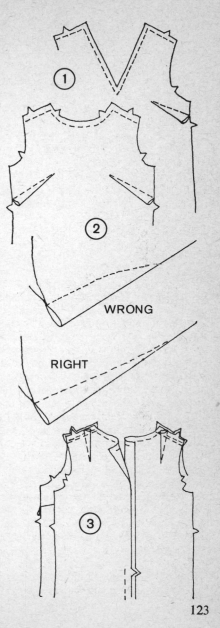

WRONG

RIGHT

marking carbon and wheel which can be bought at most sewing counters, as explained on the previous pages.

1. Stay-stitch shoulder and necklines, on both back and front sections, taking care not to stretch the edges while stitching. Stay-stitch, which is used to prevent stretching, should be made $\frac{1}{8}''$ from the seam line within the seam turning allowance, using 12 to 14 stitches to the inch and a slightly tight tension on a single thickness of fabric. Check each piece of fabric against the paper pattern for size and shape, and adjust by easing or releasing machining as necessary.

2. Machine bust and back neck darts taking care to avoid a sharp curve, which causes a bubble to form at the end of the dart – rather taper very slightly towards the end so that the last few stitches lie on the folded edge giving a flat dart when pressed.

3. If required, join centre back seam above and below zip opening, press open and then join shoulder seams matching seam ends and notches exactly.

4. Tack side seams together as for machining and tack to skirt. Fit both for width and length, noting fitting points given earlier on in this chapter. Mark the new fitting lines on the left and right sides of the dress and also on to the paper pattern for future reference.

Neck Facing

1. Machine-tack interfacing – this

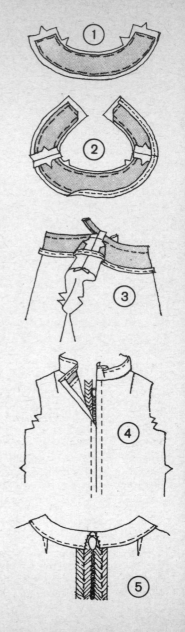

is a stiffening material, usually Vilene or natural linen canvas – to the wrong side of the neck facing pieces and trim interfacing close to stitching.

2. Join shoulder seams of facings and turn under and machine $\frac{1}{4}''$ on long facing edge.

3. Place right side of facing against right side of dress and pin facing to neck edge, matching centres, seams and balance marks. Tack and then machine. Trim seams and clip curves. Press the facing upwards with seam turnings towards facing.

4. Tack together centre back seam along zip opening and press seam open. Pin the closed zip fastener under tacked centre seam placing the stop at lower end of opening, and tack. Machine zip in, using special zipper foot as explained on page 70.

5. Turn neck facing to inside of dress, turning the centre back edges diagonally so as to miss covering the zip, and slip-stitch to zip tape, darts and shoulder seam, tacking $\frac{1}{4}''$ from neck edge to hold flat.

Armhole Facing

Armhole facings are applied in a similar way to the neck facings which have been explained above. See also Chapter 3 on basic sewing, page 63.

Pocket Unit

Patch pockets are the easiest type of pocket unit to make so we will keep to this type here. If you want to make a letter box,

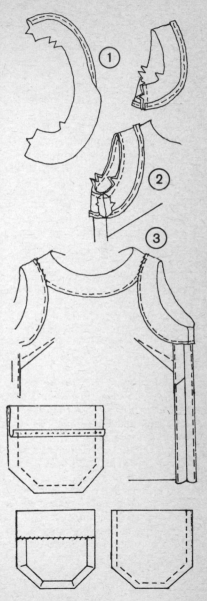

flap, welt or seam pocket, see pages 194–6. For a patch pocket first cut a paper pattern the exact size and shape required and then cut a section of fabric 2″ deeper and 1″ wider – that is with a 1½″ top allowance and a ½″ side and bottom turning.

1. Stitch under ¼″ on upper edge of patch and then turn top allowance to the outside and stitch along the seam line on all raw edges.

2. Turn top right side out and press under the raw edges on the sides and bottom along the stitching line. Slip-stitch or machine across top facing allowance to hold flat.

3. Tack patch pocket into position and machine top-stitch ⅛″ from sides and bottom edges, stitching a little diamond or square shape at the top corners for strength. Alternatively work a bar or use a decorative metal rivet, etc.

Collar Unit

1. Machine-tack interfacing to wrong side of top collar and trim interfacing level with fabric edges.

2. With right sides of under and top collar together, stitch around three sides but leave neck edge open. Trim seam and corners to ⅛″, interfacing to nothing.

3. Clip curve and turn through, rolling turnings flat, and gently press.

4. Tack completed collar to right side of bodice, and then tack bodice facings into position, having first joined the back facing section on to the front facings.

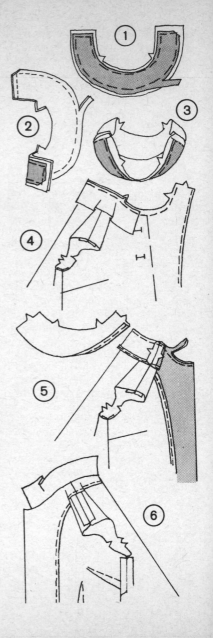

126

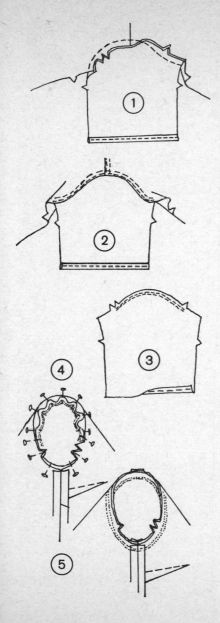

5. Machine stitch around neck edge through all thicknesses, trimming collar turning to $\frac{1}{4}''$ and facing to $\frac{1}{8}''$.

6. Turn collar and facings through to right side and then tack around the neck edge so that the turnings fall correctly. Press flat and finally stitch facings into position on shoulder seam and around the back neck (diagram 6).

Sleeve Unit

A normal shirt-type sleeve is usually joined to the bodice prior to seaming the side or underarm seams.

1. With wrong sides together and notches and balances opposite each other start pinning sleeves in. Match all balance and notch marks and tack into position. Stitch, then press seam towards sleeve, shrinking away any unwanted fullness.

2. Trim sleeve turning to $\frac{1}{4}''$, armhole to $\frac{1}{2}''$. Fold under the $\frac{1}{2}''$ armhole turning covering the $\frac{1}{4}''$ sleeve turning, tacking and completing flat fell seam. Join side seam of bodice and sleeve, pressing and neatening these seams. Neaten sleeve hem by turning under and stitching flat, or attach cuff as explained overleaf.

3. For a set-in sleeve – this is a sleeve with a curved top – first set your machine for about 10 stitches to the inch and make a row of gathering stitches on the seam line around the sleeve crown between the notches, and then another $\frac{1}{8}''$ to $\frac{1}{4}''$ above the first within the seam allowance.

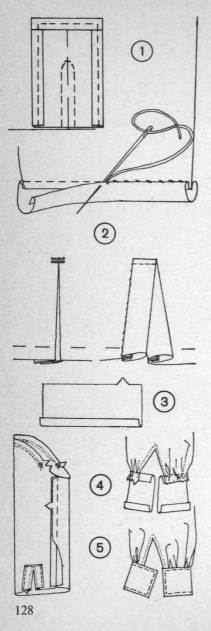

4. Join underarm seam and press open. Neaten sleeve hem by turning lower edge to inside and stitching, or attach cuff as shown in diagrams 3–5 below. With sleeve right side out and bodice wrong side out, put the sleeve into the armhole with the right sides together. Pin sleeves into position matching notches and guide marks.

5. Pull up machine gathering stitches, a little from each end until the sleeve just fits the armhole. Adjust the ease evenly, then machine sleeves into armhole, stitching a second time $\frac{1}{8}''$ away from the first row within the seam allowance. Trim close to second line.

6. Finish armhole seams by overcasting, blanket-stitch, binding in crossway fabric or with machine zig-zag stitch or overlocking.

Cuff Unit

Before making the cuff, make a simple sleeve opening following instructions 1 or 2 below or as directed in your pattern.

1. To make a faced opening first cut a fabric strip $2\frac{1}{2}''$ by $4\frac{1}{2}''$, turning in $\frac{1}{4}''$ on both long sides and across top. With right sides together, and centre line of facing strip matching sleeve opening marks, machine $\frac{1}{4}''$ each side, and in the last $\frac{1}{2}''$ graduate into a blunt point. Next cut from bottom to point through centre of sleeve and facing, turning the facing through, tacking flat and top-stitching, as explained on page 65.

2. If you prefer a continuous opening first mark and then cut an

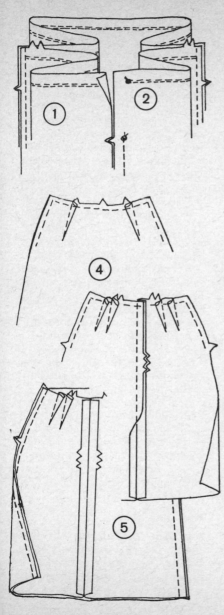

opening of the required length on the straight grain of the fabric. Cut a crossways strip double that length by 2″ wide. Next machine stitch the opening raw edge to fabric strip, with right sides together. Fold over other edge of strip and hand-stitch down, encasing all turnings. Finally stitch across top of inside fold to give strength and work a small bar across point on the right side of the fabric. (See page 66.)

3. Cut cuff section as shown in your paper pattern and then crease under the seam allowance on the long unnotched edge of cuff.

4. Pleat or gather the sleeve to size and then pin, tack, and stitch the right side of the band to the wrong side of the sleeve, checking that notches match. Next fold the wristband in half widthwise, with right sides together, machining the ends and then trimming to $\frac{1}{8}$″.

5. Turn through and tack the pressed seam allowance of band over the wrist seam. Top-stitch around the entire band $\frac{1}{8}$″ from edge.

Skirt Unit

The simplest skirt unit to make is one with a gathered waistline without darts.

1. Join centre back seam, but leave opening as indicated on paper pattern. Join side seams, then press all seams open and neaten as required.

2. On waistline make two rows of machine-gathered stitches – approximately 8 to 10 stitches to the

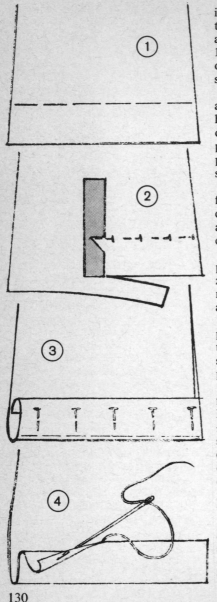

inch with a slightly loosened top tension – one on the seam line and another $\frac{1}{8}''$ to $\frac{1}{4}''$ above. Gather to 1″ larger than waist size and tack on a narrow tape to prevent stretching or sagging.

3. Fit skirt and mark a level hem as explained opposite. Turn up hem and either slip-stitch or decoratively machine stitch into place. Stitch in zip fastener, see page 70, and attach waistband as shown opposite.

4. A darted skirt is made as follows: Stay-stitch waistline and curve of hips for 9″ down. Make back and front darts and press towards centre, or snip and press open.

5. Join centre back seam and press open. Join side seams, leaving zip opening on left side above notches. Tack opening together and press side seams open.

6. Insert zipper, as explained on page 70, and then tack on a narrow tape around the waist to prevent stretching, fitting as explained opposite.

7. Turn up hem and tack $\frac{1}{4}''$ from fold. Trim hem evenly to $2\frac{1}{2}''$. Bind hem by stitching bias binding $\frac{1}{4}''$ over raw edge, and then slip-stitching. Alternatively use overcasting or blanket stitch, or any other method which gives a neat durable finish.

Hem Levelling

1. With a yard-stick and pins and the help of a friend mark a line around the hem of your skirt – when having a second fitting as explained on page 139 – the

length required. Remove the skirt and lay it flat on the table folded down the centre front and back, with side seams matching. Check to see if the pins are in an even curve, with the left matching those on the right. If there is a lot of difference, try the skirt on again to check the corrections.

2. Use a notched card hem-guide – a strip of stiffish card 6″ by 2″ with a notch the hem distance required from one end, generally about 2″. Cut away any surplus hem allowance and neaten with a narrow machined hem, turning in approximately $\frac{1}{4}$″.

3. Turn the hem up into position and pin flat. If the hem is flared or gathered either make small tucks or gatherings to reduce the fullness or use the false or taped hemming methods explained on page 62–3.

4. For a normal hem slip-stitch into position, making the stitches $\frac{1}{2}$″ long and taking only 2 or 3 threads on the skirt at each stitch. Remove all pins and tacking threads before pressing.

Waistline

1. If the skirt is to be attached to a dress bodice all you need do is machine stitch the waistlines together and neaten by oversewing or binding with a narrow tape.

2. If you are making a separate skirt cut the waistband fabric as directed on your paper pattern. Next press under the turning allowance on the long unnotched edge and trim to $\frac{3}{8}$″.

3. Pin and then tack right side

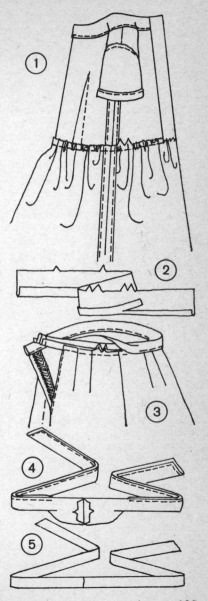

of skirt band to wrong side of skirt, matching centres and side marks. Stitch, then trim band turning to ¼″, skirt to ½″, and press seam band upwards.

4. Fold band with right sides together and stitch ends, trimming to ¼″. Turn band and tack over waist machining. Top-stitch ⅛″ from fold if required. Fasten lap end with two large hooks and bars.

If your skirt is lined, turn to page 138 for lining instructions.

Belt Unit

1. For a simple fabric tie-belt just join the belt sections together and press the seam open. Next fold in half widthways with right sides together and machine stitch along the turning allowance, leaving a 3″/4″ opening for turning the belt through.

2. Trim seam allowances to ¼″ and clip corners close to stitching. Turn belt through the opening before slip-stitching the opening edges together.

Tailoring

On the following pages we are going to explain some of the sewing techniques used in tailoring, such as pad-stitching, interlining, collar making and general methods of construction. Tailoring differs from dressmaking in that more work is put into interlining, pad-stitching and pressing.

Tailor's Pressing

This is one of the most important methods used in tailoring – it cannot be emphasized too strongly how much depends on good pressing and the art of stretching and shrinking fabric to get a tailored shape. Chapter 2, pages 40–44, covers most of the general information regarding ironing and pressing but a few of the more important methods are listed again.

Always test the heat of your iron before pressing a garment, experimenting on a cutting of the actual material so that the correct heat can be assessed. Certain fabrics scorch, harden, shrink, shrivel or even melt if the iron is too hot.

Always press on the wrong side of the fabric during making up, to avoid shining or marking the surface. If you do press on the right side when giving a final press, cover the fabric with a dryish cloth to avoid water marks.

Always press at each stage during construction as well as on completion of a major section, e.g. darts must be pressed before the side seams are joined, side seams before the hem is completed.

Always use a tailor's shape when pressing darts, shaped seams or sleeves, and always use the other aids described on pages 40–44 to prevent hem ridges, seam marks, puckering and shine, etc.

Tailored Darts

First pin the dart edges together and then tack from the point towards the edge before attempting to stitch. Always machine from the point, putting the needle down into the exact position on the folded material and then machine stitching in a smooth unbroken line to the edge. Avoid making an inward curve which causes a bubble to form at the point of the dart. Instead start the stitching so that the first few stitches lie along the folded edge thus giving a flat dart when pressed. Always tie off the threads at the point of the dart and run-stitch them along the fold to lose the ends. Finally cut the darts open to within $\frac{1}{2}''-\frac{1}{4}''$ from the ends and press the edges open. If the fabric frays easily cut only to within $\frac{3}{4}''-1''$ to avoid the formation of a hole.

Tailored Seams

Always pin seams together before tacking them and always tack seams together before machine stitching.

Always match all balance marks, dots and notches and always check that the various fabric sections being joined are facing the correct way.

Always press tailored seams open using a slightly damp cloth, and always trim the turning allowance evenly.

Always notch curved seams at regular intervals as illustrated in the diagram on page 134, and always clip away the turning ends to help minimize edge bulk.

Tailor's Interlining

Interlining is another of the very important methods used in tailor-ing and consists of the introduction of a section of tailor's canvas, Vilene, Stayflex or other specially prepared fabric, between the outside fabric of a garment and the inside facing. Its purpose is to stiffen the fabric, to add extra body and to give the garment shape. In tailoring it is essential to master the art of interlining if your coats and suits are to look professional.

The choice of interlining is important, so always spend a little time experimenting with off-cuts to make sure that your choice is not too stiff for a soft fabric, or too soft for a firm one. The types of interlining to choose from are:

Tailor's Canvas. This is the traditional interlining used in both men's and women's tailoring. Tailor's canvas can be bought in a variety of thicknesses and finishes: heavyweight with a hair weave for men's coats; medium hair for men's jackets and women's coats, medium linen for jacket fronts, stiff canvas for collars, soft canvas for cuffs, etc. We prefer to use tailor's canvas for our work, and this is the interlining we describe in the tailoring section.

Vilene. This is a non-woven synthetic fabric which comes in several weights depending on the fabric to be used. It is cheaper than tailor's canvas, but we feel that it lacks adaptability.

Stayflex. This is an iron-on interlining available in several weights. Its advantage is that provided the iron-on directions are followed it can reduce the amount of time taken on interlining. Unfortunately it tends to over-stiffen most normal tailoring fabrics, giving what we feel is the appearance of a cardboard-like finish.

Interlining Fronts. Use a medium-weight tailor's canvas.

1. Straighten the grain and shrink the canvas interlining thoroughly before cutting, and cut either with a matching or cross grain to that of the garment fabric as detailed in the paper-pattern instruction sheet.

2. Stay-stitch the garment neck edge, shoulders and armholes, and make front darts as shown on page 135. Cut and tack in the front canvas as shown on the right. To do this correctly, first cut the canvas interlining as detailed on the paper pattern and then trim the front corner as shown opposite. Next pin the canvas to the wrong side of the front, matching centres, neckline, shoulders and armhole edges. Stitch canvas to the material around the neck edge, shoulder and armhold seam lines, and $\frac{1}{4}''$ from outer front edge, trimming the canvas close to the stitching.

The extra canvas on the front edge is used to stop the fronts from stretching. Now tack-stitch the centre front line and buttonhole positions through the canvas interlining and garment and proceed to make as detailed on page 164.

Interlining Backs. Prepare the back unit as for the front, stay-stitching the neck, armhole and shoulder edges and making the back darts,

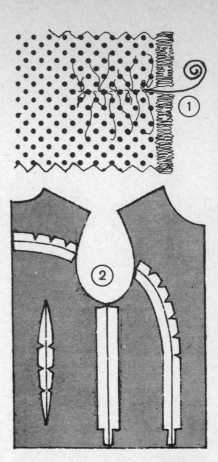

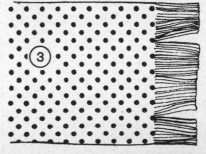

yoke seams, etc. Next cut the back canvas as shown on your paper pattern – usually a curved section 3″ to 4″ wide – and stitch into position on the seam lines. Trim canvas close to the machine lines and then join the shoulder seam, or prepare for a fitting as on page 139.

Interlining Sleeves. Cut a 3″ wide crossway strip of medium-weight canvas for attaching to the hem of sleeve. (See diagram 4 on page 137). Tack into position along the fitting lines and then catch-stitch to hold the canvas permanently in place. Turn up hem and slip-stitch on to canvas.

Interlining Collars. A slightly stiffer canvas should be used for a tailored collar, cut on the cross grain and pad-stitched to the under collar. The pad stitches should be made diagonally as in diagram 1, page 136, easing on a fraction of canvas with each stitch by slightly curving the collar with your left thumb and forefinger, to impart a natural roll. Work the stitches in rows backwards and forwards about $\frac{3}{8}$″ apart until the entire under-collar and canvas are pad-stitched together. Pad-stitch the lapels in a similar manner.

When the collar and lapels are completely padded, press them flat and then trim away any surplus canvas from the neck and outer edges.

An alternative method of hand padding is to use lines of machine stitches but the effect is not so good as this method does not give a natural roll to the collar.

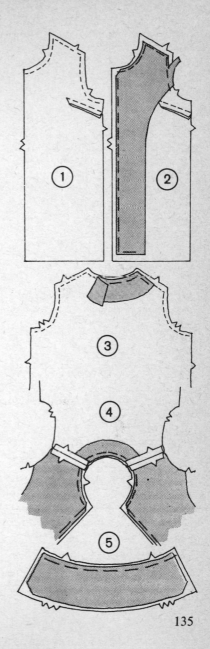

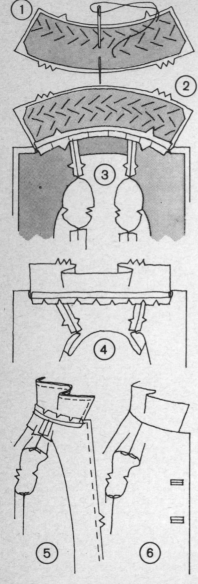

Interlining Extras. Strips of crossway canvas can also be used around the hems of jackets and coats, along the top edges of pockets, around armholes, inside belts or wherever a special tailored finish is required.

Collar Making

First pad-stitch a crossway cut strip of canvas to the under-collar as explained previously, trimming away any unwanted turnings and pressing flat. Now stitch the under-collar and garment neck edges together after joining the shoulder seams as shown in diagram 3. Press this seam open. Join and press the facing sections and top collar.

With right sides together, pin and then tack the facing and top collar unit to the body section and under-collar, matching the centre backs, fronts, seams and notches, easing the top collar on slightly to prevent drag and to allow for a natural roll.

Stitch, then finish seam by trimming facing to $\frac{1}{4}''$ and body section to $\frac{3}{8}''$, clipping close to the corners.

Turn facing and top collar to outside, rolling the seam line between finger and thumb to flatten them out neatly. Tack outside edges so that the seams roll to the underside and then press gently.

Set-in Sleeves

First make the sleeve unit: Tack the canvas interfacing on to the wrong side of the sleeve hem 1″ above the lower edge. Next make the elbow darts and then join underarm seams and press open.

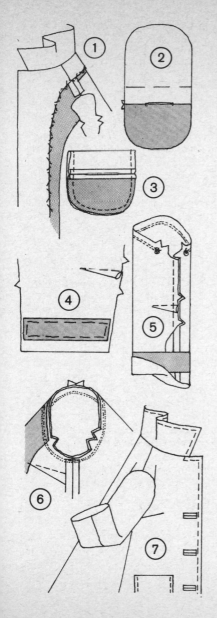

Turn up sleeve hem, tack and then catch-stitch to interfacing. Make two gathering lines around the crown of the sleeve from front to back notches as explained for a normal set-in sleeve on page 127, section 3, and pull the gathering to size. Shrink away the ease over a tailor's sleeve shaper or curved pressing board so that the sleeve is smooth and has no gathers – that is if a smooth finish is required – and then set in the sleeve as explained.

Raglan Sleeves

First make the darts on the body sections and then join the side seams together. Next join the top sleeve seam as shown in diagram 2 on page 138. If the sleeve has a shoulder dart instead of a seam then clip this dart to the point on the line indicated on the top of the sleeve, and with right sides together make top dart in sleeve. Press dart open.

With the right sides together stitch the under-sleeve seam together and then press open. Interface sleeve hem as for a normal set-in sleeve, turning cuff allowance to inside and catch-stitching into position.

To insert the raglan sleeve, place the sleeve and body sections with right sides together, matching small dots and underarm seam lines. Pin and then tack sleeve into armhole, easing sleeve to fit body section. Stitch, and then clip turnings at front and back balance notches pressing the seam open above these notches. Stitch a second line below these notches on the underarm seam $\frac{1}{8}''$ inside the first stitching. Trim underarm seam to $\frac{1}{4}''$. Proceed as for normal sleeve.

Making Lining

First cut out the garment lining as directed on the paper-pattern instruction sheet. Make darts, side seams, and shoulder seams in the same sequence as when making the garment, ironing all seams and darts as on the body section. Next iron under $\frac{3}{8}''$ on neck and front edges and $1''$ on hem and sleeve edges – or as detailed on the pattern instruction sheet. Finally attach the sleeve lining to the rest as shown in diagram 1 opposite.

Attaching Lining. With wrong sides together and the garment inside out, pin the lining to garment, matching centres, darts, notches and seams as in diagram 2 opposite. Tack around lining but on the sleeve push the lining up $\frac{1}{2}''$ to $1''$ before tacking to prevent pulling and drag when the garment is turned through.

Slip-stitch lining around neck edge and fronts, also on hem and sleeve ends, before turning through and removing all pins and tack-stitches.

Skirt Lining. Cut and mark skirt lining, stitching together as for a normal skirt, remembering to leave zip opening. Press seams open and fold up hem $1''$ shorter than the skirt. Trim hem allowance to $1''$. Fold over lining at waist and trim to $\frac{1}{4}''$. Drop lining inside skirt and pin waistlines together as in diagram 3 opposite. Slip-stitch into

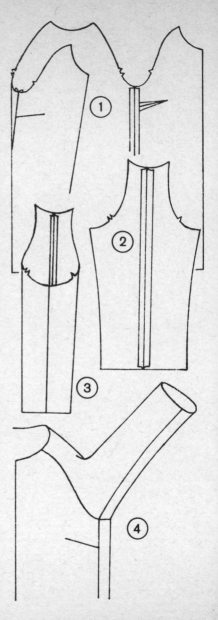

138

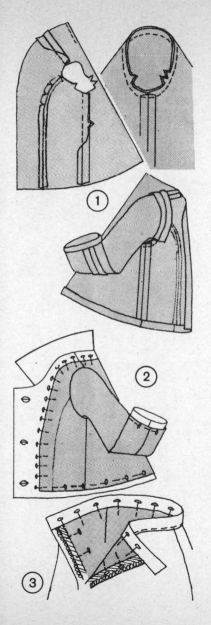

place, also stitching around zip opening $\frac{1}{4}''$ away from the teeth. Slip-stitch hem $\frac{1}{4}''$ inside hem fold or machine neaten and leave loose. Remove all pins and tack-stitches before pressing.

Fitting Notes

The fitting of a garment should only take place at certain stages in the construction. The quick little try-ons which never look right and are generally more depressing than helpful should be avoided.

If you are stock size, two fittings during the construction of a dress-made garment are usually sufficient, or three for a tailored garment. However, if you want to check the style or general fit of a garment before stitching it together then a tacked fitting can be very helpful. To do this, inside-tack your garment together ready for machine stitching and try it on both your dress stand and yourself for general fit and design look as detailed below.

If you decide to make your garment without a tacked fitting, the first fitting should take place just before joining the side and waist seams together but after sewing the darts, shoulders, collar and pockets, sleeve and centre skirt seams. The second fitting is best done just before final inside finishing, after all seams and details have been made. If the garment is being lined, as in most tailored garments, it is best to have the second fitting just prior to inserting the lining, with a final fitting after pressing and finishing just to check that all is well.

Design Fittings

This type of fitting, which is done before making up, can be very useful if you are uncertain about the fit or style of a particular garment. If you have designed it yourself, as explained later in this book, it will give you a better idea of the finished look if you experiment with mock paper buttons and alternative paper pocket shapes, etc. As this is the most interesting type of tacked fitting the rest of this section will explain what to do, and look for.

First, pin your paper pattern together on your dress stand, cutting various pocket and collar shapes, altering types of fastening, trying out different buttons or belts and generally arranging the design features within a known shape, preferably a commercial paper pattern shape that you have previously made successfully.

Having arranged your design and accurately marked the shape and placing of all the important features, cut and mark your fabric as you would normally but spend a little more time than usual, to ensure that you are accurate.

Next tack your dress together from the inside as if ready for machining, starting with the darts, then shoulder and side seams, before single-tacking over the edges of one collar piece, a cuff and pocket. Finally turn up the hem with two tack lines, one $\frac{1}{8}''$ from folded edge and the other $\frac{1}{4}''$ from raw hem edge and tack in one sleeve accurately.

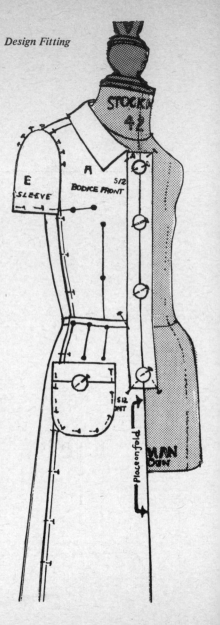

Now is the time to check the look of your design. Slip the dress on to the stand and look at the various design details and their relationship to each other, and examine the general proportions and the possibility of slight modifications before rushing into drastic changes or, what could be even worse, meek acceptance.

Fitting Sequence

Prepare your dress as explained on page 123 onwards – make front and back bodice and skirt sections, tacking these together at waist and side seams. Also tack on collar, pocket and sleeve units, etc. Alternatively tack the dress together before machining any sections as explained for a tacked fitting. Before you slip your new dress on for the first fitting, be certain that you have enough time for a good accurate fitting and preferably a willing friend to help, for nothing is worse than to be hurried. Generally twenty to thirty minutes is enough, but make sure you have prepared all your equipment and have it ready, for seams have the habit of coming undone if you have to go searching for your lost scissors or pins.

To achieve the nicest possible look, put on your best foundation garment and petticoat. Make up prettily, arrange your hair and wear shoes of the correct height. Now slip the dress on, pinning the fastening allowance accurately before looking at yourself in a full-length mirror.

Shoulder Fitting

At the beginning be a little cautious about the fit, avoid taking-in, letting-out or lifting at random for this will only lead to an uncomfortable, badly-fitting dress. Instead take a little time walking around, try sitting down or stretching – though do not try a movement for which the dress is not intended, such as a golf stroke in an evening dress, as this only shows misleading limitations.

Always fit in a set sequence, starting at the top, checking first the shoulder seam and neckline, gradually working down the dress via darts, side seam and waistline to the hem before altering the design details. The important points to look for on a well-fitting dress are that:

1. The fit of the dress is not such as to detract from the design, either by being too tight, or too loose.

2. The proportions are right, not making you look too short, too wide, or too old-fashioned.

3. The design details should accentuate the cut and fit, leading the eye around the garment and complementing your shape.

4. The seam lines should fall naturally into position, without constantly requiring attention.

5. Your ideas of fit, shape and proportion should change and progress as fashion changes so that your clothes look new and exciting and not like last year's left-overs.

Average Fitting. If your dress is a little tight across the bust, ask your friend to snip the tacking stitches on each side, re-pinning the seam

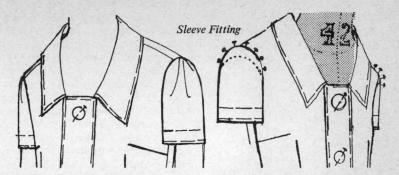

and checking that an equal amount has been let out on each piece. If the hipline is too loose pin a little in equally on both sides to keep the correct balance. However, do not fit your hip or waistline too tightly, thinking that the tighter the fit the slimmer the look, for this only causes unsightly wrinkles and creases, distorting the seam lines, and often makes you look fatter. Likewise, do not fit too loosely in the name of safety: this looks baggy and just as unattractive. After the fitting mark all the alterations as explained on page 145.

Sloping Shoulders. If your shoulders slope more than usual, causing diagonal creases to slant from neck to armhole, a small tuck of material will need to be pinned away along the seam of the shoulder line starting at shoulder point and tapering to nothing just before neck point as can be seen on the drawing opposite. Make sure you lift out creases but leave enough ease for general movement. Single-thread mark along this pin-line on both front and back pieces after the

fitting, and then re-mark the armhole using your paper pattern so that it is the correct shape and size. Adjust your paper pattern.

Square Shoulders. If your shoulders are squarer than normal causing drag lines from shoulder to bust, your shoulder tacking will need to be snipped at the armhole edge, allowing a little material to pass down equally back and front, tapering to nothing just before the neck point. Pin shoulder seam together again accurately checking that you have made a straight seam before single-thread-marking along edges to give the new seam line, noting important alterations.

Fuller Bust. If your bust is slightly larger than is allowed for in a stock paper pattern, and your dress drags across your bust causing crease lines to pull from the side seam (see diagram on page 141) your side tacking will need to be snipped at the armhole on both sides, allowing sufficient of the side seam turning to pass into the bodice, equally on all edges. Pin side seams together again, checking that you have a straight seam and not one that twists or curves, with sufficient extra over the bust, but tapering to nothing at waist. Re-mark the new side seam with single tacking after the fitting, alter your pattern and re-mark your armhole to the correct size.

Smaller Bust. If your dress is too large across the bust, pin in a small tuck starting from bust level on the armhole, taking in an equal amount both back and front on each side, tapering down to nothing at the waistline. Alter your paper pattern for future reference, re-shaping as explained opposite.

Waistline. If your waistline is either larger or smaller than that of your dress, make the necessary adjustments equally on all seams and darts, correcting your paper pattern for future reference.

Sleeves. These are generally the most difficult part of a garment to fit, so it is wise to restrict any alterations to the top or hem of the sleeve, leaving the underarm tacking untouched unless it drags badly. If in your first fitting your shoulder or side seams were altered, make sure that you adjusted the armhole so that it is the correct shape and size given on your paper pattern.

If at the second fitting the crown of your sleeve drags, causing crease lines to pull upwards in the centre of the sleeve, it means that a little more crown is needed. Snip arm-hole tacking at top of sleeve and allow a little of the sleeve turning to roll out, re-pinning and altering both your sleeves and your pattern.

If downward-curving crease lines appear on the sleeve it means that there is a little too much crown and possibly the top sleeve balance mark needs adjustment. Snip armhole tacking at top of sleeve, passing in a little of the crown until crease disappears. Pin along new sleeve edge on to armhole.

Skirts. When fitting a skirt it is important that the centre front and centre back should fall exactly straight down the centres, not running slightly to one side or twisting, so before trying on mark

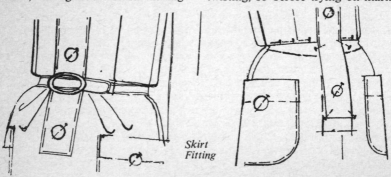

Skirt Fitting

centre lines with a simple tack line in a bright colour so that you can see if the skirt is hanging correctly.

First adjust the waistline to your size by pinning in or letting out equally on each piece, and a little on each dart if necessary. Next adjust the hip line in the same manner.

If after altering both the waist and hip lines your skirt kicks out in the front causing the side seams to swing forward, snip the front waist tacking joining the front section to bodice or waistband, and allow the centre to drop slightly. Re-pin the waist and single-tack-mark the corrections. Conversely, if the front drops causing crease-lines and a droopy hem, lift the front waist seam a little. Adjust the back of the skirt in the same way.

Marking Alterations

If after each fitting you mark along the new edges with pins on both sides of the seam, cross-pinning important balance marks, when you dismantle each piece you can easily tack mark in a different colour following the pin lines and marking the new balances, etc., before finally machining the pieces together.

Note all important alterations on to your pattern for future use. If after fitting several dresses you notice that the same alterations recur it is wise to adjust your paper pattern before cutting and marking your fabric in order to avoid fitting and altering unnecessarily.

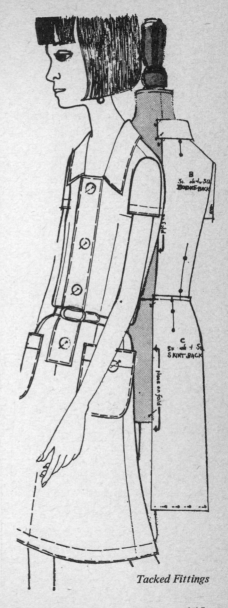

Tacked Fittings

145

6. Making Clothes

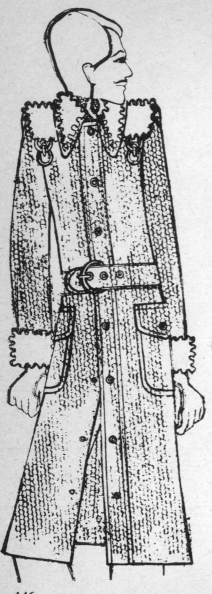

Now that you have most of the information needed for dressmaking, we feel the time has come for you to take the plunge and make your first garment, for it is then that dressmaking begins to be exciting and enjoyable.

If you are a beginner, try making several simple garments first before moving on to the more complicated tailored ones. Once you have made several garments, you can begin to make your own designs. To help you in this, and to stimulate even the most inexperienced dressmaker, we have grouped all those sewing techniques that fluctuate with fashion changes – collars, pockets, seam lines, surface decoration, trimmings, decorative fastenings, etc. – into a separate chapter called Fashion Detailing. Thus when one garment has been completed, another one using the same basic pattern but carrying many different visual ideas can be quickly made while the construction details are still fresh in your mind. If, however, you prefer to make something completely new, shop around before deciding, keeping an open mind on what you like and what is fashionable. Look at all sorts of clothes for hints on making and fashion detailing. Note down the newest shapes of collars in your scrapbook; see how hems are made in chiffon or on tweed; ask the salesgirls about the latest fabric colours and textures, and remember to keep a constant eye on current fashion magazines and newspaper articles. This will help you to keep alive to the excitement of changing fashion. For it is vital not only to wear nicely made beautifully fitting clothes in well chosen fabrics, but also that these clothes look as if they belong to today, and not as if they were yesterday's left-overs.

Garment Making

Because of their easily-understood instructions and because they can be made in the *Unit System* of dressmaking explained on page 123, we have chosen six garments from the basic range of 'Simplicity and Style' patterns which are available in many attractive designs. We have chosen a simple Blouse; classic Shirt; Skirt; Trousers; Dress and a Man's Coat because these cover most of the normal dressmaking and tailoring techniques. However, your choice is not limited to these garments as the actual making instructions would be the same for any other Style or Simplicity paper pattern, while Butterick, Vogue, McCalls, etc. are very similar.

A blouse or tunic-top made in printed cotton, gingham or cotton poplin is an ideal garment to start with. We have chosen a 'Style' pattern with an interesting collar and gathered sleeves which can be either short or long, which can be worn with the skirt described on pages 155–8 or over the trousers shown on pages 158–9. Before starting read, and always follow, the 'six-point plan' listed below:

1. Buy the right size of pattern.

Don't guess at your size, have a salesgirl or friend measure you and then insist on buying the right size of pattern. It is much easier to fit a dress or blouse if the pattern is as near your actual measurements as possible: it also saves many hours of remaking.

2. Get acquainted with your pattern. Spend a little time looking it over, reading the instruction sheet from beginning to end, becoming an expert on the garment before starting to cut out.

are given by professional dressmakers and it would be crazy to disregard their advice.

5. Pin before you tack, and tack before you machine, particularly on difficult seams and curves. It's nice to know when you are assembling a dress that one section won't turn out longer than the other, and it won't if you always pin the pieces together first, pinning both ends and working from these towards the middle, taking care to match all notches and dots.

3. Try your pattern on. Pin the pattern pieces together, pinning in the darts, etc. and then slip it on to your dress-stand or on to yourself as you would a dress. This will help you to see if it has the current length of bodice and skirt, etc. If the pattern needs altering it is far wiser to adjust now as directed on the pattern, as this will save so much time and trouble later.

4. Follow all directions carefully, marking all notches and dots, for it really is disastrous not to. Remember that the cutting layouts and the step-by-step instructions

6. If you are a beginner read Chapter 5 before starting. If you have some sewing experience then you will already know that it is wise to take your time. Always work at a brisk pace, but sewing against the clock means that either your dress or your nerves will suffer – usually both.

Cotton Blouse

Prepare and cut out your fabric. Mark each piece as directed on your pattern and instruction sheet, taking extra care at corners, darts, notches, etc., to be absolutely accurate. Marking should be made either with spot tacking as illustrated on page 122, with a marking carbon and wheel, or with tailor's chalk.

Unit 1. *Stay-stitching.* Stay-stitch shoulder and necklines, on both back and front sections, taking care not to stretch these edges whilst stitching. The stay-stitching should be made ⅛″ from the proposed seam line within the seam turning allowances, using 12 to 14 stitches to the inch and a slightly tight tension through a single thickness of fabric. Check each piece against the paper pattern and adjust by easing or releasing the machine stitching as necessary.

Unit 2. *Fronts.* Machine stitch the bust darts, taking care to avoid a pleat (see diagram 2 on page 123). Taper off the point of the dart, with the last few stitches lying on the folded edge so that you have a flat dart when pressed. Make sure that all the dots match and then press downwards.

2. Tack interfacing to the wrong side of the fronts, trimming evenly with the neck edge and catch-stitching to front fold-line. On front facing allowance turn under and stitch ¼″ seam on unnotched edge, snipping the curve so that it lies neatly. Also fold under and press ⅝″ on facing shoulder edge.

Unit 3. *Back.* Make back shoulder darts, remembering to taper the points very slightly with the last few stitches lying on the folded edge so that a bubble doesn't form at

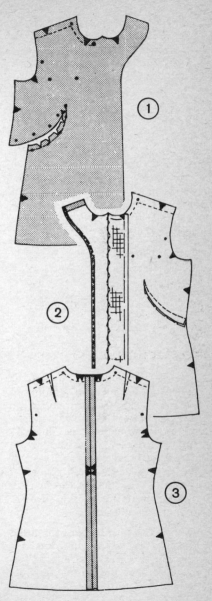

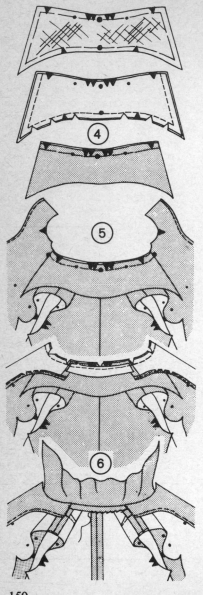

the end of the dart. Press darts towards centre back.

2. Stitch the centre back seam together taking care to match the notches accurately and take in the right amount of seam allowance.

3. Stitch the back and front sections together at shoulder seams, matching dots and notches. Press all the seams open.

Unit 4. *Pockets*, see diagram 10. With the right sides of the pocket fabric sections together, stitch around three sides leaving an opening on the fourth side to turn through. Trim seams and clip curves. Turn pocket through and press flat. Slip-stitch opening together. Alternatively use the method shown on page 125.

2. On outside of left front, pin pocket into position along marked line and top dots. Slip-stitch the sides and lower edges or surface machine into place, then top-stitch.

Unit 5. *Collar*. Tack the interfacing to the wrong side of top collar. With the right sides of the fabrics together stitch the facing to the top collar around the three outside edges, leaving the neck edge unstitched. Trim the interfacing close to the stitching and trim the fabrics to $\frac{1}{8}''$ or $\frac{1}{4}''$. Clip the curved edges at $\frac{1}{2}''$ to 1$''$ intervals and cut the corners to $\frac{1}{8}''$. Turn collar through, so that the right sides of fabric are outside and press before tacking the the raw edges together.

2. On the outside of the blouse, pin the collar to the neck edge, placing front edges to centre

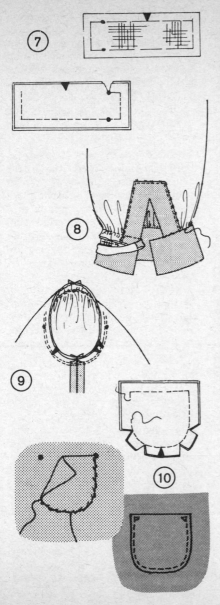

fronts, matching small dots and centre backs, easing collar on slightly to fit the neck line. Tack.

3. Turn front facings to outside along the fold line and tack to neck edge. With right sides together tack a bias strip or a 1″ wide facing of crossway cut fabric to back neck seam line, lapping over the facing $\frac{1}{2}$″ at each end. Stitch and then trim seam and clip curves.

4. Press bias and facing to inside, turning under the raw edges and slip-stitch into place, also stitching the facings to bias and shoulder seams, or alternatively top-stitch.

Unit 6. *Sleeves.* First make a simple faced opening on the bottom of the sleeve as explained on page 65 and then gather the lower edge of sleeve between the opening edges. Next tack interfacing to wrong side of cuff. With the right sides together stitch the facing to cuff around three sides, continuing up to small dot to form cuff lap. Clip to dot and trim interfacing close to stitching. Trim seam and clip corners.

2. Turn cuff through so that the right sides are outside and press. With the right sides together pin sleeve to one edge of cuff as shown in diagram 8, adjusting the gathers to fit. Tack and stitch into position.

3. Turn under $\frac{5}{8}$″ on raw edge of cuff and slip-stitch over the seam; or alternatively tack and top-stitch into position.

Unit 7. *Assembling.* Stitch back to front at side seams and press the seams open. Next insert the

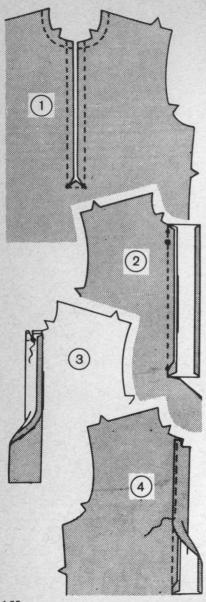

sleeves. With right sides together pin sleeves into armhole, with centre dot at shoulder seam, also matching underarm seams and remaining dots, adjusting sleeve gathers to fit armhole as explained on page 127.

Unit 8. *Finishing*. Open out front facing. Press under $\frac{1}{4}''$ on lowest edge and then press up hem, slip-stitching or top-stitching into place. Press facing to inside and slip-stitch to hem. Make worked or machine buttonholes as shown on pages 68–9 and attach buttons, etc. Finally oversew all inside raw edges or machine neaten if preferred.

Tailored Shirt

The unit system of dressmaking can also be used to make classic garments such as a man's tailored shirt. Choose a shirt which has an interesting combination of dressmaking techniques, such as front tab opening, shoulder yoke, classic collar, etc. The methods explained are also those used on a ladies' tailored blouse, smocks, cotton nighties, school shirts, etc.

Unit 1. *Front*. Stay-stitch the neckline and around front tab-line, taking care that the stitching is accurately placed. Cut down the centre front line between the stitching lines and snip diagonally into the corner marks as shown on the left, diagram 1.

2. Pin right side of front tab to wrong side of front and stitch from neck edge to point of snip with a $\frac{3}{4}''$ seam. Trim seam to $\frac{1}{4}''$ and then press seam towards band. Repeat on other side of front with second tab, as in diagram 2.

3. On outside edge of front tab, press under $\frac{3}{4}''$, then fold tab along centre line with right sides inside. Stitch neck edge to centre mark, trim seam and clip neck edge to centre as in diagram 3. Repeat on other side of front with second tab.

4. Turn bands to right sides and press top edges flat. Stitch pressed edges of band over seam edges and then tack remaining raw edges together. Top-stitch close to the folded edges, as in diagram 4.

5. On inside of shirt, lap right front band over left for a man's shirt, left over right for a lady's, matching edges. Tack bottom raw edges to shirt front, arranging the snipped point inside, and then stitch across the end through all the thicknesses. On outside top-stitch a crossed box as shown in diagram 5.

Unit 2. *Yoke.* Stay-stitch the back yoke neckline and then tack wrong side of back to right side of yoke facing, matching centres. Press under $\frac{5}{8}''$ on shoulder edges of yoke. With right sides together tack yoke to back and then stitch through all thicknesses. Trim seams.

2. Press yoke facing up. Tack wrong side of front shoulder seam to right side of yoke facing, matching balance marks. Stitch and then press seam towards yoke, trimming seam to $\frac{1}{4}''$. Pin the pressed edge of yoke over forward shoulder seams and then top-stitch $\frac{1}{8}''$ away

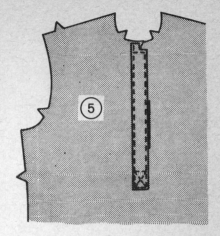

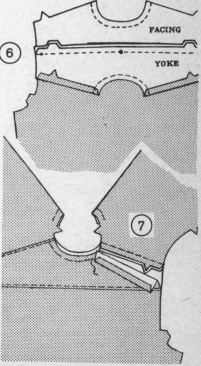

FACING

YOKE

from the edge of yoke through all thicknesses. Tack neck and armhole edges together.

Unit 3. *Collar.* Press under the $\frac{5}{8}''$ on notched edge of collar facing and then trim to $\frac{1}{4}''$. With right sides together, stitch the facing to collar around the outside three edges, leaving the notched neck edge open.

2. Clip shirt neck edge to stay-stitching. Pin collar to neck edge on outside of shirt, matching centres and balance marks. Stitch and then trim seam to $\frac{1}{4}''$, clipping curves every $\frac{1}{2}''$. Press seam towards collar.

3. On inside of collar slip-stitch pressed-under collar edge along back of seam, matching centres and balance marks. Finally top-stitch $\frac{1}{4}''$ from outer edges of collar and $\frac{1}{8}''$ in around the neck edge.

Unit 4. *Sleeves.* To make a faced opening on the bottom of the sleeve, cut a strip of fabric 2" wide and 4" long. Tack centre of strip over opening marks, right sides together, and then stitch as shown on page 65.

2. Stay-stitch along the seam lines of the body armhole edges and then clip around the curves. With right sides together, pin the sleeve to the armhole edges, matching the balance marks. Tack and then stitch, stitching a second line on the seam turnings $\frac{1}{8}''$ away from the first. Press seam towards shirt, trim and neaten.

3. Next stitch the centre underarm seam from cuff edge to armhole and then continue the stitching down

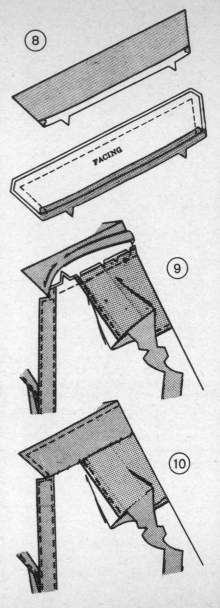

FACING

the side seam matching notches, seam lines and balance marks.

Cuffs. Gather the lower edge of sleeve by stitching along the seam line and then a second line $\frac{1}{4}''$ inside seam line between the gathering marks, using a longish machine stitch, tying thread ends together and drawing up. Alternatively, arrange cuff tucks or pleats.

2. Stitch the cuff and cuff facings together, right sides inside, around the three outside edges, leaving the notched edge open, continuing up to small dot to form cuff lap. Turn cuff and press. With right sides together, pin cuff to sleeve, matching the balance marks. Tack, easing sleeve gathering to fit. Stitch, trim and then press seam towards cuff; repeat for other cuff.

3. Slip-stitch cuff facing over seam and then top-stitch $\frac{1}{4}''$ away from all edges right round the cuff.

Unit 5. *Finishing.* Neaten side seams and stitch hem into position. Make pocket units if required, using the methods explained on pages 125 or 194. Finally make worked or machine-made buttonholes in left front; also make buttonholes in cuffs. Lap left front over right, matching centres; also lap front cuff over back, and then sew on buttons under buttonholes.

2. Finally give the shirt a press.

Wrap-over Skirt

Unit 1. *Skirt.* With right sides of fabric together and the back seam edge to edge, stitch centre back

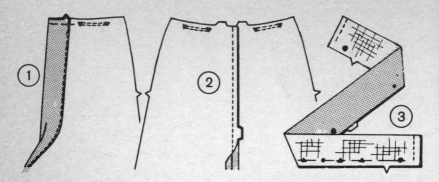

seam. Gather upper edge between triangles or machine stitch back darts. On the front sections gather upper edges between triangles and then stitch under $\frac{1}{4}''$ on front wrap edges. Omit wrap if skirt is to be plain.

2. Press front edge to inside along the fold line to form the wrap facings and tack along upper edge to hold in place.

3. Stitch back to front along the side seams.

Unit 2. *Waistband.* Tack the interfacing section to the wrong side of waistband fabric, catch-stitching to fold line. Fold waistband in half lengthwise, with the right sides together. Stitch ends to seam lines and then trim the interfacing close to the stitches. Turn waistband so that the right side is outside and press.

2. With the right sides together, pin skirt to the interlined edge of the waistband matching centres, triangles, side seams to dot, etc. Adjust gathers to fit, tack and then stitch.

3. Trim interfacing close to the stitching. Trim seam and then press up inside waistband. Finally turn under $\frac{5}{8}''$ on raw edge of

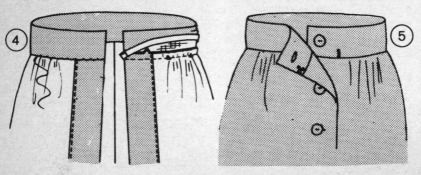

waistband and slip-stitch over the seam. If you are making a shaped waistband follow the instructions given on page 158, unit 3.

Unit 3. *Hem.* Here is the method for a plain hem. If you want a frill proceed as explained below. First fit the skirt for fit and length, marking the length accurately. Remove skirt and tack or press hem up into position, opening out front wrap facings. Mark depth of hem using a notched hem guide and then trim evenly. Stitch $\frac{1}{4}''$ from hem raw edge using a gathering stitch, pulling up the stitching so that the flared hem will lie flat. Press hem so that you shrink out the fullness. Stitch on some seam binding to neaten hem and then slip-stitch up into position. On the front-wrap corners press facing to inside and then slip-stitch to hem.

Frill. Stitch frill sections together and then stitch under $\frac{1}{4}''$ on front edges as shown on the right. Turn under $\frac{1}{4}''$ on raw hem edge and stitch, press up hem and slip-stitch. Gather upper edge of frill beginning and ending $2\frac{1}{4}''$ from front edges. Next open out the front facing. With right sides together, pin frill to skirt, matching balance marks. Adjust gathers to fit and then stitch and press with seam upwards. Finally press facing and front edges of frill to inside, slip-stitching to hem and frill seam.

Unit 4. *Finishing.* Make worked or machine buttonholes on right front and waistband. Lap right front over left, matching centres. Sew buttons

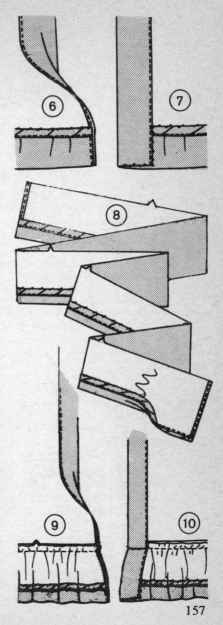

under buttonholes and then sew on hook and bar on waistband. Trim hem or frill with rick-rack braid on placement lines, arranging colours as you like or decorate in one of the many other ways described in Part Four.

Casual Trousers

Unit 1. *Legs*. Make front darts and press towards centre front seam. Make back darts and press towards centre back seam as for a skirt.

2. Stitch left back section to left front section at side seam with the right sides inside matching dots and notches exactly, then stitch inner leg seam.

3. Stitch right back section to right front section at side seam before stitching the inner leg seam.

Unit 2. *Joining*. With the right sides of the fabric together, place one trouser leg inside the other. Tack crotch seam, matching inner leg seams from upper edge at front to notch at the back. Stitch on seam line and then stitch again over the first stitching for extra strength.

2. Tack zip opening together along seam line and press open. Pin closed zipper under tacked opening with tab end 1″ below upper edge. Tack and then stitch into position using a zipper foot, as explained on page 70.

Unit 3. *Waistband*. First tack the waistband interfacing to the wrong side of the waistband section as for the shirt waistband explained previously.

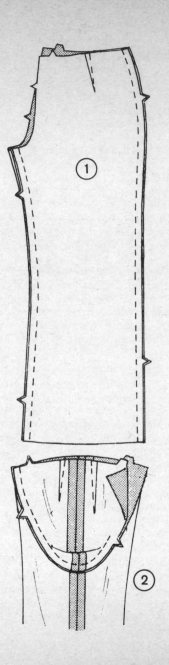

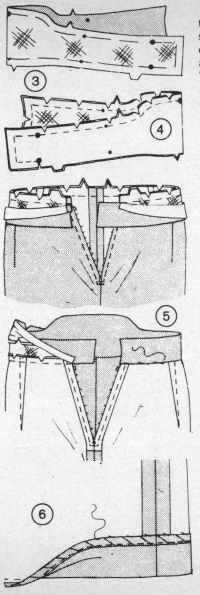

2. With right sides together pin top of trousers to the interfaced section of the waistband, matching centres, side seams to small dots and left edge of zipper to lap line. Tack, easing the trousers to fit, and then stitch. Trim interfacing close to stitching. Trim seam, clip curves, before pressing the seams towards the waistband.

3. Turn under $\frac{5}{8}''$ on the raw edge of waistband facing and slip-stitch over the seam, clipping around the curve as you go.

Unit 4. *Finishing.* Sew on hooks and bars at lap ends of waistband, or fasten with buttons if you prefer. Finish leg hems with seam binding after fitting for length in the same way as explained for a skirt hem.

Day Dress

Prepare, cut and stay-stitch the neck and shoulders as previously explained for the cotton blouse on page 149, unit 1.

Unit 1. *Darts.* Make back darts and press these towards the centre back seam. Make front darts and press these upwards.

2. Make bodice pockets as shown for a cotton blouse on page 150, unit 4. Pin pocket along pocket lines on outside of bodice front, placing upper edge between dots. Tack and then either slip-stitch or top-stitch into position.

3. Stitch back to front section at shoulder seams, matching dots and notches.

Unit 2. *Sleeves.* Mark sleeve opening

on bottom edge with tack stitches and then make opening as shown on pages 65–7. Press strip to inside and either catch-stitch or top-stitch to sleeve. Tack lower edge to sleeve.

2. Stitch underarm seam and press open. Gather top of sleeve between notches and also gather lower edge from 1″ each side of opening.

Cuffs. Tack interfacing on to the wrong side of cuff and catch-stitch to cuff fold-line as explained previously. Stitch, clip and turn cuff so that the right sides are outside and then press.

2. With right sides together, pin sleeve to interfaced edge of cuff, adjusting gathers to fit. Tack and then stitch. Trim interfacing close to stitching. Trim seam and press towards cuff.

3. Finally turn under $\frac{5}{8}$″ on raw edge of cuff and slip-stitch over the seam. If you prefer to use a two-piece cuff follow the instructions on page 151.

Unit 3. *Collar.* Tack interfacing to wrong side of top collar sections. With right sides together stitch the facing to the collar sections around three sides, leaving the neck edge open. Trim the interfacing close to the stitching. Trim seam and corners. Clip curves and turn collar sections right sides out. Press and then tack the raw neck edges together.

2. On outside of bodice, pin collar to neck edge, front edges meeting at centre front, matching small dots and centre backs.

Tack-stitch neck facing shoulder seams together and stitch under ¼″ on unnotched edge. With right sides together, tack facing to neck edge matching centres and seams. Stitch neck edge. Trim interfacing close to stitching, trim seam and clip curve. Press facing to inside.

Unit 4. *Bodice.* Stitch back bodice to front bodice at side seam.

casting, blanket-stitch or with a thin binding.

3. Also machine or hand neaten all the bodice seams.

Unit 5. *Skirt.* The directions given here are for a skirt with a front pleat. If you do not want a front pleat omit this and the next paragraph. First pin the front sections together, right sides inside, match-

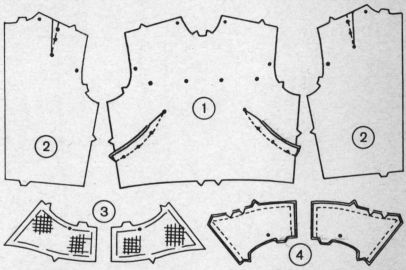

2. With right sides together pin sleeve into armhole, with the centre dot at shoulder seam, matching underarm seams and remaining dots. Pull up machine gathering stitches to fit. Tack, easing in fullness before stitching. Stitch a second time ⅛″ away from first stitching on seam turning allowance. Trim seam to ¼″ and press towards sleeve, shrinking out fullness. Neaten armhole by over-

ing dots. Tack along pleat line and stitch along stitching line. Press pleat extension open.

2. On the inside, with the right sides together, stitch the pleat underlay to skirt extension, matching dots and ending stitching 6″ above lower edge. Be careful not to stitch through skirt. Tack extension to upper edge, then topstitch ⅜″ each side of centre front from waistline to top of pleat.

3. Stitch centre back seam to notch and then stitch the back section to front section along both the side seams.

Unit 6. *Assembling.* With right sides together pin skirt to bodice, matching centre fronts, side seams and back edges. Tack, stitch and then press seam upwards.

slip-stitch. Slip-stitch facing to edge of zip tape and catch-stitch facing to shoulder seam. Attach hook and eye at top of zip.

Unit 7. *Hem.* Fit dress as explained in Chapter 5 and mark hem length. Press hem up along marking. Mark depth of hem using a notched hem guide and trim evenly. Stitch

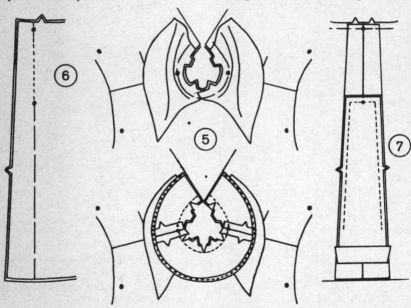

2. Open out facing at back neck edge. Press under $\frac{5}{8}''$ on centre back opening edges. Pin closed zipper under opening edges with tab end $\frac{3}{8}''$ below neck seam, having the opening edges meeting at centre of zipper. Tack. Using a zipper foot as explained on page 70 stitch zip into position. Turn under zip tape at upper end and

$\frac{1}{4}''$ from raw edge using a longish machine stitch. Pull up stitching so that the flared hem will lie flat. Press, shrinking out fullness. Stitch one edge of seam binding $\frac{1}{4}''$ over raw edge and then slip-stitch hem into position. Stitch remainder of pleat seams, stitching through turned-up hem and pleat. Re-press pleat.

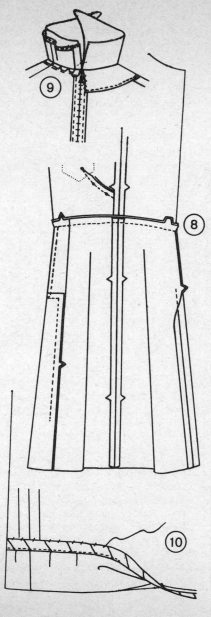

Unit 8. *Finishing.* Make worked or machine-made buttonholes on cuffs. Sew buttons to other end of cuff to correspond with buttonholes.

2. Turn lower edges of pleat seams under and overcast neatly. Also neaten waist seam with overcasting or blanket stitch.

3. Make belt as explained on page 132 and then finally add an original decorative touch such as a ribbon bow sewn to centre front neck edge, or turn to Chapter 7 for other ideas.

Tailoring

Once more we want to stress that we believe that the easiest way to make clothes is the unit method of construction. This is slightly unorthodox but it is easy to follow and helps achieve quick and good results. The unit system divides the garment into easy-to-handle units such as collar and facings, fronts, back or sleeves, and makes these in a set sequence. Once you know the sequence you always know which unit to make first and which sections follow easily.

Tailoring Patterns

Can be bought in a wide variety of shapes and sizes at most leading stores and sewing shops. There is always a wide range of designs to choose from so spend a little time browsing through the various pattern catalogues and then look around the fabric counters and find a suitable material before

163

making a decision. If you are a beginner select a simple tailored pattern with few and easy construction lines, avoiding any complicated shapes or intricately matching pieces, though this doesn't mean you can't have an interesting combination of tailored details or unusual seam lines. If you have already made several successful tailored garments turn to chapter 7 to find out how to adapt or design a garment of your own.

methods explained from page 132 onwards. If you are a beginner try making the simpler garments described earlier in this chapter.

Fitting Sequence

The fitting of a tailored garment should only take place at certain stages in the construction. As explained on pages 139 to 145, three fittings are usually sufficient if you are standard size. The first should be done just before joining

Unit Tailoring

To illustrate the unit method of tailoring we have taken a man's coat, because it has an interesting combination of tailored design details such as a shaped collar, back yoke and vent, epaulettes, bold pockets, belt and carriers, tab fastening, as well as the normal constructional points such as interfacings and lining, etc. If you decide to make a simpler design, just omit the various unit paragraphs which do not apply.

Before starting, however, you should learn the basic tailoring

the side and waist seams, but after sewing in the interlinings, joining the shoulder seams and tacking in the shoulder pads. The collar, pockets and design details should be tacked into position but not completed.

The second fitting is best done just before the final inside finishing, but after all seams and details have been completed. If the garment is being lined, have the second fitting just prior to lining with a third fitting after lining and the final press, just to check that all is well. If after fitting several tailored gar-

164

ments you notice that the same alterations recur, adjust your paper pattern before cutting and marking-up in order to avoid unnecessary fittings and alterations.

Coat Making

Unit 1. *Prepare* and cut out your fabric, taking care to cut each piece of fabric on the exact grain line required and spot-tack-marking accurately. Next stay-stitch the curved neck edges, shoulders and armholes to prevent stretching on both the front and back body sections using a slightly tight medium-spaced machine stitch.

Darts. If your garment has back or front darting, stitch these as indicated on the paper pattern, snipping the dart open to within $\frac{1}{4}$" of the points and press the turnings open over a shaped tailoring pad as explained on page 132.

Back Vent. Place centre back seams right sides together and stitch to top of vent, indicated with a small dot. Clip right back to small dot and press seam open above clip in the normal way. Press under $\frac{5}{8}$" on right back vent extension and then press left back vent extension to inside along fold line, forming facing. Tack extension to back, matching triangles. Stitch along stitching line from centre back to triangle through all thicknesses.

Back Yoke. With right sides together pin yoke to back matching centres and triangles. Tack, easing back to fit between notches. Stitch and then press seam upwards.

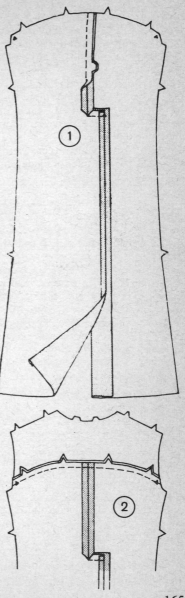

Unit 2. *Join* front panel seams and side body sections together, remembering to clip curves. Press these seams open. Do not join side seams.

Button Tab. Press under ⅛″ along tab fold line. Then with wrong side of band to right side of garment, tack band to left front at placement line, matching large dots and triangles. Top-stitch ¼″ from folded edge, ending stitching ⅞″ from upper edge. Don't if not needed.

Pockets. Make patch pockets by placing right side of patch against lining with raw edges even and stitch, leaving an opening to turn through. Trim seam and corners, clip curves. Turn pocket, press and slip-stitch opening. On outside of front section pin and tack pocket along pocket line placing upper edge between small dots. Top-stitch pocket ¼″ from side and lower edges through all thicknesses.

For the flap, stitch facing to flap with right sides inside and edges even, leaving the top edge open. Trim seam and corners. Clip curves, turn flap and press. Tack raw edges together. Top-stitch flap ¼″ from sides and lower edges. On outside of front pin top edge of flap along flap line above the patch, matching small dots, with the flap upside down. Stitch along seam line. Trim raw edges close to stitching. Press flap down into position and top-stitch flap ¼″ from seam.

If your design has a set-in welt or flap, see page 196 for instructions.

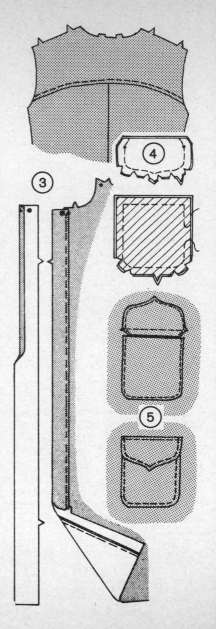

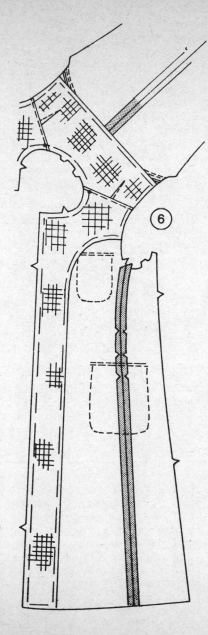

Unit 3. *Stitch* shoulder seams together, matching dots, easing back to fit between notches.

Epaulettes. If these are in the design chosen, stitch the epaulette sections together at sides and shaped end with right sides facing. Trim seams and corners. Turn through unstitched end and press flat. Tack raw edges together. Top-stitch epaulette ¼″ from sides and shaped end. Make worked or machine buttonhole at the shaped end and then tack to outside of shoulder seam, matching triangles.

Interfacing. Make darts in front and back yoke interlining if these are marked on your paper pattern by first cutting dart open along the marked solid line. Lap the cut edge of the dart over so that the seam lines meet, matching dots and stitch ⅛″ in from cut edges – darts in interlinings are generally lapped to reduce bulk, although the normal method of darting can also be used. Next lap shoulder edges of back and front interfacing, matching seam lines, and stitch along these lines. Tack interfacing to wrong side of back and front as in the diagram on the left.

Unit 4. *Stitch* centre back seam of under-collar together and then stay-stitch the inner edge of under-collar.

Collar. Lap-seam centre back edges of interfacing, matching seam line and then stitch along it. Tack interfacing to wrong side of under-collar and sew together using the

167

padding stitches described on page 136. Also tack interfacing to wrong side of collar stand if directed by the design you have chosen and join with padding stitches. Next clip around the inside curve of the under-collar. Match centre backs and small dots, tack and stitch. Press seam open, trimming under-collar seam and stand seam to $\frac{3}{8}''$.

With right sides together pin under-collar to coat, matching centre backs, triangles and small

Press seam open and press neck edge of stay down.

With right sides together, pin facing and upper-collar to the garment and under-collar, matching the centre backs, small dots and triangles. Tack and then stitch around the collar between the triangles. Cut and knot the thread ends. Next stitch the fronts from the triangles to lower edge. Clip collar to small dots. Trim seam and corners and clip curves.

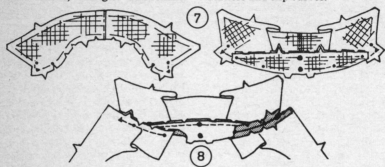

dots. Tack and then stitch between triangles. Trim seam and clip curves, before pressing the seam open.

Facing. Stay-stitch inner edge of upper-collar. Clip upper-collar to small dots and also clip curves. Attach collar stand to upper-collar in the same way as for the under-collar, trimming seam to $\frac{3}{8}''$ and pressing open.

With right sides together, tack upper-collar to front facing, matching the triangles and small dots. Stitch between triangles and small dots at the shoulder seam. Clip stay to small dots and clip curves.

Press facing and upper-collar to inside. Catch facing to back shoulder seam and sew back neck seams together. Finally top-stitch $\frac{1}{4}''$ from finished edges of collar.

Unit 5. *Stitch* back to fronts at side seams and press the seams open.

Sleeves. Tack the sleeve seam sections together, easing or darting the back edge of upper-sleeve to fit under-sleeve as directed on your paper pattern. Stitch a double line of gathering stitches around the head of the sleeve as shown and ease to size.

Pin interfacing to wrong side

168

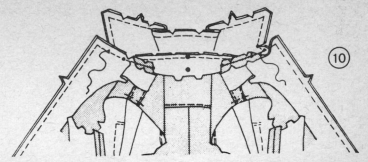

(10)

of sleeve 1½″ above the lower edge, lapping the ends at the back seam. Catch-stitch edges and ends into place. Press up hem and catch-stitch to interfacing.

Insert the sleeves. With right sides together pin the sleeve into the armhole, with centre dot at shoulder seam and remaining dots matching. Pull up machine gathering stitches to fit. Tack, easing in the fullness, and then stitch. Stitch again ⅛″ from first stitching on the seam allowance and then seam below the notches close to the second stitch-line. Press seam towards sleeve, shrinking out fullness.

Unit 6. *Fit* coat as explained in Chapter 5, pages 139–145, marking length carefully.

Hem. Check length. Open out front facing and the back vent extension and then press up the hem along marking. Mark depth of hem with a notched hem guide and trim turn-up evenly. Stitch ¼″ from raw edge using a long machine stitch. Pull up stitching so that the flared hem will lie flat. Press, shrinking out the fullness over a pressing strip. Stitch one edge of some seam binding ¼″ over raw edge and then slip-stitch hem into position. Press facing over hem and then slip-stitch in place.

If you want a slightly stiffer hem finish, attach a 4″ wide crossway strip of interfacing around the hem before turning it up, attaching this strip in the same way as for the

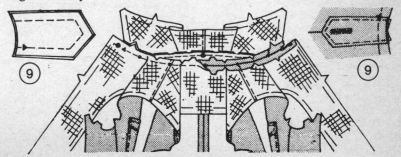

(9)   (9)

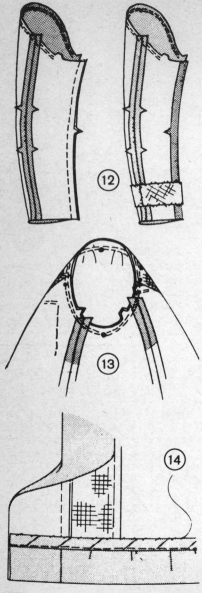

sleeve interfacing, unit 5, page 168.

Finishing. Top-stitch left front band $\frac{1}{4}''$ from front edge and across neck edge to triangle mark, connecting stitching.

Make worked or machine-made buttonholes on left front – right front if you are making a ladies' coat. Sew buttons on opposite front to correspond to buttonholes. Sew buttons under buttonholes on epaulettes. Sew buttons to dots on pocket flap. Make belt and belt carriers as explained on the pattern instruction sheet and sew these into position. Finally press your garment before lining.

Unit 7. Cut out the lining as directed on the paper pattern, reducing the hem allowance by $1\frac{1}{2}''$ to $2''$.

Lining. Stay-stitch neck edges, shoulders and armholes. Make all darts, clipping curves and waist lines. Press all darts towards centre. Press under $\frac{5}{8}''$ on left back lining edges, and $\frac{5}{8}''$ on right back extension if you have a back vent. Stitch centre back seam and press open. Stitch shoulder and side seams together ending the stitching $\frac{5}{8}''$ from front edges. Stitch seams in sleeve lining and stitch to body lining, clipping curves at regular intervals $\frac{3}{8}''$ deep.

With wrong sides together pin lining to garment, matching centres and seams, leaving lower edges free and allowing $\frac{1}{2}''$ extra lining length in sleeve to prevent tightness and dragging. Pin and then tack lower edge of sleeve lining over sleeve hem 1″ above edges. Slip-stitch lining around sleeve hems.

Tack, then hand-sew front and neck edges over facing. Now complete back vent if this applies, by slip-stitching edges of garment and lining together before loosely stitching lining to hem 1″ above hem edge.

The above method is used for lining large garments like a coat or a man's jacket. However, if you have made a child's coat or a normal jacket, use the lining method explained on page 138.

Trimmings

Braiding, leather belt and buttons, decorative fastening studs, bold zips, pocket straps with buckles, fur collar, cuffs and yoke, can be used on tailored garments as trimmings. You will be surprised how helpful these trimmings can be in giving your tailoring a new, up-to-the-minute look. Always check through the latest fashion magazines to see what the leading designers are using and note how important particular trimmings are to an otherwise simple garment. Develop your ideas in the same way as professional fashion designers do, changing your trimmings as the seasons change, experimenting with several alternatives before deciding, so that you can make the most of current fashion feeling. If you keep alive to the excitement of changing fashion your clothes will always look interesting and up to date.

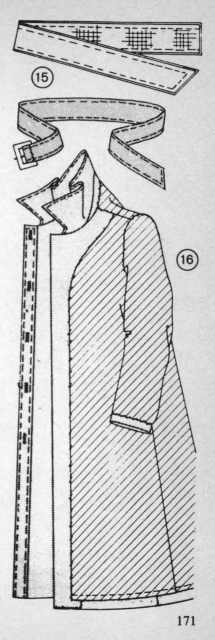

7. Fashion Detailing

If you have successfully made several garments, taken essential notes on construction and on paper-pattern alterations and fitting changes so that you have an accurate pattern to work from, the time has come for you to experiment with design changes involving 'fashion detailing'. These changes can be easily made by a change of fabric and different decorative surface and edge treatments; or by altering the functional design details such as pockets, collars, fastenings or seams as described in this chapter. Changes in design which involve pattern alterations are explained at the end of the chapter, pages 198 to 205.

Which type of detailing to use on a particular dress depends partly on one's own particular taste, partly on the fabric used, partly on the design and use of the garment and partly on the dictates of prevailing fashion. However, as the basic idea is to enhance the general look of a design, making it more interesting or adding a touch of originality, it is important to remember that it should be well made, as irregular sewing will only spoil the finished appearance.

Fashion details are continually changing in their uses and methods of application, as fashion itself changes. In their simplest forms they can be used to add a touch of informality: for example bold patch pockets on an otherwise plain dress, or a leather belt and leather buttons to give a sporty or casual look. This type of design detailing relies as much on the association of ideas as on the finished look of the garment. To use this to advantage, however, one needs to keep up to date with fashion detailing so that one can take full advantage of the nostalgic over-tones of hand-tatting or crochet used with gingham and Victorian prints, or the functional symbolism of P.V.C., studs and bold zips.

If dressmaking is thought of in this way, planning and making your own wardrobe becomes both exciting and satisfying, for the newest realms of fashion and design come within your reach. Many mass-produced clothes lack origi-nality and appeal: they may look 'in fashion' but they are often just copies of fads or gimmicks which date rapidly, or are even two seasons old fashion-wise anyway.

Appliqué

The first essential is to become really proficient at using an auto-matic swing-needle machine and to realise how it can save many hours of tedious hand-work, unless of course you enjoy this. Many interesting designs can be worked out even by beginners provided the appliqué is bold enough and the garment simple enough to be made and finished in a few days.

The ideal type of appliqué to start with is combining patterned and plain fabrics, as on a simple child's dress with a gingham flower appliqué, which is typical of the stitch and cut method explained in Chapter 14, as are the various other methods of appliqué and patchwork. These range from simple appliqué made with boldly cut areas of coloured felt attached with a few decorative embroidery stitches, to more complicated geometric patchwork made by using accurately cut lozenge, hexagonal, triangular or square shapes of fabric sewn together into a formal all-over pattern.

Ribbon Trimmings

The simplest way of using ribbon as a dress trimming is to apply it flat, singly or in bands. Several colours or shades of the same colour are often used and novelty types such as picot-edge, moiré and velvet ribbons interspersed with the plainer grosgrain and satin varieties. To apply flat bands of ribbon you first tack the upper edge of the ribbon into position and then stitch it on the tacked edge leaving the other edge free.

Gathered Ribbon. Ribbons can be gathered along one edge as shown in diagram 1, in the middle as illustrated by diagram 2 or zig-zag as shown in diagram 3. For a ribbon frill either make a hand-gathering stitch and pull up to the size required, or machine gather by adjusting the tension and stitch size to produce the right effect. For gathering in the middle first fold the ribbon in half, bringing the selvedges together and then crease to mark the exact centre.

Zig-zag gathering is done by stitching the ribbon diagonally from edge to edge as shown in

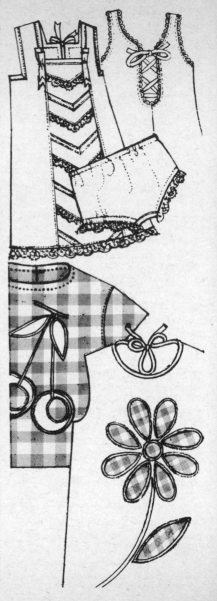

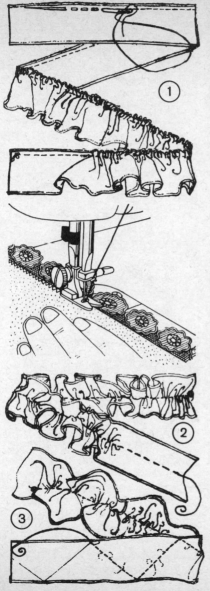

diagram 3. To ensure evenness in the gathering mark the ribbon with zig-zag creases: Lay the ribbon right side up and fold the right-hand end so that the selvedge is lying straight across the ribbon at right angles to the rest of the ribbon, creasing the fold. Now fold the end in the opposite direction so that a second fold runs at right angles to the first crease, meeting it at the upper edge, and press. Make the third fold like the first, etc. and continue until all the ribbon is marked. Gather along the creases as shown, adjusting the fullness evenly when you draw up the thread.

Slotted Ribbons, or ribbon-stitched work, is another very easy form of bold decoration, as shown in Chapter 13. Also described there are ribbon flowers, ribbon embroidery and various forms of braiding and cordwork.

Ribbon Bows can be all shapes and sizes, made in many different ribbons, and used in all sorts of ways. Try using a narrow double-sided satin ribbon made into a dozen or more small bows and scattered around the hem of a baby's christening dress, sewing them with a coloured bead or small millinery flower. Or use a wide multi-coloured ribbon tied like a cummerbund around the waistline of an otherwise simple party dress. Match a slotted ribbon dress trimming with a ribbon hair-band. Alternatively you can use ribbon bows on a glamorous evening gown or for evening accessories, etc.

175

Pleated Trimmings

These can be used in a similar way, as can fringing, *broderie anglaise*, novelty strips or lace edging. Just look around in your local shops. Choose the nicest which is available now – next time you are out looking it may not be available. Be firm when choosing your trimmings and only buy those which you really like.

Lace Insets

Mark the position with coloured tackings on to the fabric, keeping the edges on the exact grain line. Cut a strip of the decorative inset to the length required and then cut the fabric exactly between the coloured tacking lines. Fold under the surplus material and then edge-stitch the fold on to the inset strip, as shown on page 79.

Lace Edgings

These can be applied in many ways. One of the easiest methods is as follows: First neaten the garment by turning under the raw edge and stitch flat. Next place the right side of the lace against the right side of the garment, exactly edge to edge. Now overcast by hand making a stitch every $\frac{1}{4}''$. Finally press the lace edging down into its correct position.

Gathered Frills

The gathering stitches used for gathering frills can be made by hand or machine. If gathering by hand use a long thin needle and slightly thicker thread than for normal hand sewing. If you are using a machine stitch set a slightly larger, looser stitch than normally used. Space two or three rows of stitches about $\frac{1}{8}''$ apart and $\frac{1}{4}''$ in from the edge. Pull all the ends

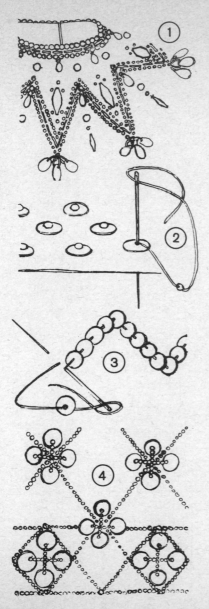

through to the wrong side at the beginning of the rows and tie them together. At the other end tie only the under machine threads or the hand gathering threads together and then pull these gently, easing the fullness evenly along the threads until the frill is the correct size. Wind the pulled out thread around a marker pin and place the frill into position on the garment, adjusting the length as required. Finally sew into place over the gathering stitches (page 77, diagram 8).

Beadwork

A seemingly unending variety of beads and sequins can be bought at most large trimming counters, ranging from simple single-holed coloured discs to multi-coloured ready-made motifs, shiny plastic, tinted crystal or fluted metal. The general method of applying them is fairly standard (see Chapter 13).

Beads. Evenly spaced beads can be easily sewn on with a normal running stitch, but for safety a small knot should be made every inch in case the thread breaks during wear. Alternatively, the beads can be applied with a back stitch as explained for sequins below. If the beads are very small then six or seven can be threaded on to the needle at each stitch, or up to an inch of beads can be attached in this way provided several inconspicuous stitches are later made across the thread on the right side, to hold it flat against the fabric.

Sequins. Single sequins can be sewn on with the aid of a small coloured bead. Use a very fine needle and bring it up through the fabric to the right side. Pass the needle through the centre of a sequin and a bead before placing the sequin into position and taking the needle back through the hole and material to the wrong side. Repeat to complete a pattern.

To apply sequins in rows you bring the needle up through the fabric and the centre hole of the sequin taking a stitch over the edge. Bring the needle up again through the fabric and another sequin $\frac{1}{8}''$ away from the first and take a backstitch to the edge of it. Repeat until all are applied.

Bead Motifs. Bead or sequin clusters are sewn on by stab-stitching with each cluster being firmly knotted at the back before starting on the next one. Ready-made motifs are generally slip-stitched on but care must be taken to secure the makers' threads on the back of the motif by knotting or with a little Evo-Stik or colourless nail varnish, as they tend to unravel.

Sequin Strips. Ready-made sequin strips can be bought in attractive patterns. Apply by catching to the garment every $\frac{1}{2}''$ with a small stitch.

Dress Embroidery

If you are experienced you can work out your own designs: if not you can buy extremely good transfer designs from most embroidery shops. These are ironed on to the fabrics as a guide to the stitching details which are fully

explained in the instruction leaflet sold with the design. They also give guidance about the various needles needed and what embroidery threads to buy. Once you have a little experience you can try some experiments, choosing different colour combinations or different thread textures to suit your own ideas. The traditional method is to use skeins of Clark's Anchor Stranded Cotton, Tapisserie Wool, or Perlita, as these can be bought at in this type of embroidery are shown in Chapter 12 and many more can be found in embroidery pamphlets and design transfers on sale at most needlework shops.

Smocking

Traditionally smocking was used on country-workers' smocks, each county or district having a distinct and characteristic style. Nowadays the style varies according to fashion but as a general rule smocking may

most shops in a wide range of colours; but it can be great fun to supplement them with knitting wools, raffia, strands of leather and plastic, ribbons, russia braids, crochet threads, rug wool, and even coloured string. Wool embroidery can be very attractive on all sorts of ready-made garments. As you will see from the illustrations, you can easily add a few decorative flowers to a pair of knee socks or fancy-knit stockings, and these can be teamed with gloves, beret, scarf or even a sweater and cardigan.

A few of the many stitches used be applied wherever there is fullness, particularly on children's clothes, lingerie or casual wear. Evenness is the key to success and this in its turn depends almost entirely on the regularity of the gathering, which must be done first, before the actual stitching is begun.

First, decide the finished depth and width the smocking is to be, cut from a smocking transfer the depth of dots required, allowing three or four times the width the finished smocking is to be, and iron on to the wrong side of the material. The gathering should also be done on the wrong side, taking up each dot with a small piece of material and securing the thread at the beginning of each row with a knot. When all the rows have been run-stitched, draw up the thread sufficiently tightly to allow the pleats to be easily worked, and secure around a pin. Now turn to Chapter 11 for stitching details.

Faggoting

This is a very traditional and extremely decorative method of join-

a pin lift out the first $\frac{1}{2}''$ of the first thread to be pulled out. Carefully pull this thread until removed, then a second and third until the required width of open work is ready for stitching, as shown on the left.

Crochet Edges

These can be made in many different designs once you have practised the basic methods explained on page 298. These can range from the finest almost lace-like edgings made in silk for evening clothes or

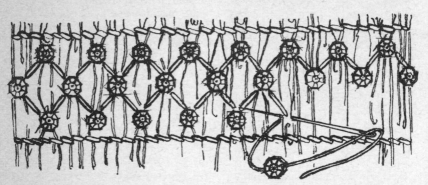

ing two pieces of fabric together.

Turn under $\frac{1}{4}''$ on both raw edges of the fabric pieces to be joined. Tack the folded edges the required distance apart on to a stiffish piece of paper, then work the faggoting stitch required, as shown opposite.

Drawn Thread Work

Many very decorative traditional stitches are used in drawnthread or open work which is usually made on linen fabrics or evenly woven material of a similar type. Using

lingerie to the boldest, chunky wool edgings or motifs for winter garments. They can also be made as separate trimmings, as on page 300, which are then sewn into position in much the same way as ready-made shop-fringes and braids, or they can be worked on to an edge as also shown. Basically, however, crochet trimmings are all made in the same way. First pick up a loop of working thread which, after pulling through, is looped many times into a regular pattern,

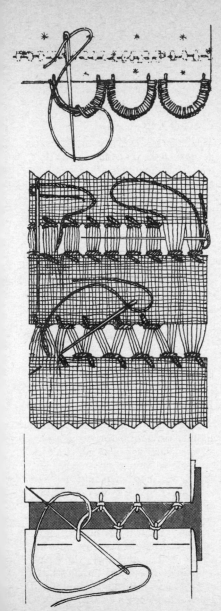

repeating the looping and pulling through at specified intervals until the pattern is completed in much the same way as knitting.

Braided Edges

Braids can be bought by the yard in many colours in silk or wool textures. First mark along the edge the depth of braiding required and then tack the braiding to this mark, right side uppermost, machining it into position as shown in diagram 1, page 183. Turn braid to the wrong side and hand stitch on to the back of the machine line as in the next diagram.

Russia braid is another decorative form of braiding generally used to outline interesting design details in the same way as top-stitching. This thin twin-corded braid is attached by either machine-stitching along the centre fold, or by neatly stab-stitching every $\frac{1}{4}''$ as for Soutache braiding on page 294. The jacket on page 183 has wool braid over its raw edges with a russia-braid inset.

Binding

This method of neatening a garment edge not only gives an interesting decorative finish but also acts as its own facing, enclosing all the raw edges. Use a bias strip of matching or contrasting fabric – cut 1″ wide for a $\frac{1}{4}''$ binding – and place this on to the edge, right sides together, stitching as explained on page 78 for a Bound Edge.

Seams

The use of different types of

181

seaming or seam placement plays an important part in fashion detailing. A Strap seam can for instance add a Safari look to an otherwise simple jacket whilst a Channel seam can be used for incorporating easy-to-make pockets.

Strap Seam. Make a plain seam on the right side of your fabric – on the outside so that it shows – press open and then trim the turning allowances to $\frac{1}{4}''$. Cut a separate strip of fabric $1\frac{1}{2}''$ wide and press under the raw edges $\frac{1}{4}''$ on both sides. Tack this strip over the seam and then machine stitch $\frac{1}{8}''$ from the folded edges through both pieces, as shown in diagram 1.

Flat Fell. First place the fitting lines of the two pieces to be joined together, wrong side to wrong side – right sides outside – and machine stitch on the fitting lines through both pieces. Press seam open and then trim one side to $\frac{1}{4}''$ and the other to $\frac{5}{8}''$. Fold larger turning over smaller one, turning the raw edge under $\frac{1}{4}''$ and machine $\frac{1}{8}''$ in from turning edge through both pieces (diagram 2 on the right).

Welt Seam. First join the fabric pieces together as for a normal seam and then press the seam open. Trim front turning allowance to a scant $\frac{1}{4}''$, leaving the back one untrimmed. Fold untrimmed turning over the trimmed one and tack flat. Turn to front of fabric and machine stitch over the tacking $\frac{3}{8}''$ from original seam line so that the back turning is joined to the front piece, encasing the trimmed turning

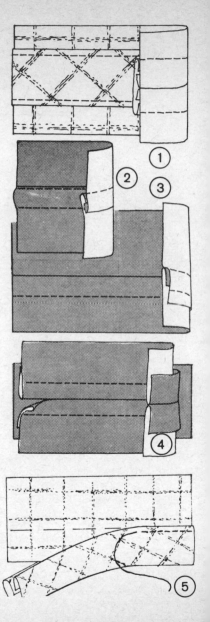

182

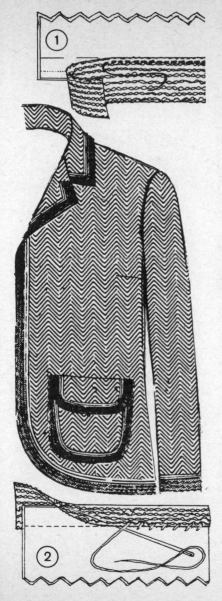

which acts as a padding, as in diagram 3 opposite.

Channel Seam. A channel or slot seam is really a double lapped seam made by turning under the seaming allowances on both the edges to be joined and then stitching them on to a separate 1″ to $1\frac{1}{2}$″ wide strip of fabric $\frac{1}{4}$″ to $\frac{3}{8}$″ in from both folds, as in diagram 4 opposite.

Lapped Seam. This is a decorative top-stitched seam made by lapping one folded edge over a normal seam allowance and machine stitching through both pieces $\frac{1}{4}$″ in from the fold.

Top-stitching

Top-stitching is both functional and decorative, for it helps to emphasize seam lines, edges or design features, and at the same time gives a crisp, neat appearance.

Edge-stitching is usually made after completion of a particular process or detail, such as a collar, cuff or pocket flap, or, if many edges are to be stitched, on completion of an entire garment. However, some top-stitching is often done even before cutting out, such as when large areas need to be quilted (see page 288), by using a layer of wadding and lining. Some top-stitching is even an integral part of certain structural seams – channel, welt, flat fell and strap seams – and is done during construction. Mark up accurately before top-stitching by using a notched guide as shown on page 184, and make sure that the stitch is perfectly set both for length and tension. Another aid to accur-

acy is your sewing machine's adjustable stitch guide that keeps the stitching a uniform distance from the edge, illustrated on page 59.

A bolder effect can be achieved by making several lines or by using thicker top thread – this requires a heavier needle and slacker tension – or two strands of top cotton through one needle; or a contrasting colour; or, if you have an automatic machine, one of the many decorative stitches; or by making a double stitch with a twin needle.

Pin Tucks

Machines using twin needles make automatic pin tucks which can also be raised and corded, or they can be made on most other sewing machines by accurately top-stitch-ing $\frac{1}{8}''$ away from a folded edge of fabric. Accuracy when marking is essential as each tuck must be on the exact grain, which is done by creasing along the mark before stitching close to the folded edge, as explained on page 79.

Cross Tucks. These are a second group of pin tucks made across a normal group of pin tucks, giving a checker-board effect. Cross tucks are sewn in the same way as pin tucks, but take extra care with the second group to avoid slipping so that each crossing is true, as explained for pin tucks on page 79.

Wide Tucks. These differ from pin tucks in that the stitching is between $\frac{1}{4}''$ and $\frac{1}{2}''$ away from the folded edge of a tuck. It is essential for each tuck to be on the exact grain, and it is wise to use a notched cardboard tuck guide as illustrated. As it is almost impossible to judge exactly how much extra material is required for a particular tucked area it is wisest to cut the material much larger than the pattern, making the tucks in the groups required before trimming accurately to shape.

Rouleaux Trimmings

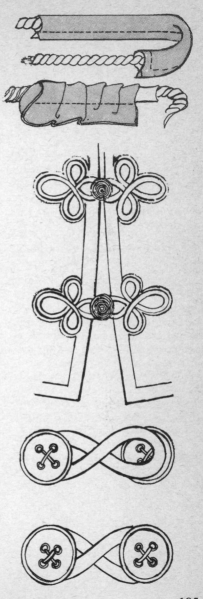

The use of bias rouleaux tubing as trimming in dressmaking is coming back into fashion for use as looped buttonholes and froggings, belts and bows, insets and set-ons, piping and edgings – the variety of uses is unlimited.

The tubing consists of crossway strips of material, cut as explained on page 73, sewn to form tubes varying from $\frac{1}{8}''$ to $\frac{3}{8}''$, depending on the type of material used. For the narrowest tubing, use fine crêpe or lawn and cut crossway strips $\frac{1}{2}''$ wide; the wider tubings of thicker fabric need bias strips $1''$ to $1\frac{1}{2}''$ wide.

To make the tubing, fold the cut crossway strip to half its width with the right side inside, and stitch $\frac{1}{8}''$ from the edge, keeping the stitching an even distance from the edge. For turning the tubing right side out, insert a flat bodkin or tapestry needle in one end, and with a fine sewing needle and thread sew the material to the eye of the bodkin. Now push the bodkin through the tube, turning the fabric right side out. If a soft cord-like

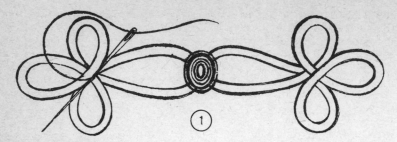

effect is required, leave the tubing unpressed, but if it is to be used as looped buttonholes or froggings as shown above or as a decorative inset as shown opposite, press the tubing, curving it to shape as you press, with the stitched edge on the under-side of the curve. See page 74 if a firmer corded rouleaux is required.

Fashion Fastenings

Rouleaux Loops. Rouleaux looped buttonholes are generally made out of soft tubing, that is without a centre cord. Cut the tubing into even lengths – 2″ long for ½″ buttons – and tack these into position at ½″ or 1″ intervals, or as required. Cover with a facing strip as for normal inset edges and then stitch through all thicknesses ¼″ away from the raw edges. Turn facing through to the wrong side

and stitch down in the normal way.

Rouleaux tabs. Many variations and designs can be made by twisting, plaiting or looping a rouleaux tube to form tab type buttonings, the simplest of which are shown on page 185, whilst the more complicated designs – known as froggings – are shown below. To make a corded rouleaux tube – that is, with a centre cord – just select a cord the width of the desired rouleaux. Next cut a length of crossway fabric as explained on pages 73–4, sufficiently wide to go round the chosen cord, plus turnings. Cut the fabric the length required and then cut the cord twice as long.

Fold the right side of the fabric over the cord, tacking the fabric edges together, and then stitch close to the cord, using a piping

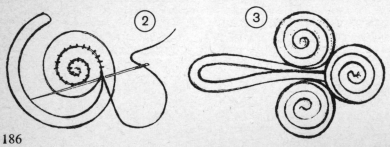

foot. Finally, stitch through all the thicknesses in the centre of the cord, so that when the cord is pulled the rouleaux turns right side out, by easing the fabric over the end stitching a little at a time. Cut to 1″ longer than required, snipping away 1″ of cord at each end, turn in ½″ of fabric and slip-stitch edges together.

To make the simplest looped-tab fastening cut an 8″ length of ¼″ rouleaux tubing and clip away ½″ of cord from each end. Tuck in fabric ends and slip-stitch the two

shape the rouleaux or ready-made fancy cord on to the paper and pin with the seam uppermost. Then tack into position. Stitch the looped crossings together securely before removing from the paper, and then neatly attach to the garment as shown in diagram 1 on the left.

If the ends consist of a tight twirl as in diagram 2, left, care should be taken to sew the edges together neatly as shown. The curves should be shaped and lightly pressed, making sure that the stitched edges fall at the back just inside the curve

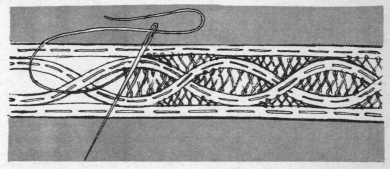

ends together. Loop the rouleaux into a figure of eight, as shown on page 185, slip-stitching the looped crossing together.

Froggings. Decorative frog fastenings can be made with soft or corded rouleaux strips, or ready-made fancy cord and braiding, by twisting, plaiting, or looping the rouleaux or cording to many different designs in addition to the ones shown opposite.

First rough out the shape you want on a piece of stiff paper;

so that they do not show when the fastening is complete – diagram 3.

Other Fastenings

A simple strip fastening is an easy way of buttoning many different types of garment is shown in diagram 1 on page 189. Cut a strip of pattern paper 1″ × 6″ and shape the ends as required. Cut two strips of fabric to this shape allowing an extra ½″ turning all round. Lay these strips face to face and stitch ⅜″ in leaving a 3″

gap along the bottom edge. Clip corners, turn to right side through gap, press, and hand stitch gap edges together. Tack along centre length and make buttonhole $1\frac{1}{4}''$ long 1" from one end. Top-stitch $\frac{3}{8}''$ from edge all round.

An alternative method is to incorporate a centre seam with a slot buttonhole. To do this first cut four strips of fabric $2\frac{1}{2}'' \times 7''$ – this allows for $\frac{3}{8}''$ seams. Place two pieces face to face and stitch along one edge leaving a buttonhole gap $1\frac{1}{2}''$ long, 1" from one end. Repeat with another two pieces and press seams open. Place both sections with right sides together and edges even and stitch, shaping the ends to a point but leaving a 3" gap in the centre of one edge. Clip corners, turn to right side through gap, press, hand stitch gap and

top-stitch $\frac{3}{8}''$ from edge all round. Finally sew buttonhole seam edges together before attaching to your jacket. Sew on the working button first, and then a correspondingly placed non-functional button through the tab as shown on the right. Single tabs are made in a similar way but instead of leaving a side gap the tab is turned through one end which is then inserted between the front and facing edges.

Decorative Buttons. These can be bought in most shops or stores in a wide variety of sizes and interesting designs, ranging from shaped metal, coloured cording, moulded glass and plastics, to jewelled and sequinned buttons. Similarly decorative buckles are also available, or button and buckle sets can easily be made by twisting, looping twirling, plaiting or knotting soft or corded rouleaux or braids and decorative cords, dyed string, pipe-cleaners or even electrical wire covering. Try several out and if they are successful hand stitch them together, concealing the stitches as much as possible.

Jewelled buttons and fancy cufflinks can also be made in the same way, as can decorative buckles, beaded belts or any number of other pretty things.

Decorative Zips. Bold novelty zip fasteners made of brass, coloured plastic, steel or see-through perspex spirals give an exciting and different look on many sorts of garments such as sports jackets, childrens' and teenage wear, jeans, or even evening casuals. If the completed design works and the effect is what you wanted then your choice was right.

Surface Studs. Use these as an alternative to buttoning in many interesting and original ways on tabs, belts, cuffs and pockets. They can be bought in a wide range of materials and sizes: the large brass or nickel ones are particularly useful.

Metal Eyelets. These are similar materials and used on the same types of garments as surface studs, and are punched on. They can also be used with lacing, or if large enough with slotted rouleaux ties as shown on page 191.

Lacing. Use ready-made corded lacing with decorative ends for

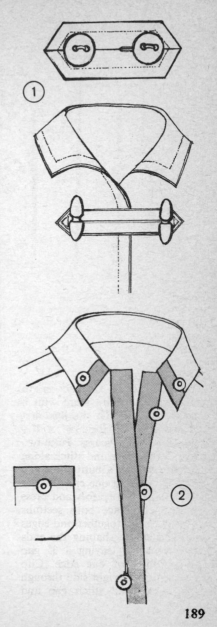

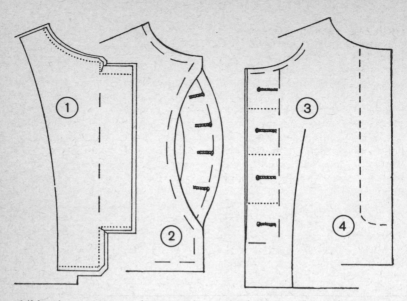

children's wear, or home-made satin rouleaux lacing for evening casuals using the rouleaux making instructions on page 185.

Fly Fastening

When cutting out, allow an extra 2½" on the front edge of the buttoning side of the jacket – right-hand side for women, left-hand side for men – in addition to the normal front overlap and turning allowances. Also add the 2½" on to the facing.

1. To make the fly fastening first tack on the facing as for a normal front, around the neck, down the front and along the hem. Next machine stitch around the neck, down the front for only 1" and then outwards to the raw edge. Now machine along the hem, up

the front for 2" and then outwards to the raw edge as in diagram 1.

2. Trim away turnings close to the machine stitching as for a normal front, also clipping corners, notching edges, and turning through. Press edges flat and remove front tacking. Tack-stitch around the neck and down the two separate front edges. Mark and make either hand or machine-made buttonholes in the facing section, finishing each buttonhole about ¾" in from the edge as in diagram 2.

3. From the wrong side tack through all thicknesses, level with the inside ends of buttonholes, and then hand stitch between each buttonhole on to the garment facing, making sure that no stitches show on the right side.

4. Turn to right side and top-stitch over guide tacking, curving the bottom as in diagram 4. Press edges flat and sew on buttons on the other jacket front which has been made in the normal way.

Drawstring Fastenings

Three methods of making decorative drawstrings – or casings – are shown below, all of which can be used with belts of various widths, fat or thin rouleaux, slotted ribbons, or simple fabric ties.

1. This is used in the middle of a garment, possibly on a dress or casual jacket. Mark position and width of drawstring with tack stitches around the garment. Cut a strip of fabric 1″ wider than marks and 1″ longer than required. Turn in $\frac{3}{8}$″ on both long sides and press these edges very flat. Make the opening on the outside of the garment evenly each side of the centre line, either making a hand stitched or fabric buttonhole or by facing-out a coin-sized circle. Tack the fabric strip along the marks on the inside of the garment turnings enclosed, and machine stitch $\frac{1}{8}$″ in from the folded edges.

2. This is for using on the lower edge of a garment, such as a blouse or casual jacket. The method of construction is the same as for 1, except that the strip is applied along the bottom edge as shown below.

3. For this method there should be an extra turning allowance along the top of a garment, in place of

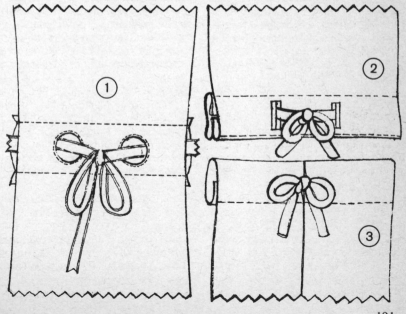

a separate strip. It can be used equally well for shorts or a casual skirt, as in diagram 3, page 191.

Fashion Belts

These come in all shapes and sizes, from thin rouleaux with knotted ends to 6″-wide ones with boned sides; made in an assortment of materials from soft chiffon to stiff patent leather; with many different fastenings from a floppy bow to a bold steel buckle. They can be worn high under the bust to low on the hips. In other words, belts are highly susceptible to fashion changes, so look around in magazines and shops before deciding which to make or buy.

Soft Tie Belts can be made from most materials. Simply cut a strip nearly three times the required finished width, fold the width in half, and stitch along the line giving the required width from fold. Press this seam open and using a safety pin turn through to right side. Press so that the seam runs down the centre inside, turn in the ends and catch the inside fold to hold flat.

Tailored Belt. Special belt kits – including stiffening and buckle – are now available to make most traditional belt shapes in your own material. Simply buy a kit the shape and size required and follow the instructions carefully.

Decorative Belts can be made with beads and sequins, curtain rings and metal loops, plaited ribbons, knotted string, couched braids, appliqués of leather and felt, etc.

Bows. The shapes, sizes and fabrics of bows vary as much as do belts. Simply try out several before deciding which is best, and then try out several more to make sure that you were right.

Collars and Cuffs

These, together with pockets, are probably the most widely used of all design features, and naturally enough are the centre of most attention, alteration and adaptation. This being so it is obvious that to get the best from your designing, your collars and cuffs should not only be neatly made and nicely finished, but that the shape and decorative treatment should be right, as well as coordinated into the design as a whole. There is little use in a nicely made, interestingly decorated collar and cuff set on a badly fitting, dowdy, old-fashioned hotchpotch of a dress.

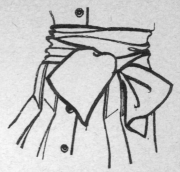

They can be made in all shapes and sizes – plain tailored, scalloped, or ruffled – in many types of materials and decorated in many ways, using slotted ribbon, bold top-stitching, embroidery with beads and sequins, or just nicely shaped buttons. In other words there are no rules so long as the collar and cuffs look right on the particular garment.

Cuff Making. Most cuffs are easy to make, either of two identical pieces of fabric, stitched together around three sides – see page 151 – or on the folded-strip-of-fabric principle, as on page 160.

Collar Making. The usual way of making and attaching a collar is shown on page 126. Several other methods are widely used, such as turning the neck edge of the collar under as on a man's shirt, page 154; using a bias strip or curved facing as on page 160; or tailored, page 167. Collar shapes and sizes vary enormously as their importance fluctuates, and it would be wrong

to be categorical about what type of collar is right for a particular garment. All that can be said is that if it looks right, it probably is right.

To help you build up a knowledge of collar shapes, roughly sketch every collar illustrated in a current magazine. You will then see the differences between a simple Peter Pan collar, a classic shirt collar, a floppy collar from the Kings Road, or a tailored collar and lapel. Notice the way they hug or stand away from the neck,

whether they have a longer, narrower look, and whether lapels are wider or more sharply notched. One year wide top-stitching looks right and the next two lines of top-stitching $\frac{1}{8}''$ apart seem better. Look, sketch, collect press cuttings, experiment and make your collar designs right for now.

at bottom. Clip corners and turn through gap. Press flat and slip-stitch gap before surface-machining into position. An alternative method for making a patch pocket is described on page 125 and the tailored method on page 166.

Pockets in Seams. There are many

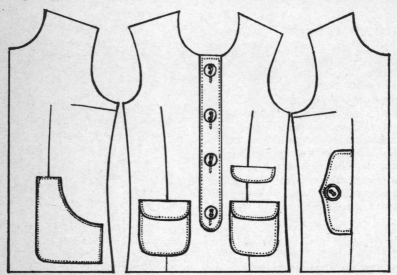

Pockets

Like collars and cuffs, pockets are constantly changing in shape, size, positioning and construction to help emphasize a particular design feeling, a new shape or a different cut.

Shaped Patch. Cut a paper pattern to the pocket shape required, and then cut two fabric pieces allowing for $\frac{1}{2}''$ seaming for each pocket. Mark and then machine to shape, right sides inside, leaving 3″ gap

easy and ingenious ways of putting pockets into a design by means of normal seam lines. If, however, you wish to introduce a special seam, simply mark its position on your pattern and cut your pattern into two sections, remembering to add turning allowances to both cut edges; mark on pocket length and machine seam together normally, leaving a gap for the pocket, then make a simple pocket bag and

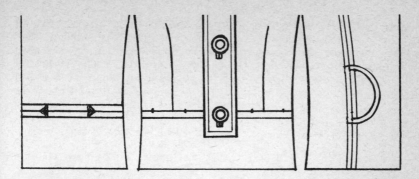

attach it by hand as for a letterbox pocket explained below.

Side-seam Pocket. This is probably the most widely used seam pocket. First stitch the seams together in the normal way, leaving a 6″ gap for pocket opening. Press seam open and then snip back turning up to machine line $\frac{1}{2}$″ above and $\frac{1}{2}$″ below pocket opening and bring this turning forward. Make and attach pocket bag as for a normal letterbox pocket, and finally work bars or arrow-heads to strengthen pocket ends.

Channel-seam Pocket. Introduce a channel seam – a double lap seam stitched on to a 2″ wide separate strip of fabric – across a garment, marking pocket lengths accurately. Lap and top-stitch the upper section on to the under strip $\frac{3}{8}$″ from edge. On the lower section fold over the seam allowance and tack $\frac{1}{8}$″ from edge, then top-stitch the pocket opening only. Next lap this on to the backing strip so that the top and bottom sections meet in the middle and top-stitch through, omitting the sections already stitched. Make pocket bag and attach to seam edges as for letterbox pocket explained below.

Letterbox Pocket. Mark a rectangle on to the front of a garment 6″ long by $\frac{1}{2}$″ wide. Cut a strip of fabric

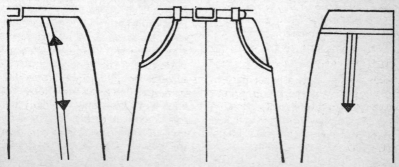

195

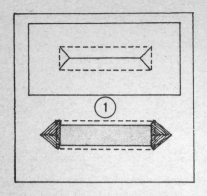

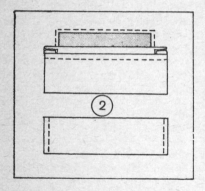

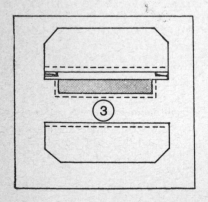

8″ × 3″ and place this over the rectangle with right sides together. Tack and machine all round, tying ends or overlapping the machining. Cut along the centre and diagonally into all four corners. Turn the strip through the hole, press flat and machine ⅛″ from edge to hold flat. Make a fabric pocket bag 6″ × 6″ and hand sew on to the back machining. Work an arrowhead at each end for a bold decorative look, as in diagram 1, or add a welt or flap as shown below.

Welt Pocket. Make a simple letter-box pocket 5″ × ½″. Cut a welt strip 7″ × 4″ on the straight or cross-grain. Fold to half the width, right sides inside, and machine across both ends ½″ in. Turn to right side and press flat. Machine the welt upside down on to the bottom of opening, avoiding pocket bag. Turn welt upright and stitch both ends into position right through the garment.

Flap Pocket. Make a letterbox pocket 5″ × ½″. Cut a paper flap shape 6″ × 2½″, and from it cut two fabric pieces, adding ½″ all round for turning allowance. With right sides inside machine stitch flap pieces together around three sides, leaving top edge open. Clip corners and turnings, turn through and press. Place flap above pocket opening so that it is facing upwards with the raw edge against the top of opening and then stitch ⅜″ from edge. Trim turnings to ⅛″, turn flap down over opening and machine stitch along fold ¼″ in.

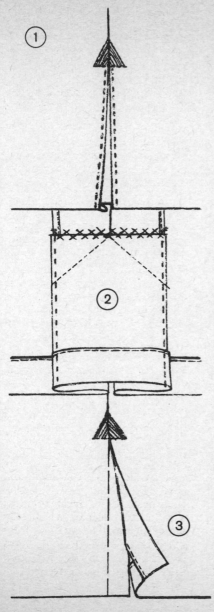

Skirt Pleat as shown by diagram 2 on the left.

1. Cut the skirt or dress with an extra wide centre back seam allowance – approximately $1\frac{1}{2}''$ to $2''$ on each side of the fitting line; stitch the back seam together in the normal way but leave the pleat length unstitched.

2. Press open the centre back seam. Now tack the pleat edges together with the hem under, not over, the back turnings. Cut an oblong of fabric $1''$ longer than the pleat opening, plus normal hem allowance, the width being the same as the pressed-open seam turnings.

3. Turn up and match the hem allowance on the oblong strip of fabric and then lay this into position over the back of the turnings, right side facing the back turnings and hems level. Machine along both sides, and $1''$ below the top of the pleat machine diagonally into the middle, as shown.

4. Neaten the side raw edges with oversewing and herringbone the top to the back of the turnings before working an arrowhead or strengthening bar on the outside top of the pleat if required.

Vent Opening as shown in diagram 3 on the left. Cut the garment with a $1\frac{1}{2}''$ allowance on the left-hand side for the vent overlap, and $2\frac{1}{2}''$ on the right-hand side for the under-wrap.

1. Machine the seam above the vent and then turn the $1\frac{1}{2}''$ allowance under along centre back line.

2. Cut diagonally in on the under-

197

wrap turning 1″ above opening and fold the underwrap forward 1¼″ and then over so that it doubles back to the centre line, tacking and pressing flat. Stitch through double thicknesses and garment to support underwrap, neaten the top and underwrap corners as explained on page 64, and then complete hem.

style lines. The second is *design cutting* which will allow more distinctive and individual effects, whilst the third method is *toile making* is explained on page 204.

You may prefer one of these methods to the other but do try experimenting with all methods, orthodox or not, as any way you

Garment Design

To anyone who has studied dress-making and tailoring the thought of being able to design and cut their own garments has an almost irresistible fascination. To be independent of commercially produced patterns, to create new ideas after the manner of the famous designers, to make individual and distinctive garments, is in fact quite possible.

The first step is *pattern adapting* in which you take an ordinary commercial paper pattern and change various design features and

find of achieving a successful design is the right way for you.

If you have read and understood the previous chapters on dress-making and tailoring, experimented and made notes as recommended, you should have enough knowledge and experience to enable you to start cutting and making your own designs, or making major design adaptations and pattern alterations.

Pattern Adapting

Having studied the functional and decorative details explained in this chapter as well as making and fitting, explained in chapters 5 and 6, you may wish to adapt your paper pattern to a variety of styles by altering the seam placements as well as the design features. The first important point, however, is to select a paper pattern which is your size and shape, preferably one you have used on a successful garment.

Bodice Adapting. The basic principle is the same for all paper pattern adaptation, whether for a bodice dart, wing seam or panelled bodice. That is, mark and then cut the new seaming required and close up the one not needed, always remembering to add a turning allowance on the new seaming line.

As a simple experiment take a normal bodice pattern. Cut a seam from the middle of the shoulder to the end of the bust dart and close the side dart by sticking it with Sellotape as in the drawing overleaf. Now completely ignore any hint of there ever having been a side dart, cut out some cheap calico, remembering to add a seam allowance to the new panel seam, and quickly machine together before fitting to check alteration.

Skirt Adapting. If you have a well-fitting, simple skirt pattern it can easily be used to cut a 'swinging flare' or a 'pleated casual'. All you need to think about is how your new design varies from the existing pattern and simply alter this as explained for adapting a bodice pattern, marking seams as needed and adding or taking away shape

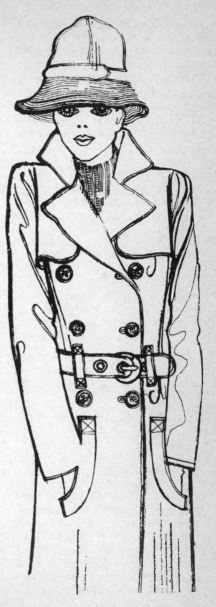

that is not required. See diagram 2 on the right.

Collar Adapting. Only the beginnings of what to do when working on new collar shapes can be explained here, as once you start to experiment you will discover many ways of making new shapes which are right for your dressmaking but would take many pages to explain.

Lay your front and back bodice patterns together along the shoulder seam lines and draw on to the paper the shape of collar required. Trace this shape on to a separate piece of paper trying out several alternatives before deciding. Next try the new collar out in calico, modifying it as necessary. When it is exactly right trace it onto paper adding the necessary $\frac{3}{8}''$ seam allowances all round plus an extra $\frac{1}{2}''$ in length and $\frac{1}{4}''$ in width for ease. See page 193 for collar making.

Pockets. As for collar shapes, anything that looks good and works is right, so when working out new pocket shapes and placings simply follow whichever method you like best. For pocket making details see pages 194-6.

Design Cutting

When starting to experiment with a new design, work from a pattern of a dress or coat that you have successfully made several times. Alternatively use a pattern which you have traced from a ready-made dress which is your exact size and shape. To do this tracing accurately,

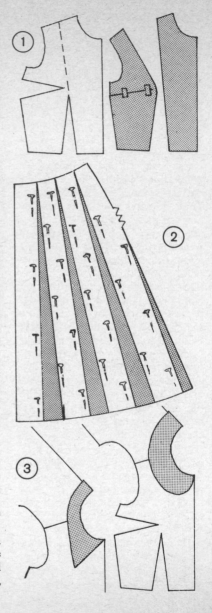

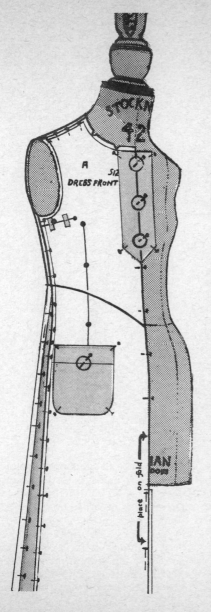

first trace-mark the exact centre front and centre back. Next unpick a few of the major seam lines – side seam, part of waist seam, darts, underarm seam but not armhole, etc. – so that you can lay the dress out flat onto a sheet of brown wrapping paper. Unpick enough to enable you to trace each section accurately, but not so much that it is difficult to re-machine again. Check each pattern piece against the dress, marking on it its position, grain lines, seam junctions, etc. before re-stitching the sample dress together again. Now proceed to use this pattern in the usual way.

Trace the paper pattern which you have decided to use on to a slightly firmer paper and Sellotape or pin it together on a dress stand. Look at the shape and cut, trying to work out new constructional lines and interesting fashion details. Decide what it is about the shape that you would like to alter, always bearing in mind that your figure is basically the same as the original pattern and that it is unwise to change drastically essential fitting points such as bust or armholes.

If you would like the design a little more flared, unpin the side seam as far as the waist, stick an extra wedge of paper on each side and re-pin. If you would like a wing or panel seam, mark it in in coloured chalk or pencil; if you would like an interestingly shaped back yoke mark that in. If below the front seam line you fancy an inverted pleat, make one the correct size in paper and stick it into position, finally for instance cutting a front tab opening and button-down patch pockets.

When you are happy with the patchwork paper result, unpin it carefully, marking all major changes and important balance marks.

Now comes the time to make an important notches, grain lines and balance marks, using a tracing wheel to mark pocket and tab placings, before finally checking the accuracy of your buttonholes.

If you would like to check your new pattern before making it in an expensive material, buy some cheap calico, cut out the new shape,

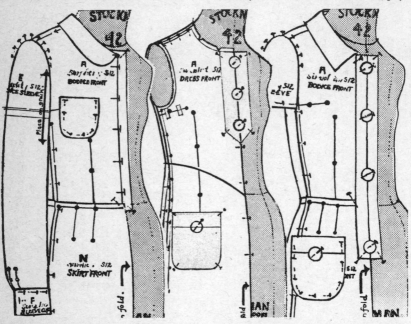

accurate new pattern, so before any of the side flare comes unstuck or the front pleat gets lost, simply cut along the final design lines in a continuous smooth line, and on to each of the new edges attach a turning allowance of $\frac{5}{8}''$ or $\frac{3}{4}''$ as allowed on commercial patterns. Next trace accurately on to another piece of paper, marking all im-

pencil-mark all important points and quickly machine major seams together with a largish stitch. Do not face neck line or armholes, simply mark on the correct shape in pencil on the right side, cut away turnings to $\frac{1}{4}''$, pin up hem and pin on mock paper tab, pockets, buttons, etc. When fitting this trial dress, note essential alterations, adjusting the pattern accordingly, and you will save many hours of fitting and altering and possibly the need for a first fitting.

If your design is more complex or asymmetrical you should trace both the left and right sides of the pattern onto a sheet of firmish

choose from, that you can decide which one is most successful.

Major Points

After experimenting with a paper pattern check each piece carefully, marking on the various names of each section – such as side body, back, sleeve, etc., as well as grain

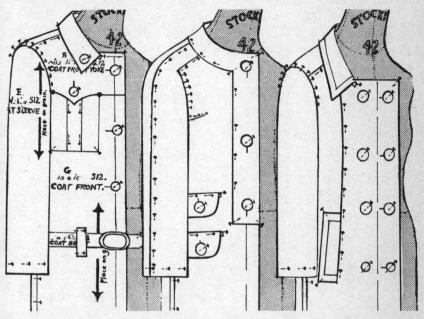

paper. Proceed as before, Sellotaping or pinning the pieces together to make a complete replica of the original design. Slip this paper shell onto your stand and draw on your chosen design. Do not automatically accept your first try as correct – it is only by trying several times, and therefore having several alternatives to

lines, balance marks, easing, dart positions, etc. Finally make sure that you haven't overlooked any of the following major points:

1. Mark out both the left and right side of your pattern on to a slightly firmer plain paper.

2. Sellotape or pin together accurately before placing on to your dress-stand.

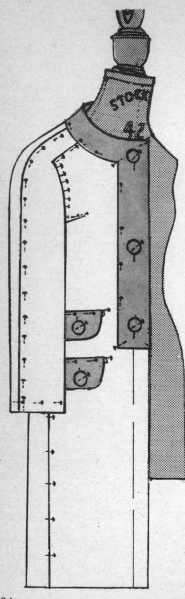

3. Draw on your chosen design and cutting lines, but experiment with several alternatives before choosing the most successful one.

4. Balance-mark all curved lines, seam junctions and important details before cutting along the new design lines.

5. Trace on to some more clean paper so that seam allowances, hems and facings can be added like those on a commercial paper pattern.

6. Check each pattern piece carefully, marking its junction lines, grain lines, balance marks, darts, easing, etc. before cutting out.

Toile Making

Toile making, like design cutting, is an exciting and interesting skill: the one is used to complement the other. If you have cut a new pattern in paper and would like to check it in calico to see if you can improve the hang or change the shape, simply cut the right half in calico, choosing a weight that is approximately the same as the material you intend to use, and mark the seam allowances in HB pencil before pinning together. Put the half toile on to your dress stand, checking that it balances correctly before pinning the centre lines of the toile to the centre lines of the stand.

With your half toile on the stand you can start experimenting by changing dart positions. Unpin any you do not like and repin them in a better position, shaping a little more under the bust or side seam, but always remembering that you are modelling on a static dress form, whereas you yourself are softer and can move about, so the toile should not be too tight. Leave sufficient slack for normal movement as most professionals do. They also re-mark their armholes from their basic paper pattern if a sleeve pattern is being used. As most professional toile makers work in their own particular way very little technique need be explained. They all agree, however, on the following basic principles, so you would be wise to keep them in mind.

1. Use calico that is of a similar weight to the intended fabric.

2. Prepare your calico as with a normal fabric by straightening the grain and ironing flat.

3. Always cut on the correct grain paying particular attention to centre and hem lines.

4. When starting always use a paper pattern that is close to your intended design, developing and adapting from that pattern as necessary.

5. Always centre your toile correctly on the stand and never pull it off balance.

6. If you are not happy with a particular shape, unpin it and start again.

Finally. When you are experimenting, keep your scrap-book of fashion ideas and photographs handy so that you can try out some of the latest designs and ideas.

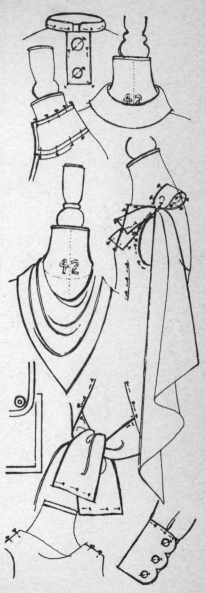

Part Three   Fashion Furnishings

This section is divided into three chapters which cover many aspects of household sewing from cushions and curtains to bedspreads, garden hammocks and table linen, with lots of nursery things added for good measure. The first chapter deals with decorative things for beginners, as these give a grounding in the sewing methods needed to tackle the more advanced household articles in the following two chapters. As in the rest of the book, the methods used are intended to be freely interpreted with an emphasis on ease and enjoyment which will help even inexperienced sewers to produce successful work.

8. Making Decorative Things

The following twenty-three pages are intended as an introduction to sewing for the home. The items featured have been designed around a decorative theme so that they are fun to make, but in addition they also give a good introduction to the sewing methods used in more advanced work. In this chapter we will explain how to use pretty coloured cotton prints for trimming sheets and pillow-cases and how to make a lampshade to match; or you can try some holiday things such as a beach rug and a garden hammock; or you may prefer to make something for the nursery. Whatever your choice, however, do remember to be a little more adventurous with each item, adding some extra decorative detailing or using unusual colouring, as this is what makes sewing interesting and exciting. If you are making or decorating some new sheets or pillow-cases spend a little time looking at the latest Swiss embroidered ones in a quality shop. If you are making some nursery cushions or a nightie case look through those in a big store to see how they are made and decorated. If you are making a tablecloth don't just make it from the same fabric you always use; instead spend a little time looking through various fabric shops, comparing colours, textures and prices. When you have gained enough experience to attempt some curtains and blinds look at some recent magazines to help you sort out your thoughts, adding articles about furnishing trends and interesting

photographs to your scrap-book as explained on page 7, as this helps to increase your awareness and keeps your imagination alive to change.

The Bedroom

Sewing for the bedroom is probably the most exciting and personally rewarding type of sewing in the home – you can make so many pretty decorative things without having to compromise too much on their functional use. You can also try out extra decorative detailing or unusual colouring without having to change everything else in the room, using a pretty coloured cotton print for a bedroom chair, making a dressing-table valance to match; gingham curtains with cotton lace edges to match bindings on blankets, sheets and pillow-cases; window blinds made out of the same material as your bedspread, or decorative cushions teamed with a decorative lampshade.

Decorative Sheets

Plain everyday bed-linen can be simply made by using a bought sheet or pillow-case as a pattern for cutting out and finishing some pretty fabric you have chosen. Or you can add a decoration to bed-linen you have already bought. The first thing is to decide what effect you would like to achieve. A few such effects are shown here, but many more can be seen in most big stores or magazines and newspapers.

One of the simplest and most

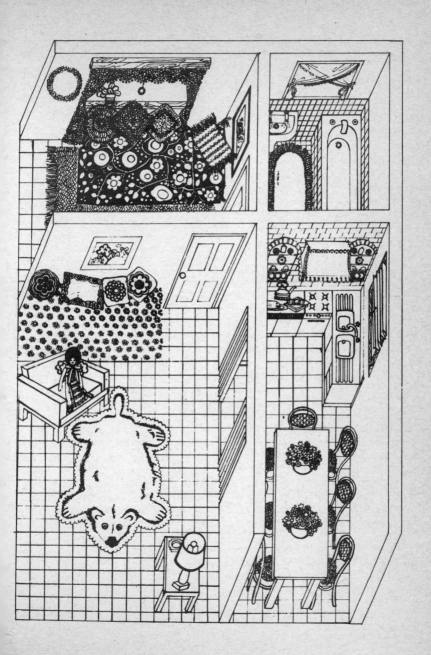

feminine decorations is a gathered frill of printed cotton added to the edge of the pillow-slip and a deep turn-back added to the top sheet. Another is to add a scalloped edging of *broderie anglaise* to both slip and sheet, while a more masculine way would be to stitch on a section of madras cotton to one side of a pillow-slip and a matching strip of striped madras to the top sheet turn-back. Other ideas are appliquéd initials, crossway bindings of checkerboard cotton, asymmetrical designs in colour and white with braided seamings, or set-in edges with dyed pillow-slips.

Adding Decoration. The simplest method of adding a decorative sheet turn-back is to cut a rectangle of coloured cotton 24″ by the width of the top of the sheet, unpick the sheet hem, press the turnings flat, and lay the coloured strip face down on to the right side of the sheet. Stitch through the three outside edges, starting and finishing $\frac{1}{2}$″ above the coloured fabric's lower edge. Turn through so that the right sides of the turn-back are outside, turn $\frac{1}{2}$″ along coloured raw edge, and tack flat before machine stitching through a scant $\frac{1}{8}$″ from fold. If you are not sure how to add a crossway binding, frill or edging, turn to page 78.

Other things such as decorative cushions, valances, roller blinds and curtains as illustrated here are explained in the following two chapters.

Decorative Rugs

These can be made in many ways for bedroom, bathroom or nursery.

Pom-pom Rugs can be made out of colourful pom-poms – page 303 – of rug wool, knitting wool, ribbons, $\frac{1}{2}''$ wide strips of cotton fabric or many other materials. The pom-poms are arranged to form a symmetrical or random pattern on a canvas or felt backing. The thread used to wind round the pom-poms should be threaded through the backing and tied neatly.

Fringed Rugs can be made by stitching strips of cheap string fringing onto a soft canvas backing. They can also be made by using a rug needle and string loops, which are knotted through a rugmaker's canvas backing. All these items can be bought at notion counters in the larger stores or specialist shops.

Rag Rugs are made from small strips of fabric – $\frac{1}{2}''$ to $1''$ wide and $3''$ to $4''$ long – which are looped at $\frac{1}{2}''$ intervals through an open weave canvas with a rug needle and the ends then passed through the loop and pulled tight, in much the same way as the fringed rug.

Plaited Rug. A traditional American Plaited Rug is made from long fabric strips, $1''$ wide, which are plaited together and then stitched through each plait to form an ever-increasing spiral. Repeat the plaiting and stitching until the

required size is reached before sticking and stitching onto a backing of canvas or felt.

Lampshades

Most lampshades are very simple to cover, requiring no more than an evening's work, and no special tools – just sharp scissors, dressmakers' chalk, needles and pins, a little Evo-stik or Copydex, sufficient fabric for covering, and some matching tape or bias binding.

1. Cut tape for covering the side

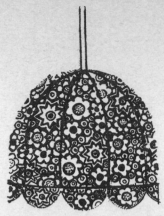

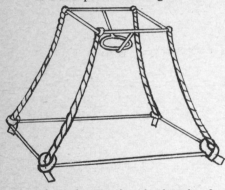

spokes about twice the length of each and bind from top to bottom, slot-knotting neatly at the base as shown in the diagram above. Cut a piece of tape about three times the top ring length and bind as for spokes, binding the bottom ring in a similar way and enclosing all the tape ends.

2. Next cut a rectangle of fabric on the crossway grain large enough to cover one section of the frame, allowing an extra 2″ all round. Pin fabric to spokes and pull firmly to shape along each side and

then pin the fabric to the taped top and bottom rings, again pulling tight. Mark round all the lines of pins with dressmakers' chalk. Take out the pins and then cut the shape, leaving ½″ turning allowance all round.

3. Cut remaining sections using the chalked shape as a guide, and then stitch together using a simple, flat or zig-zag neatened seam. Place cover over the frame, pulling and

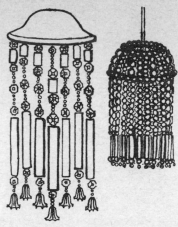

lampshades is to make an elasticated tube of fabric as follows:

1. Cut a rectangle of printed cotton fabric 3″ deeper and 3″ wider than the circumference of the lampshade frame.

2. Join the side seams to make a fabric tube which should fit over the frame quite easily. Neaten top and bottom by first creasing under $\frac{1}{4}$″ and then folding under another $\frac{3}{4}$″ turning, stitching through all thicknesses $\frac{1}{8}$″ from creased edge, top and bottom, to form an elastic casing.

pinning firmly into position, and making sure that the seam lines are running evenly with the spokes. Turn in the top and bottom raw edges and sew these firmly and neatly to the frame.

4. Add any braid or fringing, sticking with Evo-stik or Copydex before neatly sewing.

Elasticated Lampshade. An alternative method for covering simple

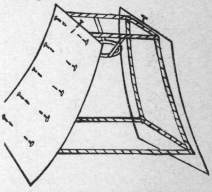

3. With the aid of a bodkin slot a length of narrow elastic into the top and bottom casings. Slip cover onto lampshade and tie elastic ends together so that they pull in the fullness, but allow the cover to be removed for laundering.

4. Trim with fringe or braiding, fabric scallops or beads, appliqué or ribbonwork, as explained elsewhere in this book.

Other easy lampshades include those covered in raffia or ribbons, paper or parchment, beads or crochet. Others can be decorated with various stick-ons of coloured pieces of plastic, sequins and felt shapes, dried flowers, lace motifs, embroidered cordings, appliqués, bobble edgings, coloured fringings, tassels – or indeed anything which looks interesting and decorative.

Beading is a simple form of decorative sewing which achieves interesting effects by random colourings and unusual textures. Unfortunately new beads are rather expensive so to begin with use old beads purchased in a street market or back-street junk-shop. The most

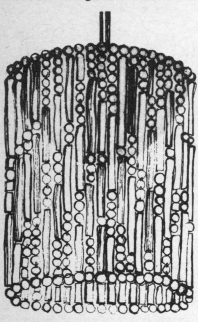

Decorative Beading

This is another easy way of making things for the bedroom, ranging from a beaded arch, as shown opposite, which can be used in a bedroom window, doorway or as a decorative bathroom screen, to beaded lampshades as shown below. (See page 268 for beaded curtains, 337 for a beaded blind hem; and the index for other beaded things.)

useful type to look out for are those used on old lampshades or curtains. They are usually very chunky and boldly coloured which makes them ideal for re-stringing. First of all clean them thoroughly, washing them in mild soapy water, with a soft scrubbing brush to get into the corners and grooves, before drying them with a soft towel and a hair drier. They are then ready for re-stringing on

214

upholstery twine, using beeswax to get a point on the twine rather than a needle, as a waxed thread without a needle is easier to manage. Beeswax can be bought at most needlework counters, and you simply rub the thread through the beeswax several times to give it a firm end.

bead – and tie the unwaxed end of the twine round it. Arrange the pattern of beads on to a convenient work table and slip the waxed thread through the beads one at a time. When the last bead is threaded – again a chunky round one – the thread is tied around it. Similar strings of beads can

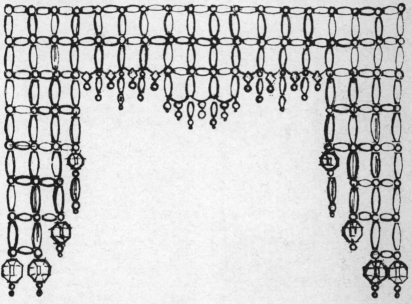

Hanging Beads. To make a string of hanging beads for use on a valance, lampshade or curtain first cut a length of upholstery twine or linen carpet thread about 12″ longer than the beading length required. Rub one end through the beeswax to give a firm threading end.

2. Thread an end stopper-bead on first – this is a chunky round

then be made and used as required.

3. If you are working on a particular design or sequence of beads you will find a strip of corrugated cardboard very useful for arranging the pattern. Lay out several areas of beads using the corrugated grooves to keep each line in place. This was the method used to arrange the elephant lampshade shown opposite.

215

Beaded Arch. These are usually made in the same way as the beaded curtains shown on page 269 except that each string of beads is a different length – the shortest ones hung in the middle and the longest at each end.

A beaded hem for a window-blind can be made by threading several chunky beads onto a length of twine, followed by a larger bead, then looping back through a coloured drop, metal section, wooden novelty or glass bugle bead as required before once again threading the waxed tip of the twine through several more chunky beads, and repeating the sequence until the beaded hem is complete.

The Bathroom

Many things can be made for the bathroom, including colourful checker-board towels with a matching flannel glove, comfortable bath head-rests, matching cushions and seat covers, bathroom tidies, curtains or decorative rugs. Just a few ideas are shown but many more can be designed and made by those who enjoy this kind of sewing.

Decorative Towels

Make these out of pretty coloured towellings, which you buy by the yard at most fabric counters. These towels may be as complex as the beach towel shown on the left, or plain-coloured with a deep string fringe stitched at each end. A matching hand flannel can also be made by stitching an 8″ by 10″

216

rectangle together so that it fits on the hand, rather like a child's mitten, and adding a coloured hanging tape or cord.

Head-rest. A simple rectangular head-rest, similar to the one shown top left, can be made out of a large bathroom flannel or 12" square of towelling.

1. First seam two parallel sides of a flannel together, the right

form into the head-rest and close tube by stitching 1" from end. If you are using a cut square of towelling instead of a flannel neaten the flange side with blanket or machine zig-zag stitch.

3. Finally, fix four rubber suckers to the back of the 1" end flanges.

Seat Covers

These can be made to fit over most bathroom chairs, stools, or

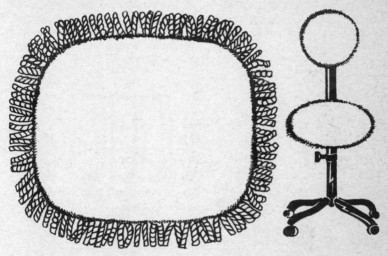

side inside, and then turn through to form a tube. One inch from one end stitch the tube edges together to form a fixing flange.

2. Next fill a 10" polythene sandwich bag with foam pieces and seal up the end with Sellotape. Slip this into another polythene bag, then into a third, reversing the open ends each time so that the filling is waterproof. Slip this inner

a w.c. lid. Generally they are best made in terry or stretch towelling, although other soft fabrics could also be used.

1. First cut your fabric shape 2" to 3" larger all round than the seat to be covered, then either crease over $\frac{1}{2}$" and stitch flat, or, if the fabric is too thick, bind in bias strip as explained on page 78.

2. Next, fold over 1" all round

217

and tack flat, easing in any fullness evenly before stitching $\frac{1}{4}''$ from inside edge right round the shape, but leaving a 1" gap at the back.

3. Slot a length of $\frac{1}{4}''$ or $\frac{1}{2}''$ elastic through this gap with the aid of a bodkin or safety-pin and pass right round inside the turning, taking care not to snag the fabric pile.

4. Place cover in position and draw out enough elastic to hold the cover there firmly before knotting the elastic ends. To remove for washing simply pull off, unknotting and removing the elastic if necessary.

Bathroom Rugs

Make them out of a simple rectangle or oval of thick terry towelling backed with a sheet of $\frac{1}{2}''$ thick underlay polythene foam or latex, and edged with a string fringe, as shown on page 217.

1. Cut a rectangle or oval of $\frac{1}{2}''$ polythene foam underlay – which can be bought by the yard at most large stores – and also cut a section of terry towelling the same shape.

2. Tack the towelling and polythene together edge to edge and then bind with a wide bias strip of cotton fabric.

3. Tack, then hand stitch, some string fringe around the shape so that the fringe webbing covers up the bound edge.

Bathroom Cushions

A great variety of fabrics can be used for bathroom cushions though they should be in something practical such as shiny plastic, sailcloth, linen or towelling. They can match curtains, seat covers, bath towels or a rug. The cushions should preferably be made around an inner waterproof shape, which can be bought ready-made at most stores; alternatively the filling can be packed inside several layers of sheet polythene or polythene bags before slotting into the cover.

Children's Rooms

Many functional as well as decorative things can be made for children's rooms; particularly toys, fun cushions, bedding and bed covers, curtains, wall-hangings, hot-water-bottle covers, pyjama cases, etc. Some of these are detailed on the following pages, while many more are explained in other chapters of this book.

Nursery Rugs

Rugs can be made out of colourful fur fabric trimmed with a contrasting fringe as shown opposite, or you can cut the fur fabric into an animal shape as shown on the following page.

Bear-skin Rug. To make this rug you must first cut a brown paper pattern to the size and shape required, experimenting with several patterns before cutting the fur fabric. From this pencil the shape onto the plain back of the fur fabric and then cut it out, using just the tips of the scissors to avoid cutting the pile. An alternative method is to cut out with a metal-backed razor blade, again using just the point.

Cut two ear shapes and a tail from the fur fabric scraps and sew these into position before trimming off the excess felt with pinking shears, or scalloping the edge as required.

3. Finally sew on a dark nose patch, two beaded eyes and looped rug-wool claws.

Coat-hangers

These can be made for children in gay and colourful designs, as can be seen by the illustration

2. Next, make a small oval pad for the head out of calico with rag stuffing, which should be about 2″ thick and ¼″ smaller all round than the head. Place the bear-shaped fur fabric and oval head pad onto a rectangle of coloured felt 3″ larger than the bear all round – remembering to allow for the tail – and hand stitch them together around the body shape.

opposite, by decorating plain hangers with pieces of brightly-coloured felt and fabrics. Stick these into position with Uhu glue, adding pieces of ribbon, beads, etc., before finally securing with a few hand stitches for strength.

Nursery Cushions

Follow much the same making and designing techniques as those used for animal and toy cushions,

220

explained on pages 14 and 15, and for normal cushions explained in the following chapter. However do avoid using any easily detachable trimmings which could be dangerous if swallowed.

Nursery Cases

The basic method for making a hot-water bottle or nightie case, or travelling nappy-holder is the same.

1. Cut a rough paper pattern to the size required, using a hot-water bottle or a folded child's nightie as a guide. Next add 1″ all round the basic shape, without bothering to copy the exact shape of the stopper or other intricate detail, as for this you need only draw a smooth curve.

2. For an average-sized hot-water

bottle cover, or decorative nightie case, the material needed is $\frac{1}{4}$ to $\frac{1}{2}$ yard of terry towelling, needlecord, velvet curtaining, corduroy or something similar, and an 8″ to 10″ zip. In addition several pieces of coloured felt, small pieces of lace or crochet, coloured embroidery silks, odd lengths of ribbon, or indeed anything you choose, can be used for decoration.

3. Cut two identical pieces of fabric to the size and shape of your pattern. Lay these edge to edge, right sides inside, and stitch $\frac{1}{2}$″ in along three sides, leaving the bottom end open. Next, turn the case right sides out, and firmly sew in the zip across the bottom, turning the edges under so that they do not show.

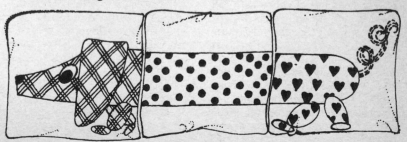

4. Cut pieces of coloured felt to shapes required – for example, two penny-sized pieces of blue felt for the eyes, and two ten-penny-sized pieces of red felt for cheeks – and stick and stitch these into position. Next, cut four ovals for ears, joining two together to make a pair, with a little lightweight stuffing sandwiched in between, and stitch these firmly to the side seam.

5. Make simple legs and arms; stitch on rug-wool hair, woollen poms-poms, lace edging, gay ribbon, etc., and embroider a mouth and any other features or decorations as required.

Nursery Pictures

Wall hangings can be made in many designs ranging from the simple felt stuck-and-stitched picture shown opposite and on page 363 to an intricately worked family portrait, as shown on page 375. The materials include a mixture of coloured and textured fabrics and felts with braids and beads, raffia, oddments of wools and strands of leather and plastic, in fact, anything that takes your fancy. There are no hard and fast rules; only those you care to make for yourself.

Garden Things

When sewing for out-of-doors you can try out bold decorative detailing or unusual colouring which, in a room, might be too dominating. You can use a pretty coloured cotton print for some garden seats;

or some striped towelling with a deep cotton fringe for a beach towel, with matching bikini, beach-bag and cushion; you could make a play tent out of the same material used for a kite; or a decorative garden swing to match a garden hammock.

Outdoor Cushions

Garden, picnic or beach cushions follow much the same principles of construction as those already explained on pages 14 and 15. However, certain types of fabric are obviously more suited to out-door use, such as deckchair canvas, PVC, sailcloth, bold checked linens or plastic coated fabrics. Water-proof cushions are especially useful for the garden; towelling is ideal for the beach provided a water-proof inner shape is used. Remember that the cushions will only be as practical as the fabric used.

Cushion Seat

A useful cushion-cum-seat can be made around a ready-made foam rubber square. Cover as for a normal square-gusseted cushion by cutting two sections of attractively striped or patterned towelling for the top and bottom, leaving 1″ seam allowance on all sides, plus a long gusset strip as explained on page 234. Stitch these sections together, including the gusset, $\frac{1}{2}$″ in from all edges, but leaving one edge completely open for turning through and for slotting in the inner foam shape before stitching up the gap. Alternatively a zip fastener

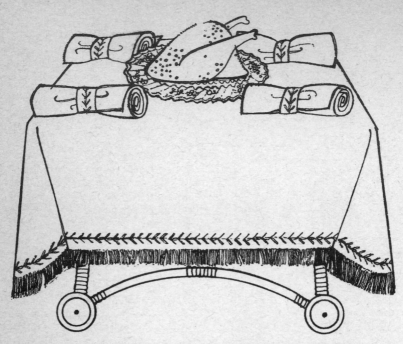

can be inserted to allow for easy removal for washing or drying.

Garden Tablecloth

Many of the decorative techniques explained in this book can be used on table linen for casual entertaining, outdoor picnics, barbecues or formal dinners.

1. Buy a piece of even weave fabric the length required – generally 3 yards of 54″ wide fabric is sufficient for a 6 ft table as this allows for 18″ to hang down all round. If the selvedge is tight and tends to hold in the fabric trim it away ½″ in from both edges. Also trim across both cut ends exactly on the grain. Crease over ¼″ to

wrong side all round and machine stitch to hold flat.

Next fold and press the hem 1″ in all round. At corners fold inwards diagonally on the 1″ crease line and then cut away the corner, leaving ¼″ seam allowance.

2. Refold the hem at the corners, tack up into position and then slip-stitch the diagonal mitre together as on page 64. Stitch hem into position by machining ⅛″ from both the creased and folded edges, or by using a decorative embroidery stitch.

3. For a simple embroidered hem finish, use the fern stitch shown on page 313. This is simply three straight stitches of equal length

radiating from the same point. You could also use one of the other stitches shown in Chapter 12 on Embroidery Stitches.

4. If you want to add a fringe, simply attach by first pinning the fringe accurately into position and then slip-stitching or embroidering it on with a chain stitch or similar embroidery stitch.

5. Finally, make some matching table napkins out of an extra length of fabric – six out of 1 yard of 54″ fabric cut into equal 18″ squares – stitching and decorating them in the same way as the tablecloth.

Decorative Swing

A garden swing can be made to look very decorative. The one illustrated on page 226, for instance, is a normal Galt play swing which can be purchased with all the necessary fixing points, side ropes and wooden seat; or the swing could easily be made at home by your husband if he felt so inclined.

1. Start by fixing the swing into a suitable position – under a tree, on a patio or in the corner of your sitting room. Make sure that the top fixing loops are screwed in correctly and that the side ropes are properly secured.

2. Start by decorating the side ropes with pretty ribbon, colourful braids, millinery flowers, beads and other attractive things, adding

several bows at the top and bottom of the side ropes.

3. Next cut a 2″ thick section of polythene or latex foam padding to fit on to the seat and form a cushion. Cut two rectangular sections of pretty printed cotton fabric, ½″ larger all round than the polythene shape. Next cut a side gusset section 3″ wide – that is 1″ wider than the foam shape – to go right round, plus extra for side seams.

4. Join all these sections together as for an ordinary cushion leaving one side open for slotting in the polythene shape.

5. Attach this cushion to the swing with ribbon side tapes which should be tied into bows around the side ropes.

Garden Hammock

Materials required: 2½ yards of strong striped deckchair canvas; 7 yards of carpet webbing for binding, coloured, striped or plain; 10 yards of strong upholstery webbing for end-hanging supports or some strong rope; two 2″ solid metal rings from an ironmonger's, a box of 1″ upholstery nails, two 1¼″ hardwood dowels the same width as the deckchair canvas; a heavy-duty machining needle, size 18 or 19 for most makes; some strong matching thread, either heavy-duty mercerized or six cord No. 24; a carpet needle; and linen carpet thread.

1. Bind the two long sides of the deckchair canvas with the carpet webbing, using a strong machine thread and heavy-duty needle. To bind accurately first cut a $2\frac{1}{2}$ yard length of webbing and press the width in half right along this length, making sure that the edges meet exactly all the way along. Slot the deckchair canvas in between this fold, first tacking and then machining right through $\frac{1}{4}''$ from inside edge.

stitched three or four times and then overcast is strongest.

3. Stitch on a piece of carpet webbing next to the end dowel casings so that they lie against the turned-in raw edges on each end, but leave $2''$ protruding each side as in diagram 3, page 229. Turn in this $2''$ allowance at each end and

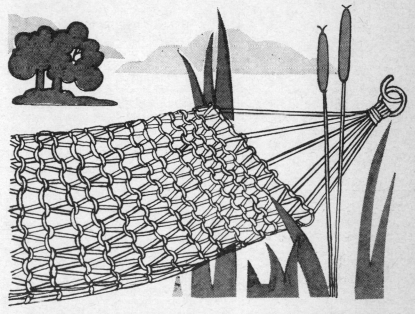

2. Turn over $2\frac{1}{2}''$ at each end of canvas to form the dowel casing and then machine stitch $\frac{1}{2}''$ from the raw edge right through both thicknesses as far as the webbing edges but preferably hand stitching both sides where the webbing overlaps to avoid breaking the machine needle. You will find that a carpet needle and linen thread back-

then turn webbing over to cover stitches, thus forming a flange.

4. Insert the dowel into end casing. Now cut the upholstery webbing into four equal sections $2\frac{1}{4}$ yards long. Turn in $1''$ at both ends of each piece and stitch down flat.

5. Take one of the prepared upholstery webbing strips and tuck one end under the carpet webbing

227

flange 1″ in from the edge. Using four strong upholstery nails, nail through the flange, upholstery webbing, and the canvas into the centre of the dowel. Similarly attach the three remaining pieces of upholstery webbing to the other corners, using four nails for each piece.

6. Next take the left-hand webbing strip and slot it through the special 2″ solid metal ring, then nail it with four nails into position 2″ beyond the exact centre of the dowel. Take the right-hand webbing and slot it through the metal ring, nailing it 2″ beyond the other side of centre so that the webbing strips cross each other but lie flat as they pass through the loop. Nail the gaps flat every 2″ between each strap.

7. Edgings. The easiest of all edgings to attach is a simple string fringe, which can either be bought by the yard or made, as illustrated on page 305. Other decorative edgings can also be used – scallops, dagging or tasselled edges, bobble fringing, cotton crochet, dried seeds and beads, appliquéd and bound sections, looped tassels, felt stick-ons, etc. See index for page numbers.

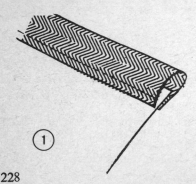

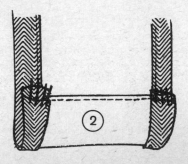

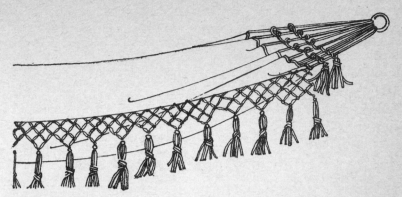

8. Make two bolster cushions from an extra length of matching or contrasting fabric, following the instructions on page 236. Finally loop the end rings safely between two suitable trees or other firm fixings.

Holiday Things

Striking beach towels and matching cushions as shown on the following page; a comfortable beach mattress with soft plastic filling and waterproof back, teamed with a matching bikini, as also shown; decorative beach-bags as explained on page 92

– together with many other things – can easily be made.

Beach Rug

This can be made out of plain and patterned terry towelling together with matching beach cushions and a towel set.

1. To make a beach rug with matching cushions and towels as illustrated on page 230, buy three 2-yard lengths of different towellings – plain, striped, patterned – 6 yards of 3″ bold string fringing, matching sewing threads and two medium-sized air cushions or poly-

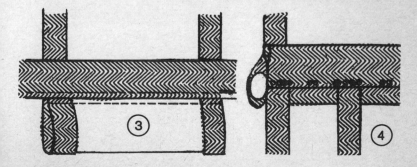

thene foam or latex cushion shapes.

2. First cut a long strip from the plain towelling 24″ wide, using the full length of the fabric and incorporating the neat selvedge edge. Next cut another long strip from the printed towelling 8″ wide, again incorporating the ready-neatened selvedge edge. Finally, cut a 16″ long strip of striped towelling.

3. Allowing ¾″ for seaming, join the raw edge of the 24″ strip to the 8″ strip selvedge edge, and then the 8″ strip raw edge to the 16″ strip raw edge. Press these seams open and then stitch each seam turning flat all the way down on to the main section ¼″ from seam line. On most towelling this is sufficient

neatening, although the turning can be cross-stitched down.

4. Turn in ½″ at each end and stitch flat. Finally cover the raw edge with the fringing strip and stitch into place at each end.

5. If you are making a pair of beach rugs then cut three more sections in the same way for the second rug, but using the contrast towelling in place of the plain one, the striped towelling in place of the contrasting one, and the plain towelling in place of the striped one. Seam these together as shown below. If, however, you prefer to make matching beach towels, proceed as follows:

6. To make a pair of matching

beach towels cut a rectangle of striped towelling 56″ long by 28″ wide, and a similar rectangle from the contrasting towelling. Turn under ½″ all round and stitch flat – preferably using a machine cross-stitch – before attaching the fringing strip at each end.

7. Use the remaining sections of towelling to make a beach cushion – the 28″ × 16″ rectangles for top and bottom with the long plain towelling cut into two 8″ wide lengths as gussets – or if you have three long sections left, seam these together and use them to cover either a pair of blow-up cushions or a foam shape.

Beach Bed

A simple beach mattress like the one on the right can be made from 2½ yards of towelling, 2½ yards of waterproof canvas or plastic, and 2¼ yards of 1½″ thick polythene foam or a blow-up beach mattress. Make the cover in exactly the same way as for a large cushion and then make a matching cushion and a bikini to complete the set.

Beach Tent

A beach tent for the children to play in can be made by following the instructions given on pages 103–4. Use bold designs with unusual colouring and exciting textures, freely interpreting the general methods of sewing given throughout this book so that you have fun developing original ideas of your own.

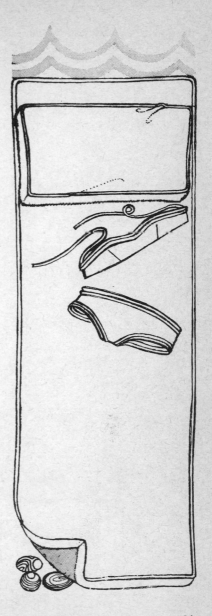

9. Cushions and Chair Covers

Buying Fabric

When choosing fabric for a set of cushions or loose chair covers always take a little time to browse around, visiting several shops and comparing snippets until you find something suitable, not only in colour and design, but also correct in type for the particular job. This last point is most important, as many of the disappointments in loose covers are due to choosing the wrong type of fabric. Before buying be certain that you have the necessary skill to handle the fabric chosen. If you are unsure of a particular fabric buy just a quarter of a yard to test your sewing skill. If it has a predominant pattern that requires matching then buy extra yardage or ask the salesman to reserve a length until you have cut and matched all the pieces required. Avoid choosing the same fabric you have always used just because you know how to handle it and how well it wears. Remember to be on the look-out for new ideas when making, as explained on page 7.

Finally, if you are a beginner, choose a fabric and something to make that is within your capabilities, for many unhappy and soul-destroying hours lie before the unwary beginner who foolishly attempts to make a tailored cover for an antique wingbacked chair before covering a simple contemporary chair first. Success on simple things leads to the confidence needed when tackling a more sophisticated task.

Trimmings

The choosing or making of trimmings for cushions or chair covers is as important as choosing the correct type of fabric, so be sure to buy or make trimmings as well and as imaginatively as you can.

Which type to use on a particular design depends partly on one's own particular taste, partly on the fabric being used, partly on the usability of the trimming or decoration and partly on the prevailing decorative trends. However, as the basic idea is to enhance the general look of the

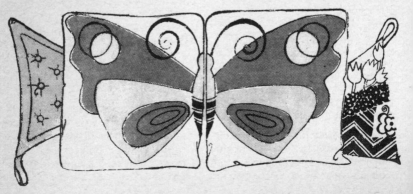

232

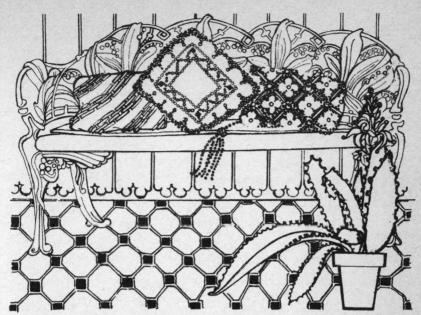

design, making it more interesting or adding a touch of originality, it should be well made and nicely finished.

Fringing. Many types of ready-made fringing are available for use on cushions or loose covers. The most popular is the chunky string fringe which is hand-stitched on flat around the edge. An alternative is a bobble edging stitched on to a scalloped or interestingly shaped edge. The best thing to do is to look at other chairs, see what can be bought over the counter, and choose what you like best.

Edge decoration, such as cording, braiding, top-stitching, couching and even lace edging or crochet can be used on some decorative chairs or cushions, particularly those used in a bedroom or bathroom.

Surface Decoration. A wide range of embroidery stitches can be made on most automatic or swing-needle sewing machines whilst many more hand stitches and traditional motifs can be worked by those who have both the time and patience – see chapter 12 for details. Among the materials which can be used are string, braids, leather, raffia, plastic, beads, sequins, ribbons and many other novelties.

An alternative to embroidery would be patchwork with a choice between the classic geometric style explained in chapter 14, which is made by using lozenge, hexagonal, triangular or square shapes, and

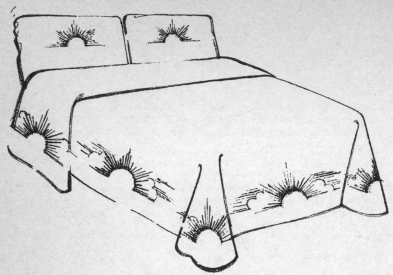

crazy patchwork if you want to use various pieces of interestingly overlaid coloured and decorated fabrics in random shapes and sizes. Appliqué patchwork can also be used, as could appliqué itself. The first essential however is to become really proficient at using an automatic swing-needle machine unless you enjoy working by hand.

Other suggestions include crochet, quilting, cording, couching, ribbon work, or tufting. Look around and choose the most interesting method for your cushion design.

Cushion Making

To make a flat square cushion cut two identical squares of fabric and lay them together face to face with edges exactly matching. Stitch all round $\frac{1}{2}''$ in, leaving a turning-through opening 6" long in the middle of one side. Turn cushion

through this gap so that the fabric is right side out and then slip in ready-made inner cushion or fill with kapok, polythene cuttings or similar inexpensive filling before slip-stitching gap edges together.

Foam Shapes. Several types of foam rubber or expanded plastic cushion shapes or pieces for cutting are sold by the leading stores and draper's. They should first be covered in a cheap cotton or calico and then covered in fabric in the normal way, and be either detachable, using Velcro or a zip fastening – see pages 70–72 – or permanently stitched as for normal cushions.

Gussets. A cushion with a side gusset is best made to fit an existing shaped inner cushion or a polythene or latex foam shape. Cut two sections of fabric of the required shape $\frac{1}{2}''$ larger all round than the

234

inner shape, for the top and bottom of the cushion. Now cut a gusset section 1″ wider than the depth required, and long enough to go right round, plus extra for side seam allowances.

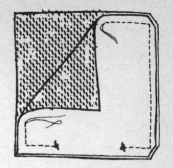

Measure the exact length round the cushion shape and then join gusset sections together to this size. Pin gusset to base section, face to face and edge to edge, snipping gusset at ½″ intervals around the corners. Stitch ½″ in from edge and then attach top section in the same way, leaving one end open for inserting the inner shape before finally slip-stitching the gap together.

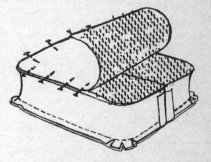

Piped Edges. Piped cushions are made in exactly the same way as ordinary ones except that a piping section is placed between the fabric pieces to be joined together.

First cut several lengths of 1″ wide crossway strips from the fabric you are using as explained on page 73, and join these together to form a continuous strip a little longer than the length of piping you need for the cushion. Fold this strip around a piping cord so that the raw edges meet, then tack-stitch through the turnings so that the cord is pushed tightly against the folded edge. Using a piping foot machine-stitch close to the cord.

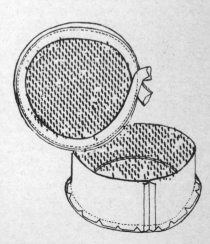

To apply the piping, simply pin, tack and then machine the piping into position as you make the cushion seams with raw edges of piping matching raw edges of fabric, joining the piping as shown

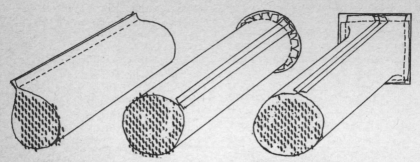

on page 244 and then proceed as already described.

Inset Edges. A cushion with an inset frill or bought inset edging is made in exactly the same way except that the inset section is placed between the top and bottom fabrics in much the same way as attaching a piping section, as shown below.

Soft Bolsters

For a 7″ high bolster, cut a rectangle of fabric the length required plus 6″, and 24″ wide. Fold the width in half so that the two long edges meet, with right sides facing, and stitch ½″ from edge leaving a 6″ gap in the centre for turning through. Run a double gathering

stitch 1″ in from each end, pull in tightly, and then fasten securely, stitching through gathered turnings for added strength. Turn through central gap and stuff with kapok or other inexpensive filling before slip-stitching the gap together.

Shaped Bolsters

Make a long tube as shown above for a soft bolster, but allowing only 1″ extra in length. Cut two circles of fabric 8″ across and stitch these into each end, remembering to snip the tube end turning allowance at ½″ intervals as shown. Turn through central stitching gap and fill with stuffing before slip-stitching gap together.

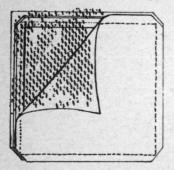
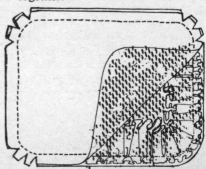

Round Cushions

Cut two round pieces of fabric the required size, adding a $\frac{1}{2}''$ seam allowance all round using a large meat plate as a guide. Apply piping right round one side, clipping piping turnings every $\frac{1}{2}''$. Place over the other fabric circle, right sides together, and stitch right through

cross tacking. Thread four thicknesses of strong linen carpet thread on to a long darning needle and tie all the ends securely to the metal shank of a self-covered or matching button which has a shank and then sew through the cushion. Pass needle through the shank of the second button and then pass it back through the cushion under

on top of piping stitches, leaving a 4″ gap on one side. Turn through gap and stuff before slip-stitching edges together. Finally sew a covered or decorative button in the centre as explained below.

Buttoned Cushions

Mark the exact positions of the buttons on to the finished cushion with white tailor's chalk or with

the first button, pulling tight. Cut, leaving 5″ of thread for tying off. The four strands are then divided into twos. Pass two strands around and under one side of the first button and two round and under the other side, knotting them tightly three times where they cross, and again on the other side of the button, before cutting away the thread ends.

Hanging Cushions

Tapes, ties, strapping or rouleaux loops can be used to fix most specially shaped cushions into their correct positions, and can also add an interesting design feature to a particular chair, such as the bolster-shaped cushion shown on page 240, which has leather straps attaching it to the back of a modern cane and wood armchair, or the suspended rectangular foam-covered cushions with fabric rouleaux loop fixing at the top, shown opposite. Hanging cushions are made in exactly the same way as the shaped cushions already described, the only difference being that the method of fixing must be considered as an integral part of the general construction. Also make sure that the fixing is strong enough to support the cushion in use.

Slot-in Cushions

Some chairs have specially constructed recesses in their framework into which shaped cushions 'slot in', as in the chair on page 240. These cushions are constructed in the normal way but special care should be taken that the fit is accurate. Slot-in cushions should not be confused with detachable seats, which are made on a wooden frame as shown on page 243.

Notched Cushions

Some chairs have fitted cushions with notched-out corners which fit snugly around the arm and back supports. Care should be taken when making or re-covering these cushions to fit these areas accurately but apart from this they are made in the normal way.

Outdoor Cushions

For garden, picnics or beach use follow much the same principles as for indoor cushions. However, certain types of fabric are obviously more suited to outdoor use, such as deckchair canvas, sailcloth, terry towelling, PVC and plastic-coated fabrics. Remember that the cushion will only be as practical as the fabric used.

Couch Cushions

Cushions for couches are very much the same as the chair cushions previously described, except that they tend to be slightly larger with a more robust construction. Also the grouping of three or more together does present an interesting possibility for some original design ideas, possibly along the lines of those shown on the left, which have been decorated with appliqués of coloured felt, pieces of PVC and cording.

Grouped Cushions

As shown opposite and on pages 221, 232, 361, etc., they follow much the same principles of making as ordinary cushions, but the actual size and shape of the groups to-gether with the decoration depend as much on the inventiveness of the maker as on their intended use. When starting it is best to rough out the intended shape on a sheet of firm paper in much the same way as explained for decorative nursery cases on pages 221–2 with single designs varying from an owl, pig, lion, to cow-shapes grouped into a zoo, or square cushions decorated as the head, body and legs, etc.

Pillows

The distinction between pillows and cushions is very difficult to define, as you will see by the illustrations on the previous six pages. In fact, pillows for studio couches often double up as cushions during the daytime. Generally pillows are softer than cushions, being fitted with feather-filled inner pillows which are usually bought ready-made. But apart from that their covers can be constructed in

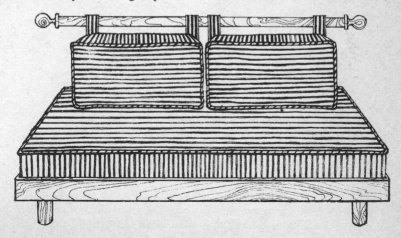

any of the ways described. If your pillows are used during the daytime, make some detachable covers to put on top of the pillow-slips, as explained below.

Cushion Covers

Detachable cushion or pillow covers can be made to fit all shapes and sizes simply by making the cover $\frac{1}{4}''$ to $\frac{1}{2}''$ larger than the original cushion or pillow, with a large enough opening gap to slip over the cushion easily. This gap is fastened with a zip or press studs as explained on page 249.

Applied Decoration. Many sorts of applied surface decoration can be used for making simple-shaped cushion and pillow covers attractive and original. Other possibilities also present themselves when the covers are made in unusual shapes, such as the animal cushions and nursery cases. The border line between fantasy and possibility is your choice, so spare a thought for the decorative as well as the functional use of your cushions.

Covering Chairs

Making a loose cover for a simple chair is very much like making cushion covers. Many types of chair coverings can be made, apart from the traditional fully upholstered easy-chair ones, so if you are a beginner it is better to try

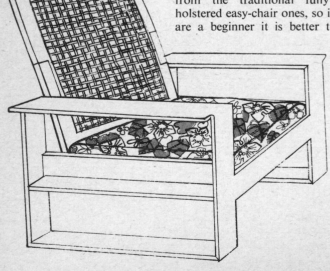

those described on the following pages before attempting the more complex shapes. The first thing you need to do is to select the right fabric for the cover and estimate accurately the yardage required.

Fabric

A wide variety of fabrics suitable for chair covering is on sale at most furnishing-fabric counters in the larger stores or specialist shops, ranging from the traditionally patterned natural fibre fabrics to the newest ranges of stretch synthetics. It is wise, however, to shop around comparing snippets and prices before deciding which is the best for a particular chair. On page 232 are some notes on buying fabric and trimmings which you might find helpful; also see page 53.

Yardage. If your chair is as simple as the one shown on page 242 then the measuring method is quite adequate – you measure the seat depth from front to back, plus the back height, plus an extra half yard for underlaps and turnings, of 48"/54" fabric. If, however, your chair is more complex, then the paper pattern or pinned-on calico methods are best used (see page 247).

Before starting to cut and make

a loose cover, spend a little time reading the general cutting information given in Chapter 3, testing your fabric for ironability and tendency to fray, as well as testing your machine tension, stitch size and needle thickness. Make sure that all your equipment is at hand and arranged for ease of use as this will save much time when actually sewing.

Chair Backs

Chair backs, as shown opposite, are simply made from a square or rectangular cushion with the addition of a back-hanging flange which is made 6″ to 8″ deep. This is then sewn on to the back of the cushion and fitted over the top of the chair back. Alternatively, hanging straps can be used as shown on page 240.

Detachable Seats

Many types of chair have detachable seat sections, as distinct from fitted cushions. These wooden-framed and webbed seats are much easier to cover than most cushions if the webbing and stuffing are reasonably intact.

1. Cut a square of fabric allowing 4″ turning-under allowance on all sides, and making sure that any design motif is centralized. Turn in ¼″ all round and stitch. Place the seat in the centre of the wrong side of the fabric and pull the edges, pinning the trimmings firmly to the under-canvas or webbing. Next pin away the surplus corner fabric into large mitres before hand stitching into position as shown.

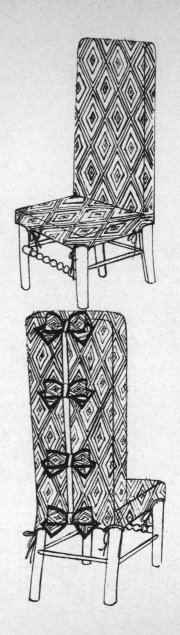

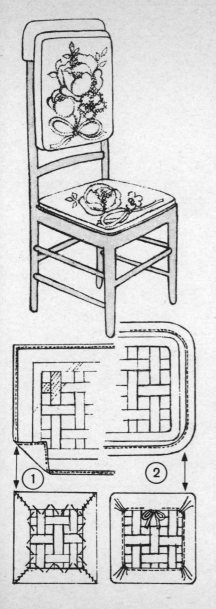

2. For detachable covers cut fabric as above, rounding off the corners with a saucer. Crease under $\frac{1}{4}''$ and then turn in $\frac{3}{4}''$, stitching $\frac{1}{8}''$ from crease edge, leaving a $2''$ gap at the centre back for slotting through the fixing tape. After inserting the tape, place the cover over the seat, centralizing any design motif, draw up tape ends and tie securely.

Sewing Methods

On the following two pages are shown a few of the sewing methods used for making pipings, corners, or for fastening chair covers. Other methods such as seam finishing, machine stitching and edgings are given in Chapter 2 on basic sewing methods, whilst surface decoration is dealt with in Chapters 12 to 14.

Piping Strips are cut on the true crossway grain which runs diagonally across the fabric. This diagonal line can be found by folding the corner of the fabric over so that the cut end runs parallel to the selvedge edge. Crease along the diagonal fold and then cut along the crease line. Cut several strips parallel to the diagonal cut and then join these together along their straight grain lines as shown in diagram 1, page 244. Press each seam open to obtain a continuous strip. Alternatively cut a single strip of fabric which is wide enough for several piping strips and seam together before cutting into a continuous strip as shown on page 73, diagram 2.

Corded Piping. Cut a length of cord ½" longer than the length required and place it on to the wrong side of the bias strip. Fold the strip in half so that the raw edges meet and tack-stitch through the turnings so that the cord is pushed tightly against the folded edge of the binding as in diagram 2. Using a piping foot machine stitch close to the cord over the top of the tacking.

Joining Piping. Cut along the exact grain lines of piping pieces to be joined so that they are complementary diagonals. Cut the cord of one end ¾" short and fold under a ¼" turning, leaving the other cord end protruding ¼" as in diagram 3. Slot in so that the fold covers the raw edges and then slip-stitch together.

Piped Seam. Lay the piping on to the seam so that the raw edges are together, and the piping-stitch line exactly matches the fitting lines. Tack piping into position before adding the other section which is to be joined. If there is a square corner, snip the piping turnings as shown in diagram 4 so that a neat corner can be made.

Curved Piping. If a curved seam is to be piped then the turnings of the piping will need to be snipped at ½" intervals, as shown in diagram 5 on the right. The piping is then attached in the normal way.

Mitred Corner. Turn the hem up on to the right side of the fabric

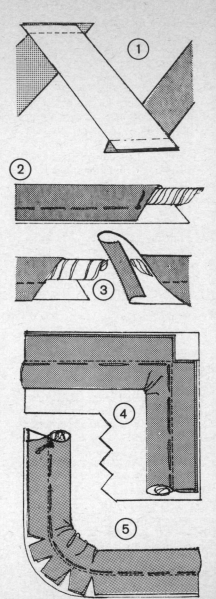

and then turn edge also on to the right side. Even out the corner pleat so that a matching diagonal line runs from corner to edge junctions and mark with a crease line. Run-stitch along crease line as shown in diagram 1 on page 64 before cutting pleat away, leaving $\frac{1}{4}''$ turnings. Turn corner through so that the hem and side allowances are now in their correct positions before slip-stitching them neatly.

Lapped Corner. First turn up and tack hem into position in the normal way. Next fold over the side turning into its correct position, marking with chalk exactly where it laps over the hem. Trim away the overlapped section to within $1''$ of chalk line and $\frac{1}{2}''$ from bottom edge before lapping back and hand sewing as shown in diagram 2, page 64.

Round Corners. A separate facing is required when neatening a round or curved corner. Pin, tack, and machine stitch the facing into position and then trim turnings to $\frac{1}{4}''$. Notch the turning around the curve as shown on the right before turning through and tacking flat, as in diagram 3 on page 64.

Velcro Fastening. This is a strip fastening which can be bought in various lengths and colours in the same way as a zip fastener. It is made from two strips of tape covered in hundreds of tiny plastic hooks which interlock the tapes together. One tape is stitched to the

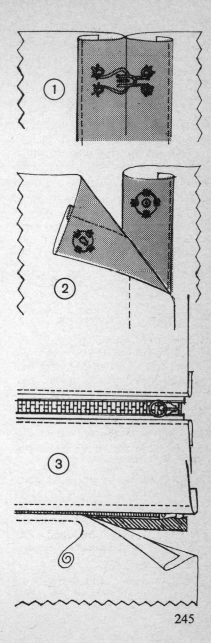

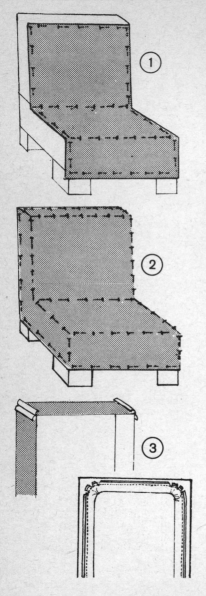

underside of an opening, while the other is stitched to the surface of the underlap. When pressed against each other the Velcro strips fasten together.

Hooks and Eyes. Sew the hooks on the inside turning of a simple opening so that the hook end is level with the edge. Sew the eye section on to the opposite turning so that when they are hooked together the seam edges meet as shown in diagram 1, page 245.

Press Studs. Always make sure that the ball and socket sections are sewn on so that they are opposite each other. Sew the ball section on first, then place the underlap into position and press so that the ball makes an impression for placing the socket correctly.

Exposed Zip. Cut along the grain in the exact position where a zip fastener is required. Crease under a $\frac{1}{4}''$ turning along each edge of the cut and then pin the closed zipper in position, laying the crease lines $\frac{1}{4}''$ away from the centre of the zip teeth. Tack flat, and then attach a zipper foot to the sewing-machine and stitch a scant $\frac{1}{8}''$ away from the crease line.

Lapped Zip. Turn under the edges of the opening, tack, and press into position. Pin the closed zip fastener under the tacking, making sure that the centre-line of the teeth is exactly under the centre of the fold and that the zip top is $\frac{1}{2}''$ away from the end turning allowance. Tack zipper into position $\frac{1}{4}''$ from the edge of the teeth. Attach zipper foot to the sewing-machine and adjust to a medium stitch before stitching over the top of the tacking lines.

Chair Covering

If the chair you wish to cover already has a loose cover then it is an easy job to trace out the various fabric pieces on to a sheet of brown wrapping paper which you then use as a pattern. If your chair does not have a cover then, before cutting out your fabric, you should make a paper pattern as follows:

1. Cut square shapes out of cheap brown paper, taking the sizes from exact measurements of your chair, and allowing 1″ to 2″ for turnings – these are later trimmed to ½″ after a pinned fitting of the fabric. Label each pattern piece according to its position and check each one against the chair for reasonable accuracy. Where you have two identical sections, such as a left and right side panel, then two patterns should be cut with the correct side of the fabric marked on for left and right. Lay all these pattern pieces onto a carpet to find out the exact length of material required. Remember to fit the pieces into a normal 48″/54″ width of fabric and make sure that each piece is laid facing the correct way, so that the pattern or pile is running all the same way when cut. Measure the total length and add on an extra yard for pipings, under-flanges and forgotten allowances.

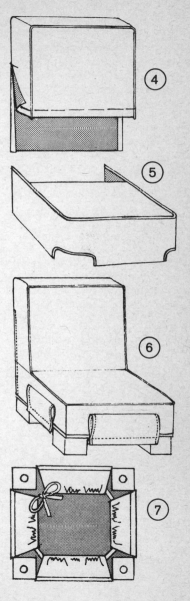

2. Having placed your brown paper pattern on the fabric with all pieces correctly laid for pile as detailed, cut the fabric required making certain that any bold design feature is centralized on the larger pieces.

Place the fabric on to the chair, pinning accurately along each seam. Allow ½″ seam allowance everywhere, but leave 2″ on hems, and cut away excess fabric, marking pin line with pencil or chalk.

3. Start making by stitching pipings to the seat and back sections and joining top gusset seams to form side shaping.

4. Stitch front and back sections each side of top shaping, taking care to match corners correctly and leaving the last 8″ of the outside back as a zip opening.

5. Stitch seat to side shaping and join seat to back section along 'waist' line. Slip cover over chair to check fit, adjusting where necessary, and mark leg cut-outs. Pipe or turn back along these marks. Next stitch in matching coloured upholstery zip as shown on page 245.

6. Cut the under-fixing flanges 8″ wide by the length between legs on all four sides, allowing ½″ seam allowances. Turn in this allowance and stitch flat. Fold the 8″ width in half right sides outside and stitch to hem 1″ from edge.

7. Fit the cover on to the chair, checking the fit after centralizing all panels and seam lines. Turn chair upside-down and slot some strong tape or string through the

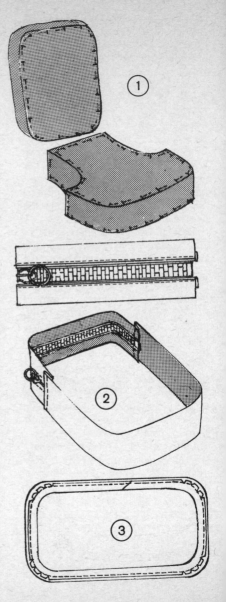

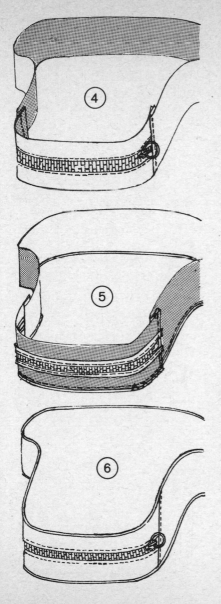

under-fixing flanges, and tie tightly as shown on page 247.

Fitted Cushions

When you are covering a chair with fitted cushions it is essential to obtain an accurate pattern. If the cushion has a loose cover, use this as a guide by placing it flat on to a sheet of brown paper and tracing round it, and then adding on $\frac{1}{2}''$ for turnings. Measure the gussets and cut your pattern accordingly. If there is no loose cover, then:

1. Lay the cushion on to a sheet of thin brown paper and trace round it, adding on $\frac{1}{2}''$ turning allowances. Pin this shape to the cushion to check accuracy.

2. Cut two fabric pieces using the pattern and then cut the gusset sections by measuring each gusset accurately, then adding $\frac{1}{2}''$ for each seam. Pin all the sections together over the cushion to check fit.

3. Cut the back gusset section in half widthways and crease under $\frac{1}{4}''$ along the cut edge. Lap this crease on to a zip of the correct length and colour so that the fold is $\frac{1}{4}''$ from the centre of the teeth. Tack into position and then tack on the other side in the same way. Attach a zipper foot to the machine and stitch a scant $\frac{1}{8}''$ away from crease lines as shown on page 245, diagram 3, for an exposed zip.

4. Lap-stitch the side of the gusset section over the zip section, creasing under the end allowances before stitching through $\frac{1}{8}''$ from crease line, as in diagram 2.

5. Stitch the pipings on to the

249

major cushion sections, remembering to attach the piping foot and to snip the piping turning allowance every $\frac{1}{2}''$ round the curves and at corners as explained in the basic piping method on page 244.

6. Tack and then stitch the completed gusset section on to the piped body section, right sides inside, remembering to centralize the zip. Tack and then stitch on the other body section.

7. Turn cushion cover through and check that its shape is true and not twisting to one side: this will happen if you have not centralized the sections correctly. Slip in the cushion shape, zip up, and check the fit.

Armchair Covers

Use the brown paper pattern method described earlier in this chapter, and place the paper pieces against the chair to check curves, difficult corners or odd angles. This paper pattern, however, is only used as a rough guide for cutting a calico shape, which is then pin-fitted on the chair for the correct pattern shaping.

1. Remove the fitted cushions and look at the method and seam placement used in their construction. If they have zip-on covers these should be removed as an accurate flat pattern can easily be traced from them. If, however, the cover is permanent you should lay the cushion on to a sheet of cheap brown wrapping paper and trace round the shape to make a pattern, also measuring the side shaping

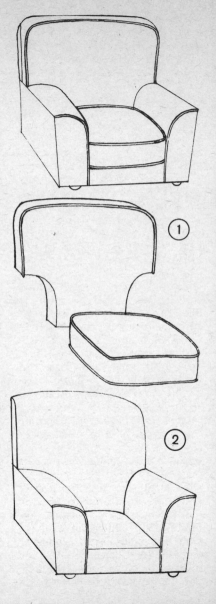

width and length from seam to seam, cutting corresponding pattern pieces as explained above.

2. With the cushions removed inspect the chair for seam placement, tuck-ins, difficult shaping, easing or darting, etc., adjusting the paper pattern accordingly.

3. Using cheap calico, preferably of medium weight with a slightly firmish feel, cut out the various chair sections with the paper pattern as a guide, but allowing 1″ to 2″ for a pinning and alteration allowance. Pin each piece accurately along each seam line, then cut away the excess, leaving 1″ seam allowances everywhere. With an ordinary pencil draw along each pin line and mark notch lines at seam junctions, easing allowances and curves. Mark the fabric grain lines on to each pattern piece with a line indicating any surface texture or design feature. Lay all the calico pattern pieces on to the floor, arranging them in jigsaw fashion to find out how much fabric is required, remembering that of several sections you need a left- and a right-hand side, for which you use the brown paper patterns as duplicates. Fit all these pieces into the intended fabric width, making sure that each piece is laid facing the correct way, so that the surface design or pile will all be going in the same direction. Measure the total length, adding an extra $1\frac{1}{2}$ yards for piping, extra hemmings, and forgotten allowances. Also add on a length for cushions if required.

4. Using the calico pattern as a

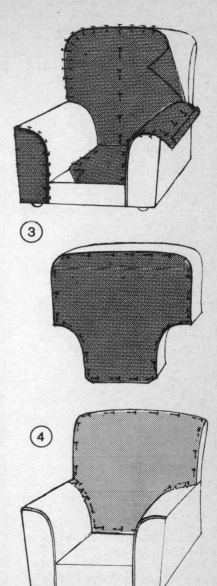

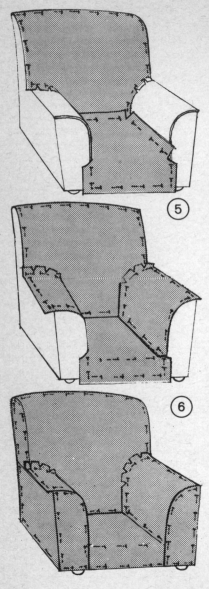

guide, cut out the various fabric pieces, again making sure that the grain and design arrows are all facing up the length of fabric, but add an extra 4″ to 6″ tuck-in allowance on all inside seat seams, inside body and inside arm pieces, and 6″ for hems. With the right side of the fabric facing the chair – except for very boldly designed fabrics which have to be centralized and seam-matched – pin each piece into position, starting with the inside back section. At the crevice at the bottom of the inside back a tuck-in allowance of 4″ should be left, while the other edges should be cut to a 1″ allowance. Using pencil or chalk, mark seam lines, dart positions, seam junctions and easing allowances.

5. Next pin on the seat section, again placing the face of the fabric against the chair. Start by pinning the centre of the seat into position, smoothing out the fabric towards the edges and over front spring-edge. Pin along each side of the seat and across the back, trimming these tuck-in allowances to 4″. Bring the fabric down over the front spring-edge and pin each side to the seam line and also along the hem. Cut the side front seam allowances to ½″ but leave maximum for hem allowance – approximately 5″ to 6″. Pin the inside top arm sections into position and check that the grain lines are running correctly and that any design motif is properly centralized. Cut seam allowances to ½″, notching into that allowance at the inside

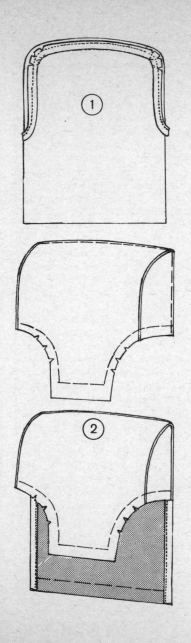

back of arm curve so that the fabric lies flat, but remember to leave a 4″ tuck-in allowance along seat edge.

6. Pin side panels into position, leaving maximum hem allowance but trimming the rest to $\frac{1}{2}$″ for normal seaming. Similarly attach and trim the front arm sections and the small side back sections. Mark all the seam allowances with chalk or pencil, together with extra notches at seam junctions, darts, and easing or curve positions.

The last piece of fabric to pin into position is the back section. Take extra care that it hangs correctly and that the grain lines are not forced out of shape.

If there is any particular difficulty in matching an area or curve on the chair, it is wise to spread the seam lines open and chalk-mark on the front of the fabric each side of the seams so that these chalk marks can be easily matched when seaming together. Finally mark the opening length on the back and side sections with surface chalk-marks, the length being about 4″ to 6″ above arm seams.

Making up. Start by making the covers in the same way as the fitted cushions explained on page 249, taking care to fit these accurately. During the cushion making, note any peculiarities of the fabric, and any tendency to fray or shrink. Check your sewing machine, insert a new strong machine needle, and thread with strong enough thread – needle 14 or 16 and thread 40 are correct for most domestic sewing machines. Adjust stitch length and tension before starting and also make sure your iron is clean – see pages 37–9.

1. Unpin the entire cover, checking marks and allowances as you go, to make sure that nothing has been forgotten. Then stitch the piping to the small upper side sections and then to the back section, curving the piping out at arm seam notches. as in diagram 1, page 253.

2. Start putting the main body section together by first stitching the piped upper side sections to the front of chair back section, being very careful when rounding the curve so that just the right amount of ease is allowed. Next join the top back section to the front section (diagram 2). Turn in the side seam allowance of the back section, below the stitched sections, and tack flat ready for inserting the two zip fasteners – these should be medium weight zips, the exact length of the openings, and a good colour match – , or alternatively use Velcro strip, or hooks and bars and press studs.

3. Stitch the corded crossway piping on to the front arm sections. snipping the piping turning allowance around the curves and in the corners. Join inside arm section to side panel section along their top edges and then seam on to the front arm section. This particular seam is a little tricky so be very accurate with matching your balance notch-marks and giving just the right amount of ease around

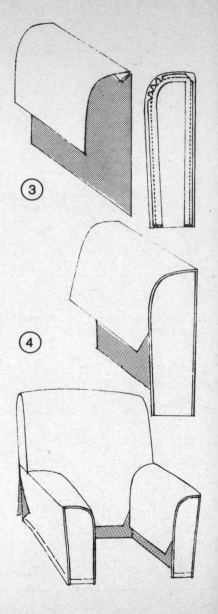

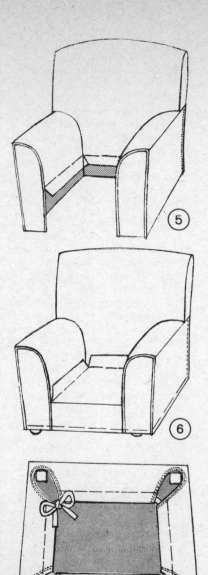

the curves and in the corners. Also remember to stop your stitching at the inside arm tuck-in allowance marks – see diagram 4 opposite.

4. Put back section on to the chair and check fit and seam placement angles. Also check arm sections in the same way and see that the proposed seam line joining the arms to the back fits together neatly. Remove cover from chair and seam arm sections to the back, leaving side seams open for zip or Velcro insertion.

5. Insert zip fasteners as shown on page 245 for a lapped zip opening.

Fit the cover back on to the chair and check fastenings for fit. Tuck in the 4″ tuck-in allowance and then lay on the seat section, checking that the seam edges will fit together accurately. Remove cover and seam the seat section to the body and then put on chair again for a final check.

6. To make a plain tailored finish to your chair see whether most of the 6″ hem allowance is still in place. If the cover is 'pulling up' because the fit is too tight, some of this allowance may have disappeared. If between 4″ to 5″ is still hanging below the chair line, then make a tailored hem, but if not, add either an extra taping flange as detailed on page 248, or a frill, scallop, or pleated hem as shown on pages 256–7. For a tailored hem, turn the chair upside down and pin the hem allowance firmly to the bottom canvas. Using either tailor's chalk or a pencil,

255

mark round each chair leg before cutting surplus away, remembering to leave $\frac{1}{2}''$ for turning allowance. Remove the cover from the chair and turn in the $\frac{1}{2}''$ seam allowance around shaped leg cut-outs, stitching twice to hold them flat. Alternatively, bind or face these edges, using a crossway strip, before stitching them flat. Turn back a hem of about 1" along the four remaining bottom edges, and then use this as a tape casing. Slot a strong tape through the casing and then slip the cover on to the chair, pulling the tape end tight and tying ends together very firmly, as shown in diagram 6, page 255, and tuck the surplus tape under the hem allowance.

Decorative Hems

The bold 'Pullman' armchair shown on the previous six pages is best left with a simple tailored hem as the designers intended. If, however, your chair is of a different shape, then a decorative hem finish could be applied. Make your loose cover in exactly the same way but allow an extra 1 to 2 yards of fabric, depending on the shape of hem required.

Frilled hem. Measure the depth of the frill required from the bottom edge of the chair to the required distance from the floor – generally between 6" and 8" – adding 2" for hem and top turnings. Cut strips of fabric this depth, twice the chair circumference. Join all the side seams together into a continuous strip. Turn up a $1\frac{1}{2}''$ hem and stitch flat.

If the chair sides are equal, divide the frill length into four sections by folding in half and then folding again, marking each fold with a pin. If the sides of the chair vary, modify the pin markings accordingly.

Cut the back section along the folded lines and then neaten the cut edges by turning under and stitching flat. Next gather each of the marked sections separately along the fitting line $\frac{1}{2}''$ from the top edge as for the dressmaking frill illustrated on page 157. Pin the marked folds on to the four corners of the chair cover and draw up the gathering threads, distributing the fullness evenly. Pin to the cover at 2″ intervals. Remove the cover from the chair with the frill still pinned in place, carefully unpinning each section and turning upside down so that the frill and cover are face to face ready for stitching. Re-pin frill so that the gathering threads match the bottom edge of the chair cover and then machine stitch into place along the fitting lines. Stitch a second line $\frac{1}{8}''$ nearer the raw edges for strength.

Pleated Hem. A pleated hem is made in a similar way to the gathered hem explained above, using the same depth of fabric but varying the length of the strips according to the pleats required –

generally two to three times the perimeter is needed. Join the side seams together, neaten the hem, and then divide into four sections as previously explained. Arrange the pleats as required – knife edge, box or inverted pleats – or have the hem section permanently pleated. Attach to hem as explained above.

Scalloped Hem. Many differently shaped edges can be added to the hem of a chair. These edges are made from strips of fabric cut 2″ longer and 2″ wider than the finished sizes required. Mark, stitch and turn the edges through – as explained on page 75 – and then stitch these to the chair cover in the same way as a frilled hem.

10. Curtains and Bedspreads

In this chapter we are going to explain the simplest ways of making several basic curtains, some decorative swags, pelmets, window blinds, bed drapes and bedspreads. Beginners should tackle the simplest curtains first before attempting the more complex swags and drapes for the pleasure of finishing and hanging your first simple curtains will be much more rewarding than the disappointment of uneven drapes due to inexperience.

Curtains

The variations of curtain styles are infinite, as are the fabrics. You can use plain and printed cottons, voile, velvet, organdie, spot muslin, terylene, wild silk or rayon, cotton rep, thin tweeds and tartans, cotton lace, net, and even knitting and crochet: for styles ranging from the straight up and down to festoons, cascades and swags enriched with pleats, ruching, fringes and tassels. All these are explained in the first part of this chapter, as well as pelmets, valances and blinds.

Fabric Requirements

As the choice of fabrics is so wide – ranging from plain terylene net to intricately patterned silk brocades, with lots of pretty cotton fabrics in between – the first thing to do is to estimate accurately the yardage required for a particular set of curtains. To measure the windows correctly, start by measuring from the top of the curtain track, rod or wire – these should extend 2″ to 3″ beyond the window frames on each side – to just below the sill for short curtains, or just clear of the floor for long ones. Allow a further 6″ to 8″ for hem, heading and possible shrinkage. The width of the curtain

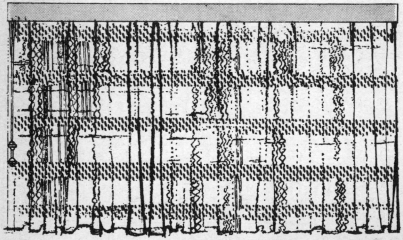

should be at least 1½ times the finished width – preferably twice the finished width – plus 1″ for each seam when the width is such that seams are necessary, and 1″–1½″ for each side turning. Write all the measurements down correctly together with a rough plan of the proposed curtains so that you will know you are buying the correct amount of fabric.

If you have chosen a boldly patterned fabric a little extra should be allowed for wastage when matching seams, and the left hand curtain to the right-hand one.

Also allow an extra 1″ for every 2 ft of curtain length, using this extra length for a deeper hem which should be unpicked before laundering to allow for shrinkage.

Simplest Curtains

These are best made in simple, fairly lightweight materials without hook tape. The fixing is over a narrow curtain rod or dowel. They are suitable for small windows in the kitchen, bathroom, bedroom, etc. When measuring your window remember to check that the rod or wire extends 2″ to 3″ beyond each side of the window-frame, with the width of the curtaining required being 1½ times to twice the width of the window plus seam and side-turning allowances, as explained above.

1. Cut a rectangle of fabric the length required retaining the full width complete with selvedge edges down both sides. Fold over 1″ on to the wrong side of the fabric, pin and stitch ⅛″ away from both inside and outside edges.

2. For a plain casing which goes over a rod or wire, crease over the top and stitch as for the side turnings. See diagram 2 on the following page.

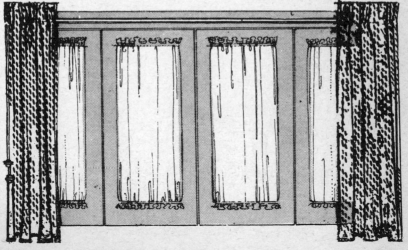

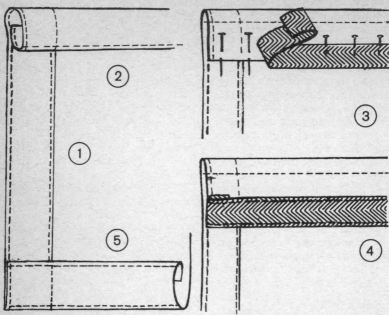

3. For a headed casing – this is a decorative finish above the fixing rod or wire – fold over the $1\frac{1}{2}''$ top allowance and stitch $\frac{1}{2}''$ in from top fold. Cover top raw edge with a strip of $\frac{1}{2}''$ wide tape – as shown in diagram 3 – pinning into position and turning under $\frac{1}{2}''$ at each end.

4. Stitch $\frac{1}{8}''$ in from each edge of tape through all thicknesses as in diagram 4. Alternatively, omit the tape, fold under $\frac{1}{4}''$ along the raw edge and stitch flat a scant $\frac{1}{8}''$ from folded edge through all thicknesses.

5. Slip the curtain into position and mark the exact length required. Crease in $\frac{1}{2}''$ from the bottom raw edge and then pin and stitch hem to exact length $\frac{1}{4}''$ below crease, and again $\frac{1}{4}''$ from folded edge as shown

in diagram 5. Remember to allow for possible shrinkage, adding an extra $1''$ for every 2 ft of curtain length. Use this extra length for a deeper hem which should be un-picked before laundering.

Net Curtains are made in the same way, except that as the net can be bought in a great variety of widths, from $36''$ to $120''$, they can be made with the minimum of stitching as no seams are required. When estimating multiply by 2 or 3 times the width for correct fullness and buy the width nearest to your calculations.

Unlined Curtains

These can be made of printed

cotton, gingham, cotton rep, etc., and are made with Rufflette tape for hanging from a curtain track.

1. Cut a rectangle of fabric 1½ times or twice the width required, measured from the width of the track and not the window width, with 1½″ each side added for turnings; the length is also measured from the track, with 6″ to 8″ added for heading, hem and possible shrinkage. Cut a length of Rufflette curtain tape the curtain width. Unthread 1½″ of cord at each end of tape and tie one end into a knot on the underside of tape, but leave other side-end free. If the selvedge edge is tight, cut away about ½″ along both sides.

2. Crease over to the wrong side ¼″ of each side seam allowance and then fold over 1″–1¼″ more, pinning and stitching ⅛″ from both creased and folded edges. Turn down the curtain top to the depth of heading required – 1½″ has been allowed, but more might be required if you are making a tall heading – and pin flat. Turn in the Rufflette tape 1½″ end allowance so that the knot end is covered, but leave the cords at the other end free. Place the wrong side of the tape to cover the turned-down heading raw edge, with the fold-ins level with the curtain edge, and stitch right round the edge of the tape, outside the cords, leaving an even 1″ between top of tape and curtain top, or more for a special heading.

3. Tie the two free cords together and pull the fabric along the cords until it is all packed at one end.

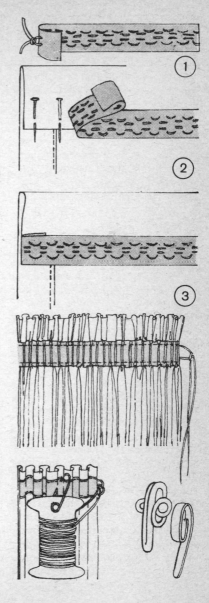

Next, pull out the fabric again to the required width and knot the cords to hold it at this width, distributing the fullness evenly. Do not cut off the surplus cord: instead wind it around a cord tidy, as shown on the previous page, and safety-pin this out of sight. Insert hooks and hang curtains into position.

4. Accurately mark hem length required. Remove curtain and crease over $\frac{1}{2}''$, then pin and stitch hem to required length, using mitred or lapped corners if required, as shown on page 64.

5. For a tall heading a layer of dressmaker's Vilene or horsehair stiffening should be tacked to the top turn-over and stitched, to just short of the top and side edge lines, as shown by diagrams 6 and 7 opposite. Alternatively, use the special Rufflette tape and hooks, which are put on and used in a similar way to the standard tape.

Lined Curtains

These are made from velveteen, cotton rep, tweeds and jacquard fabrics, etc.

1. Cut a rectangle of curtain fabric exactly as for a normal unlined curtain. Cut a rectangle of lining fabric 6″ shorter and 2″ narrower. On the lining turn up a $1\frac{1}{2}''$ hem and stitch $\frac{1}{2}''$ away from the raw edge.

2. Lay the curtain fabric face up and roughly fold in a 4″ to 6″ pleat down the middle. Lay the lining face down over the curtain fabric so that the hem is 6″ above curtain

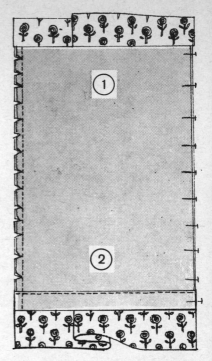

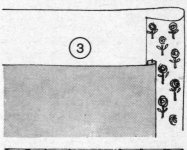

hem and the top 1½″ below the curtain top, with the sides edge to edge, and pin these into position. Stitch ½″ away from outside raw edges and then snip turnings at 1″ to 2″ intervals to prevent seam tightness which causes puckering – see diagrams 1 and 2.

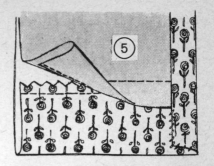

3. Turn curtain through so that the right sides are outside and lay out flat so that the smaller lining section can be centralized. Turn down top 1½″ allowance, angling away the corners slightly, and tack right through all thicknesses, as in diagrams 3 and 4.

4. Cut the Rufflette tape 3″ longer than the curtain width, and first unthread 1½″ of cord at each end and tie one end into a knot on the underside of the tape. Next turn in the tape 1½″ end allowances, covering the knot at one end but leaving the cords free at the other. Place the tape over the turned-down heading raw edge, level with the curtain edge, and stitch right round the edge of the tape, keeping outside the cords, and leaving 1″ of heading above the top of the tape.

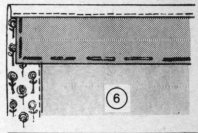

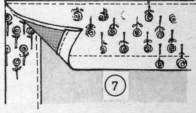

5. Knot free cord ends together and draw up cord, knotting and winding round a cord tidy before inserting hooks at 2″ to 3″ intervals. Hang curtains in position and mark hem accurately. Remove curtains and neaten hem by tacking it up under the lining, as shown in diagram 5, and then hand stitching the corners neatly. Before finally finishing the hem it is wise to leave the curtains to hang for a few days, as they may drop slightly. If they

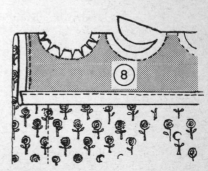

do, then it is a simple job to re-level them before loosely slip-stitching the lining and curtain hems together.

Decorative headings

If a stiffened or special heading is required, then an extra allowance should be made when cutting out – double the heading required – i.e., for a 1½" heading, allow 3" when cutting. Cut a strip of stiffening – dressmaker's Vilene or horsehair stiffening – 1" less than the curtain width and the same depth as the heading design. Tack this on to the top of the curtain ½" away from all edges. Crease over the top ½" allowance so that the stiffening is

tight against the fold, tack, and stitch ¼" in. Turn the heading down over the stiffening, tack and then stitch around the rest of the stiffening, as in diagram 7, page 263.

An alternative method for headings is to use special Rufflette tapes and long-stemmed hooks available at most sewing centres.

Shaped headings. If you wish to shape the top of a headed curtain, then fold the top stiffened allowance to the outside of the curtain so that the fabrics are face to face, and pin down. Next mark on the shapes required – possibly scallops, as on page 263, which were pencilled on to the stiffening with the aid of a conveniently sized jar or lid,

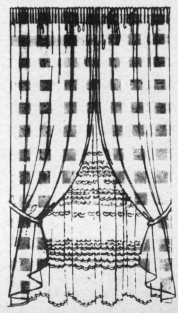

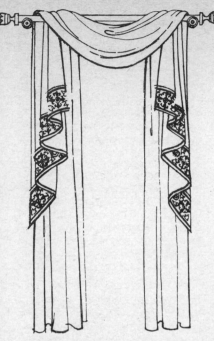

is inevitable. Generally the amount required is between two to three times the finished curtain width, i.e. for a window which is 4 ft wide with a drop of 8 ft, you require three 3-yard lengths which equals 9 yards of 48/54″ material. Prepare the curtain top in the way just described for stiffened headings, or use Rufflette deep pleat tapes and the special long-stemmed pleat-forming hooks.

Pencil pleats, diagram 1, page 266, are regular pleats which must be evenly formed. The best method is to use the special Rufflette Regis tape, which is attached in a very similar way to the normal Rufflette tape described on page 263.

leaving 1″ gaps between. Stitch around each shape, fastening the thread ends securely. Cut the surplus stiffening very close to the stitched scallops and then cut the fabric leaving $\frac{1}{4}$″ turning, snipping around the curves at $\frac{1}{4}$″ to $\frac{1}{2}$″ intervals–diagram 8, page 263. Turn top edges and then complete the heading in the normal way.

Pleated headings can be made in a variety of styles ranging from simple pencil pleats to the more complicated triple pinch or box-pleated designs, but do remember that each sort of pleat requires different quantities of fabric so a certain amount of trial and error

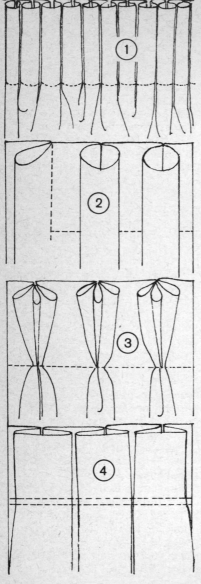

Organ pleats, as shown in diagram 2, are bold single pleats which can be formed by hand stitching the pleating allowance together, above the heading allowance stitching-line. A little padding or stiffening can then be dropped in to the top of each pleat to hold out the shape. Sew on a hook or ring to the back of each pleat just above the inside lower turning line, for hanging.

Pinch pleats, diagram 3. These are evenly spaced groups of pleats which can be formed by Rufflette Deep Pleat tapes and Triple Pleat hooks. Alternatively stitch by hand in a similar way to organ pleats, adding several extra hand stab-stitches to form the divisions of the pleat waists near the top.

Box pleats, diagram 4. Exactly three times the curtain width is required, which should then be divided into exactly equal sections according to the number of pleats required. Arrange the pleats evenly and double stitch right through along the pleat waistline. Hang from individual hooks or rings sewn at the back of each pleat onto the waistline machining.

Cartridge pleats, diagram 5. Make as for Organ pleats but stitch down and draw in each pleat, giving a gathered waist.

Tie-backs

Simple curtain tie-backs can be made out of straight strips of matching or contrasting fabrics, which can be decorated with braid,

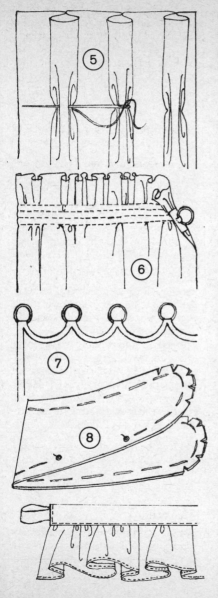

ribbons, fringing or frills. These strips are then fixed to the edge of the window frame, looped around the curtain and tied to hold the curtain back. Curved tie-backs are a little more complex, and can be made in several ways. First cut a reasonably curve-shaped pattern. Cut a curved strip of brown paper the approximate length required – generally 16" to 18" long and 2" to 3" deep – and test it for shape against the curtains. Using this curved strip as a guide, cut another paper tie-back but this time one that is more accurately shaped. If this one still isn't quite right, cut a third, and even a fourth until it is the shape you want.

1. Cut two curved pieces of fabric – using the brown paper pattern as a guide – leaving $\frac{1}{2}$" turnings all round. Lay the two pieces face to face and stitch round $\frac{1}{2}$" in, leaving a 3" gap along the bottom. Cut end curves to $\frac{1}{4}$" and notch out every $\frac{1}{2}$" as shown in diagram 8 on the left. Turn through gap right way out and slip-stitch remaining edges together before pressing and sewing on fixing rings or loops.

2. If the fabric is slightly stiff or thick, then a bound or lined design would probably be easier. Make the bound one with two layers of fabric cut to exact size and placed back to back and edge to edge so that the raw edges can be bound in braid or tape in the same way as tailored braiding as shown on page 183 or normal binding on page 78. Lined tie-backs require

267

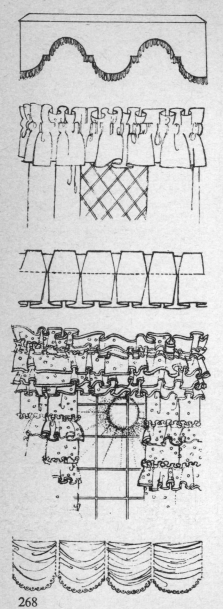

only one layer of fabric with one of lining, the fabric and lining being made up as for a normal curved tieback.

3. Hanging rings or loops should be fixed at each end so that when they are in position around the curtain they can be easily fixed on to their fixing hooks.

Valances

These are the unstiffened version of a pelmet explained opposite made over a wire track or frame instead of a board. Valances are really a shortened version of curtains and can be made plain or with frills, pleats and ruffles. Make them in exactly the same way as normal curtains out of the same or contrasting fabrics, using the normal Rufflette tape or the deeper self-pleating tapes to attach them to the valance rail.

Cotton flannelette is often used to add body to a thin fabric which is being used for a valance. Cut this flannelette exactly the same size as the fabric, laying the two together right sides outside. Tack all round to hold them together and then make up as one fabric with a lining in the normal way. A matching valance for a dressing table or vanity shelf can be made in much the same way as a curtain valance, varying the depth to suit the particular piece of furniture and fixing into position with decorative tacks or covered drawing-pins.

Beaded Valances, beaded curtains or decorative drapes made of beads can be used in hallways, windows, doorways, or as a decorative bathroom screen, etc. They are very easy to make, with many interesting and exciting effects to be achieved by using random colouring and mixing unusual textures and sizes. If you become interested in the more complicated techniques, many other elaborate designs can be worked out. As new beads are expensive, old beads purchased in a street market or back-street junk-shop are the best buys. Before re-threading they should be cleaned thoroughly, as explained on page 214. They can then be re-threaded as also explained on page 337.

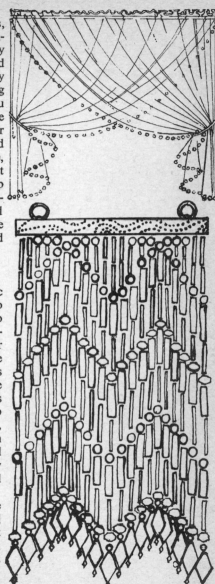

Pelmets

These are a stiff section of fabric which is hung above the curtains to conceal the curtain track and to help balance the window proportions. They can be starkly simple or intricately decorated, and can be used to connect several windows together, combining them into one scheme. Pelmets are fixed by means of a pelmet board, which is a strip of wood $\frac{1}{2}''$ to 1″ thick, 4″ to 6″ deep, and 2″ to 3″ longer than the curtain track. This strip of wood is fixed just above the curtain track by pelmet supports bought and fixed with the track.

1. Measure around the outside edge of the pelmet board from wall to wall, to get the exact pelmet length. Cut a brown paper pattern, experimenting for various shapes as explained for tie-backs on page 267, until the shape is correct, folding in

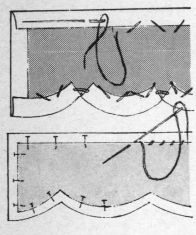

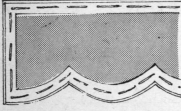

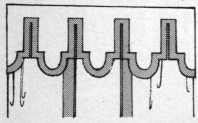

half to check for detailed accuracy and correct shaping.

2. Cut the exact shape required in pelmet buckram, and then cut the outside fabric 2″ larger all round. Normally the covering material is cut the same way as the curtains, which may mean joining two sections together for a long pelmet. Lay the fabric face down and centre the buckram shape on to the back of the fabric, checking that any design feature is evenly placed.

3. Turn the fabric edge allowance on to the buckram, snipping into the corners and curves as for normal sewing, sticking into position with a little Evo-Stik until you have secured the turnings with shallow catch-stitches, as shown on the left.

Alternatively the buckram can be dampened: the glue which is used to stiffen the buckram will hold the fabric in place, but this method is not suitable for thin fabrics unless the fabric is mounted as already explained for valances on page 268.

4. Stick and stitch any decorative braid or fringe trimming into position on the pelmet fabric before lining.

5. Cut a strip of lining $\frac{1}{4}$″ larger all round than the pelmet and lay over the wrong side of the covered pelmet, smoothing the lining so that it lies flat. Fold under the lining edges $\frac{1}{2}$″ and slip-stitch or stick to the pelmet turnings. Fix pelmet to board with $\frac{1}{2}$″ tacks, covering the fixing tacks with stick-on braid or decorative motifs.

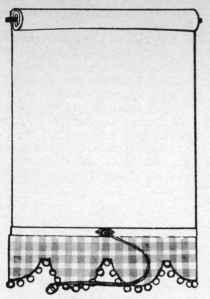
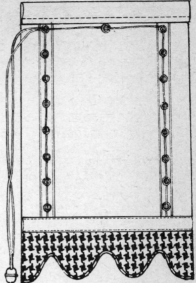

Window Blinds

Window blinds are becoming popular both functionally and for decoration. Slatted Venetian blinds are bought ready-made, but the various types of fabric blinds can easily be made by anyone moderately skilled at sewing.

The traditional fabric to use for roller blinds is heavy glazed cotton; however, colourful prints and unusual edgings can be very attractive. Roller blinds can be bought at most curtaining shops and stores to be covered in your own choice of fabric – formal chintz or shiny modern print – or you can buy a roller blind which is covered in the traditional plain-coloured glazed cotton holland and add a shaped

strip of fabric to match your curtains, as shown above, or you could add a decorative hem as shown overleaf.

Pull-up Blinds

1. Cut a rectangle of fabric 4″ wider than required and 8″ longer. Turn in 2″ to wrong side of side edges, cover the raw edges with Rufflette tape and stitch each side $\frac{1}{8}$″ from tape edges, finishing the tape 3″ from each end.

2. Turn up bottom $2\frac{1}{2}$″ and stitch $\frac{1}{2}$″ from fold. Crease over $\frac{1}{2}$″ of raw edge and stitch $\frac{1}{4}$″ from crease through blind.

3. Next crease over $\frac{1}{2}$″ on top allowance, then fold over 2″ and stitch $\frac{1}{4}$″ from crease line.

4. Buy two strips of wood 2″

271

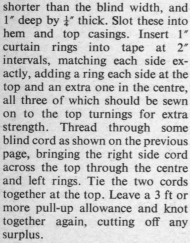

shorter than the blind width, and 1" deep by ¼" thick. Slot these into hem and top casings. Insert 1" curtain rings into tape at 2" intervals, matching each side exactly, adding a ring each side at the top and an extra one in the centre, all three of which should be sewn on to the top turnings for extra strength. Thread through some blind cord as shown on the previous page, bringing the right side cord across the top through the centre and left rings. Tie the two cords together at the top. Leave a 3 ft or more pull-up allowance and knot together again, cutting off any surplus.

5. Finish hem by sticking and stitching on a decorative fringe. Finally nail or screw the top

wood-stiffened section to the window frame or architrave. Pull knotted cord to raise the blind. Fix a small hook on to window frame over which the knotted cord is tied, and adjust the cord and knots for even hang.

Decorative Hems can be made in many different ways; a few ideas are shown on the right. The simplest method is to stick and stitch a ready-made string fringe or decorative bobble fringe on to the blind end, while the more adventurous scalloped and tasselled ends can be easily made from separate strips of matching or contrasting pieces of fabric.

Cotton lace and crochet can be used on most blind hems: 6"-wide cotton lace edging, decorative doilies cut in half and joined into a long strip, or hand-made crochet. Attach to the hem of the blind by lap-stitching $\frac{1}{4}"$ in from bottom folded edge with the raw edge of the strip under-lapping $\frac{1}{2}"$ on to the wrong side of blind.

Fringing and cording can be stuck or stitched directly to the bottom folded edge of a blind, or applied to separate strips of double or stiffened fabric which is then lap-stitched to the blind as explained for scalloped and tasselled ends.

Decoration, such as appliqué, embroidery, lace motifs, looped rosettes and even felt stuck-ons, all of which are described in other sections of this book – see index –, can also be applied to the simpler blinds, as can many other ideas seen in magazines and newspapers.

Draped Curtains

Drapes, festoons, swags and scarves, are formal treatments for elegant window-dressing, ideal for classical rooms or rooms with character. These curtains should be made in a rich-looking fabric such as velvet, plush, shot silk, moiré or brocade so that the richness of the drapes can be embellished with ruching, fringing, pleating, or braiding as well as tasselled and decorated tie-backs.

Mock-up. In order to plan accurately and to save much unnecessary expense and wasted time, it is wisest to start experimenting for

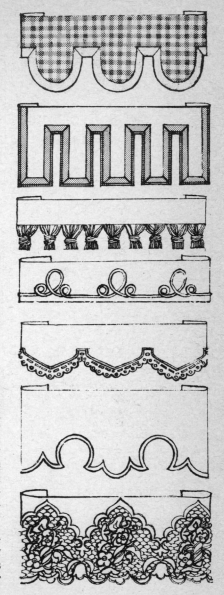

suitable draperies or swags by cutting and trying out calico mock-ups until you learn how to obtain the right effect. Washed calico or cheap cotton flannelette are best as they can be bought at most shops and stores for a few pence. Choose the sort which is nearest in width to the fabric you plan to use.

Swags

Swag drapes, which are illustrated on the left, are best cut on the true cross. Following diagram 4 on the right, measure the finished width required, i.e., the outside edge of the pelmet board or valance frame, A to A. A to B on each side is 18" to 24", flared out 4" to 6". B to C to B is a curve dropping 10" to 12" in the centre. Drape a mock-up as shown in diagrams 1 or 2, taking careful note of each fold, marking it accurately so that it can be reproduced in the proper fabric and repeated for several windows if necessary.

If the swag is to be lined the lining should be cut to fit the finished shape without any drapery or fullness.

Festoon Pelmets

Cut in exactly the same way as swags, but in order to get the triple swagging, curtain tape is stitched onto the back of the fabric forming the divisions required as shown in diagram 6. The cords are knotted at one end, pulled out at the other, and tied together to hold the required shape. The back is lined to the finished shape without any drapery or fullness. Bows, fringing, cording or braids are stuck and stitched on as required, and then fixed to the pelmet board with tacks.

Side Tails

Cut as shown in diagram 5 they are usually used in conjunction with either a swagged or a festooned pelmet. A to B equals the drop required, A to C is either a half or the full width of the curtaining fabric, C to D is the drop required before cascading and D to B is an even curve. If the cascading tail is to be lined, cut the lining the same size and place it face to face on to the fabric. Stitch $\frac{1}{2}''$ in around the three lower edges, leaving the top open for turning through, arranging pleats and hanging as shown on the page opposite.

Scarf Drapes

Drapes like those shown on page 265 can be made by measuring the depth of the drop required each side, adding on the top span of the draping rail and then allowing an extra length of 12″ to 18″ for the swag or looped draping required. It is advisable to experiment first in calico or cotton flannelette, as explained, so that the right effect can be achieved in a cheap fabric, and then an accurate and economical yardage bought of your final fabric. The exact shape and size of each scarf varies from window to window, but generally they are made from a half width of curtaining fabric with shaped ends of a similar size to the side tails.

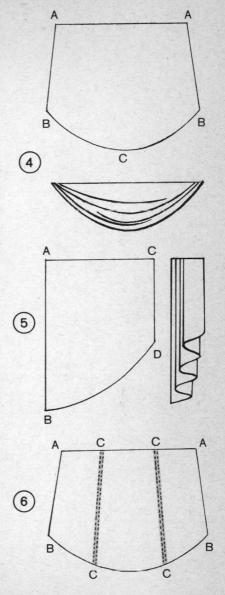

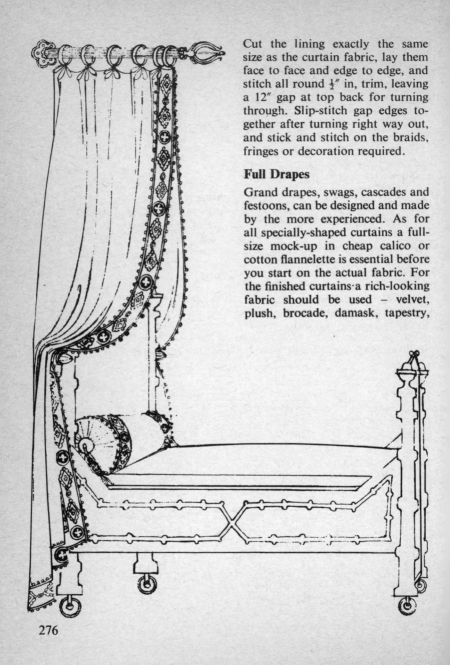

Cut the lining exactly the same size as the curtain fabric, lay them face to face and edge to edge, and stitch all round $\frac{1}{2}''$ in, trim, leaving a 12'' gap at top back for turning through. Slip-stitch gap edges together after turning right way out, and stick and stitch on the braids, fringes or decoration required.

Full Drapes

Grand drapes, swags, cascades and festoons, can be designed and made by the more experienced. As for all specially-shaped curtains a full-size mock-up in cheap calico or cotton flannelette is essential before you start on the actual fabric. For the finished curtains a rich-looking fabric should be used – velvet, plush, brocade, damask, tapestry, moiré, etc. – which can then be embellished with fringing, braiding, ruching, or cording as well as tasselled and decorated tie-backs, etc.

Bed Drapes

Side or back drapes, or full draped curtains, can be made for most beds provided the design fits in happily with the rest of the bedroom. Generally these drapes are used with a simple canopy or with a pelmet as for normal curtains. However, if you have a particularly nice fixing pole and ring set you can make the sort of draping that is shown on the left.

Bed curtains and drapes should be made in the same way as window curtains, but as they are generally decorative rather than functional, the minimum amount of sewing to give the effect required should be your aim.

Bed Canopies

Simple bed canopies are made in exactly the same way as curtain valances, and are attached above the bed-head to a valance board or metal track. This board or track should be 4″ to 6″ wider than the bed with a depth of between 6″ to 8″, and is fixed either to the wall or to the ceiling, arranged so that the fixing is covered by the drapes. Make the valance as explained on page 268 and attach it with drawing-pins concealed under a fold of fabric, or with curtain hooks.

Bed Valances

These are made to fit between the mattress and the bedsprings and are intended to be used in conjunction with a tucked-in decorative blanket or fitted bed cover.

1. To make a simple gathered

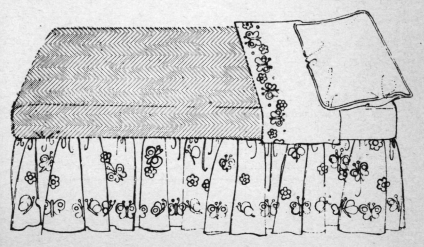

valance – page 277 – cut strips of fabric the depth of the side drop to be covered, adding on an extra 2″ for the hem and top allowances. The total lengths should be nearly double the bed circumference. For an average 6′ 3″ by 2′ 6″ single bed this would be approximately 3 to 3½ yards of 48″ fabric cut into 14″ strips giving between 10 to 12 yards

for the gathered frill. Also required is a rectangle of calico the size of the top of the bed plus 1″ all round.

2. Stitch all the side seams of the strips together to make one long strip. Machine-neaten hem in normal way using 1″ to 1½″ allowance. Mark the strip in sections to correspond with the edges being covered – if a double length of material has been allowed, then each section should be double the measurement of the side to be covered. If less has been allowed, mark correspondingly less. Run a double gathering stitch ½″ from top edge of each section and pull into the correct size. If you prefer pleats, then measure and arrange each pleat so that it is the size required.

3. Cut the rectangle of cheap calico 1″ larger than the bed dimensions, double turn in edges and stitch to exact size. Remove the mattress and lay the calico on to the middle of the springs and then pin gathered edge on to calico ½″ in all round. Next tack-stitch the gathering to the calico, arranging the depth and corners correctly before machine-stitching.

Simple Bedspread

For a simple 'throw-over' bedspread 5 yards of fabric is generally enough for a medium-sized double bed. Allow an extra ½ yard if you wish to pipe the seams.

1. From the length of fabric cut two pieces exactly 2½ yards long.

Cut one of these in half along its length giving two pieces of 2½ yards by 24″/27″ wide. Lay one of these strips on each side of the wide piece – right sides together and selvedge edges exactly matching. Stitch ½″ in from both selvedge edges so that you have a very wide spread which is 2½ yards long. If the cover is for a single bed, you should reduce the centre panel to the width of your bed before attaching the side pieces.

2. Piping can be incorporated into the panel seams if required. The piping should be made from the off-cuts of fabric, or from an extra half yard. Cut crossway strips 1½″ wide, joining them together and stitching over piping cord as explained on page 244. Stitch the piping on to the centre panel before joining this to the side panels.

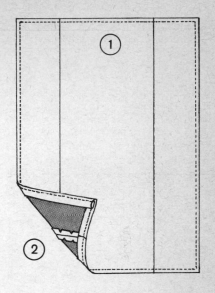

3. Press seam lines open and try half-made cover on top of made-up bed – this is important as it affects both the size and hang of the bedspread. If the seams tend to drag then the selvedge edge needs snipping at 2″ intervals. Leave length as long as possible but adjust width so that it just clears the floor, removing an equal amount each side, but remembering to leave 1″ turning-in allowance for edge finishing.

4. Turn in ¼″ on to wrong side all the way round the cover and stitch flat. Turn in another ½″ all round and again stitch flat. Alternatively use a hemming attachment.

5. Round ends are an easy alternative to the square ones

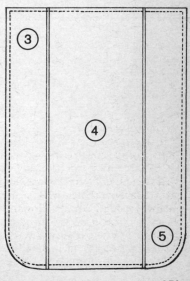

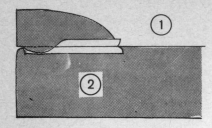

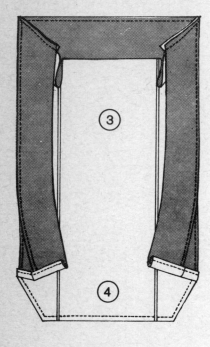

already explained. Mark off the round corners before turning in – a large meat plate is a good guide for marking the curve – and then make and complete the edges in the normal way.

Fitted Bedspread

This sort of cover should be made out of fairly firm, medium-weight, crease-resistant fabric. Between 6 and 7 yards of 48″/54″ wide material is required for most double beds and 5 yards for most single beds.

1. Cut a rectangle of fabric the size of the bed when made, allowing an extra 12″ to 18″ in length for pillow rise and tuck over, and the normal seam allowances on both sides. If the fabric is not wide enough, join a strip on each side, reducing the centre panel slightly to give a balanced panel seaming. Remember to measure the size required over a fully made-up bed, as the sheets, blankets and pillows make quite a difference for an accurate fit.

2. Cut two side strips the length and depth of the made-up bed, plus 2″ allowance in length and 4″ in depth. Cut a foot-of-bed panel the same depth by the width plus extra allowances. Cut two pillow gussets as shown in diagram 1, basing their size on the width and height of the pillows – generally a curving 6″ to 8″ high gusset 16″ to 18″ in length. Seam these on to the top end of each side gusset, making a left- and a right-sided panel.

3. Turn in $\frac{1}{2}$″ on pillow gusset end of side panels and stitch. Turn in another ½″ and stitch flat. Join other end to foot panel. Make piping as shown on page 244 – approximately 6 yards will be needed. Stitch piping to three sides of top panel – the two long sides and across the foot end. Lay the side sections on top of the top panel with right sides of fabric facing, edges meeting and curved edge of pillow gusset about 18″ away from the top edge – this is the tuck-over allowance. Stitch sides to top panel, having first attached piping foot to the swing-needle machine so that the stitching can be tight against the piping cord.

4. Fit half-made cover on to made-up bed to check. Measure and mark the side depth required and angle the top tuck-in allowance so that it is easy to manage and doesn't show. Trim hem level all round and then remove cover from the bed. Trim pillow tuck-over allowance by angling edges 2″ to 4″ off the straight grain. Turn in ¼″ all round tuck-over and stitch flat; then turn in ½″ and stitch again. Neaten all inside raw edges by automatic cross-stitch, overcasting or bias binding. Finally, neaten hem with a double turn-in and machine top-stitching or by attaching a decorative fringe.

Shaped Bedspread

The shaped bedspread shown below will require between 6½ and 8 yards of fairly firm medium-weight crease-

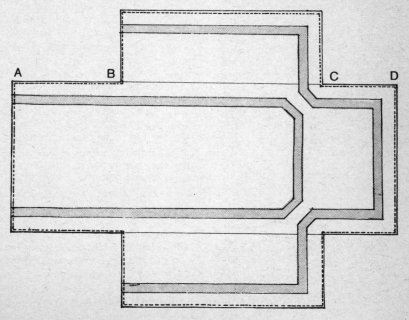

resistant fabric 48″/54″ wide for a normal double bed.

1. Cut a rectangle of fabric 12 ft long by the width of the properly made-up bed. If the fabric is not wide enough, join on two narrow 12-ft long strips, one for each side, reducing the centre panel slightly to give a balanced panel seaming as for a fitted bedspread.

2. Cut two side panels the exact length and depth of the made-up bed, plus 2″ allowance in length and $1\frac{1}{2}$″ in depth.

3. Measure and mark the 12 ft long top strip as shown previously: A to B = 4 ft for pillow cover; B to C is the exact length of bed; C to D is what is left, generally 12″ to 18″.

4. Neaten the two short edges of the two side panels by double turning-in and stitching flat, and then neaten one long edge of each panel for the hem. Join the un-neatened edge to the top section between points B and C. Turn under and neaten the remaining edges and ends.

5. Place on some decorative braid as shown, or decorate in one of the many ways explained throughout this book. Simply adapt the making instructions to the design required.

6. Corner pleats can be introduced at the foot of the bed if there is no foot board. To make these pleats, the foot end drop section C to D must be the same as the side panels – this may mean starting with a longer top section. Make the bedspread as before, but inset two 12″ inverted pleats into the bottom corners.

Quilted Bedspread

Cut a rectangle of top fabric and another of cotton lining, both 4″ longer and 4″ wider than the top of the bed. Lay these fabrics together, right sides outside with a layer of terylene wadding sand-

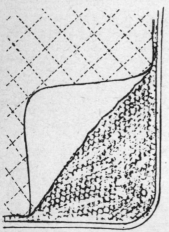
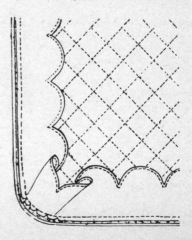

wiched between them. Using a long sharp needle tack through all the thicknesses and then mark out the quilting stitch lines required in a similar way to that described on page 288. Machine stitch and then remove the tacking stitches. Cut to 1″ larger than the made-up bed size and then continue making as for a fitted bedspread just described. Alternatively make narrower scalloped sides over a pleated valance as illustrated on the right.

Covered Bed-head

1. Cut a rectangle of fabric the full length of the bed-head by double the depth, adding an extra 2″ all the way round for seaming allowances and for the thickness of the bed-head.

2. Turn under ½″ and neaten the two long edges and then fold in half so that the two neatened edges are together with the right side of the fabric inside. Stitch the folded raw edges together ½″ in. Turn right way out. Place over bed-head, adding the tapes in the centre and 4″ from each end of the cover-opening to secure into position.

3. If you want to decorate the cover, you should do this before stitching, but remember that half of the cover is for the back of the bed-head.

4. An alternative method for cutting the bed-head cover is to cut two long thin sections – one for the front and the other for the back – which are seamed together on the sides and top. Add decoration to the front section only.

Part Four   Decorative Sewing

In the following four chapters we are going to explain how to master
many attractive decorative techniques using simplified methods, which
are slightly unorthodox but easily understood and will help you to
achieve quick and attractive results. The variations in Decorative Sewing
are infinite, but we have tried to cover most of the basic principles in
these four chapters. The first chapter – Chapter 11 – covers an assortment
of decorative methods from Smocking to Macramé, whilst the other three
chapters deal with Embroidery Stitches, Bead and Ribbon Work, Appliqué
and Patchwork. A few ideas on how to use these methods have also
been given, but in general these four chapters are intended to be used in
conjunction with the rest of this book.

11. Smocking to Macramé

Smocking

A very attractive way of decorating gathered fullness. It consists of working various ornamental stitches into geometric groups on top of the small tucks formed by gathering-stitches. The use of smocking varies according to fashion, but as a general rule wherever fullness is shown smocking may be applied, with a small stitch evenly across the fabric. Secure the thread at the beginning of each row with a knot and leave ample thread at the other end for pulling up. When all the rows have been worked, draw up the threads sufficiently tightly to allow the pleats to be stroked into place with a pin so that they lie evenly and can be easily smocked. Secure the ends around a pin as for

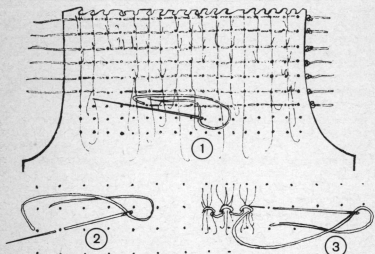

particularly on children's clothes, lingerie or casual and holiday wear.

First decide on the depth and width the smocking is to be, and then cut a section of smocking transfer dots, which can be bought at most sewing shops, to the chosen depth, allowing about three times the finished width of smocking required. Iron these dots on to the material and gather it as shown by the diagram, taking up each dot

a gathered frill, shown on page 77.

Finally, work the smocking-stitches to make a decorative pattern before removing the gathering-stitches.

Cable Smocking. Working from left to right over a line of dots on top of regularly gathered pleats, bring the thread up through the first dot, as in diagram 2 above, picking up next dot with thread above the

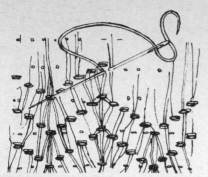

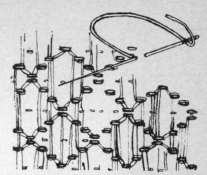

needle and draw up, as in diagram 3. Pick up the third dot with thread below the needle, repeating the cable stitch with the thread alternating above and below the needle.

Patterned Smocking, such as the zig-zag and diamond designs shown above, can also be easily worked in smocking as can the butterfly pattern shown below.

The zig-zag pattern is worked in lines ½″ apart, and each line is made by making four, five or six stitches up and then the same number of stitches down, each stitch taking up one pleat.

The diamond pattern is made by working four stitches up and then four stitches down, each stitch taking up one pleat. The second row which forms the lower half of the diamond, is worked so that the upper point of the groups of stitches will touch the lower ones of the previous group.

The butterfly smocking is a free adaptation of traditional smocking combined with some of the embroidery stitches shown in the next chapter. Many other stitches can be used. If you are interested in learning more about smocking, write to The Sewing Group, Coats Patons Ltd, 50 Bothwell Street, Glasgow, G25 PA for details.

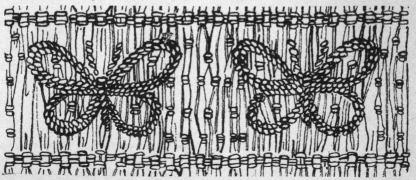

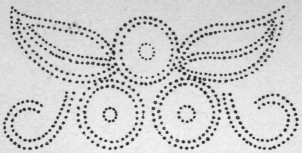

Shirring

Made by machine stitching using a special elasticated shirring thread on the spool. Adjust the stitch length and the top tension as explained on the shirring elastic information sheet, and then test the stitching on an off-cut of fabric before stitching the actual area required.

Gauging

Or decorative gathering can be made with hand or machine gathering stitches. The lines of stitches should be evenly spaced every $\frac{1}{4}''$ to $\frac{1}{2}''$, using a notched guide to keep them even as shown for tucks on page 78. Decorative stitches can be worked on top of gauging if required.

Quilting

This decorative technique is usually used for bedding, as in the cot cover opposite, but it can also be used on clothes, as seen in the recent vogue for quilted evening skirts in colourful fabrics, etc.

1. Cut two pieces of fabric 3″ to 4″ larger than the finished size required. Lay these fabrics together with the right sides outside and sandwich between them one or more layers of terylene wadding. Using a long needle tack through all thicknesses 2″ in from the edges, right round the shape.

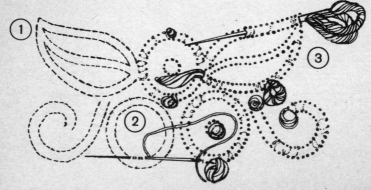

2. Using white dressmaker's chalk, mark on the quilting shapes required. The cot cover is criss-crossed with the diagonal lines 1½" apart. Tack along each line accurately, or, if you are experienced, pin and tack only alternative lines.

3. Machine stitch along each line, adjusting both the stitch tension and foot pressure as directed in your sewing machine manual and

Italian Quilting

This consists of making two parallel lines of stitches ¼" apart through two layers of fabric and then slotting thick wool between the layers, to raise the quilted design.

1. Mark your design on to a soft piece of backing fabric which is not too closely woven – cheesecloth is ideal – and then tack the marked

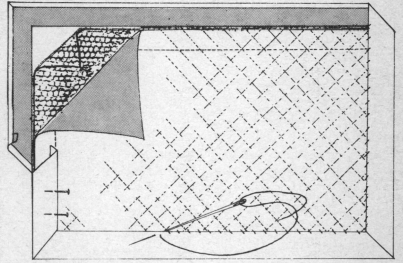

on page 38, to prevent drag and puckering. Remove tacking stitches and then cut to the exact size and shape required.

4. For the cot cover, use two rectangles of fabric 3" larger than the cot size and quilt-stitch as above. Next cut to exact size. To bind the edges cut a 4" wide crossway strip long enough to go right round, plus about 6" – see pages 73 and 78 for details.

material on to the wrong side of the top fabric which should be of a much closer weave. See top diagram on the opposite page.

2. Make small running-stitches ⅛" away from the marked outline and a second row a scant ⅛" on the other side, so that there are two parallel stitch lines ¼" apart right round the design.

3. For the padding or raising of the design thread a blunt-pointed

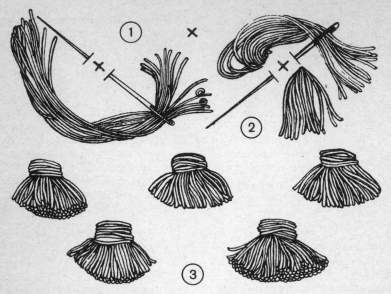

large-eyed tapestry needle with thick soft knitting wool, matching the colour if possible, or using a bright contrasting colour if a shadow effect is required. From the back, slot the needle between the stitched layer, making long stitches where possible, but bringing the needle out at the back when a curve prevents you from going any further. Insert the needle again in the same place and proceed as before, leaving small loops between the stitches so that the padding is not drawn too tightly. Do not use knots: simply clip away any unwanted ends after completing the padding – see bottom diagram on page 288.

Maltese tufting

This is the formal use of regular

tufting stitches to give small tassels, similar to those shown above. The material used for trying out this stitch should be a fairly firm linen, or cotton rep, with Anchor Stranded Cotton for the tufts. Once you have tried it out you should experiment with other fabrics and threads so that you can combine it with other techniques. This stitch is particularly suitable for covering large surfaces, as it is quick and easy to do.

First mark the positions for the tassels with a small tacked cross or chalked spot, following a traced-on pattern if you like. Begin on the right-hand side, using a large-eyed embroidery needle and some stranded cotton embroidery thread used double. Make a slightly diagonal stitch to the left ¼" long and $\frac{1}{8}$" up (diagram 1 opposite), and then make a second diagonal stitch over the first, $\frac{1}{4}$" long and $\frac{1}{8}$" down as in diagram 2. Pull the stitch taut and clip the ends to $\frac{1}{2}$", arranging the threads as shown in diagram 3. Repeat the stitches in formal single patterns, in groups, as a tassel border or combined with any of the other methods illustrated. This stitch can also be used to make a small rug or decorative pram cover.

Tufted Flowers

Make them over a cardboard template of stiffish card – a cereal packet is ideal – to the size and shape required. If you are making an irregular random design then templates cut free-hand are used, but if you are planning a formal arrangement an accurate template is necessary. The template shown below was cut from a 6" square of card, with 2" flower petals shaped diagonally and a 1" hole in the centre. Try making several experimental shapes and then try them out in coloured wool on a firm fabric before deciding which to use for an ambitious design.

1. Place the card template into position and stitch over the edge and through the hole to secure it firmly into place with coloured wool.

2. Work first along one petal making $\frac{1}{8}$" wide stitches, first on one side looping across to the other side and then back again until completely covered.

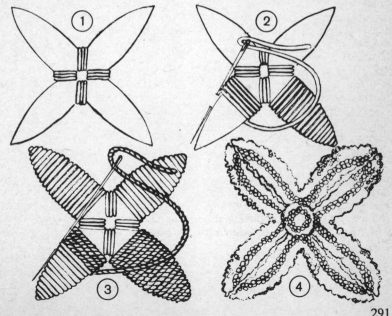

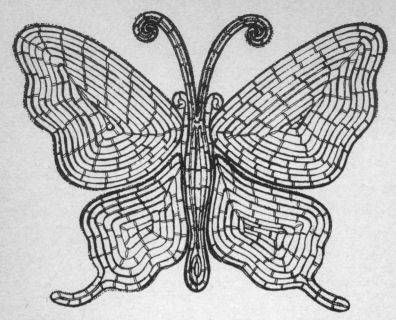

3. Work another colour over the top in a similar way.

4. Starting from the centre of the template cut the different coloured wool loops along the centre of each petal so that the strands open out like the petal of a flower and the template can be removed.

5. The tufting strands should be secured from behind with some hand stitches, using matching coloured cotton either before or after removing the template. Evo-Stik can be used in moderation instead of the securing stitches, but this method is only suitable for heavier fabrics where the slightly stiff effect caused by the glue is not noticeable.

Couching

Couch-stitched embroidery work

is a very decorative bold cord work which is both simple and quick to do. Thin cord, braid, or special couching threads are used with embroidery stitches and these can then be combined with looped ribbon work as shown in Chapter 13, soutache work overleaf, appliqué work in Chapter 14, or any of the other methods of surface decoration explained in the other chapters of this or our other books.

When working this type of bold cord decoration, the outline of the design must be couch-stitched first. This consists of applying a coloured cord or bold thread around the edge of the design and fixing it by means of small stitches of finer thread made across the cord. These stitches are usually planned to show and

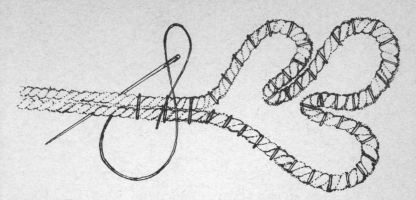

may even be of a contrasting colour. After stitching the cord around the outline of the design the cord can either be couched in ever-decreasing spirals as in the stylized butterfly, or the inner shapes can be filled with loops of ribbon, beads and sequins, or embroidery stitches as required.

1. To apply the couching cord, first lay the cord or heavy thread on the line to be followed, making regular straight stitches over it as above, or a blanket stitch as below. The stitches should be evenly spaced approximately every $\frac{1}{2}''$ to $\frac{3}{4}''$ and

made with a matching or contrasting thread as the design requires.

2. Leave about 1″ of cord at the beginning of the design and 1″ beyond the end of the line worked so that the threads of the cord can be neatened by taking them through to the wrong side. Either thread them through with a large-eyed darning needle or make a hole in the material with an embroiderer's stiletto, being careful not to break any threads, and then draw the heavy thread through with a small crochet hook, securing with a few extra stitches.

3. Couching is also used in appliqué work for attaching shapes of coloured fabric and at the same time concealing the raw edges, as can be seen on page 354. Another alternative is to combine it with braid embroidery as in the flower illustration on page 349. Whichever way you decide to use this bold decorative technique do remember that the stitches are meant to show so work them neatly at regular intervals.

Soutache Braid Embroidery

This is another very decorative type of bold stylized embroidery. The work is easily done and very effective when used in dressmaking, on cushions and bedspreads, or stitched on to net as blind lace.

The outline cording on the blind edging is made by sewing the cord or braid around the outline of the traced design. The stitch used is either a machine stitch if you can hold the braid accurately and stop it stretching; a small back-stitch $\frac{1}{8}''$ long and worked every $\frac{1}{8}''$ in the centre of the cord; or a simple running-stitch. At the curves of the design ease the braid smoothly around the shape so that the inside edge is slightly full. This fullness can then be pressed to shrink the braided curve into shape. As explained for couched embroidery on the previous page the ends of the braid must be threaded through to the wrong side of the fabric with the aid of a stiletto. To do this make a small hole with the stiletto and using a crochet hook draw the

braid through, securing the ends with a few hand stitches.

Soutache braid embroidery on net also makes very effective trimming for valances, curtain edgings, or dresses. Net of any kind can be used, with braid in a corresponding or contrasting colour.

The design chosen is first copied stitches tightly as this tends to pucker the braid. When all the outline has been stitched, cut the tacking threads and remove the backing paper, re-using the design for the next section of net to be decorated. When complete, press the back of the lace with a moderately warm iron and trim away any

on to a strip of stout brown paper, then the net is carefully tacked over the pattern. Next place the braid over the outline of the design and sew to the net, using a normal machine stitch, stitching through braid, net and paper. Alternatively, stitch by hand, using an even running-stitch through the centre of the braid and net, but avoiding the backing paper. Do not pull the unwanted net close to the braided outline. Finally, decorate with a few crochet motifs or embroidery stitches if required.

Faggoting

A much-neglected yet extremely decorative method of joining two pieces of fabric. The edges to be joined are first neatened by folding under the seam allowance. They are

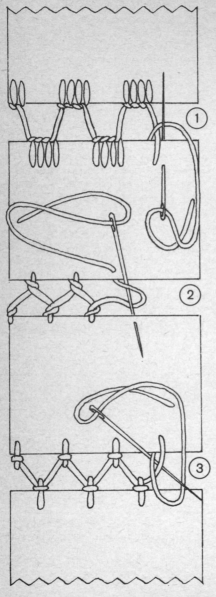

then tacked on to a strip of stiffish paper the required distance apart – between $\frac{1}{4}''$ and $\frac{1}{2}''$ – and then one of the following stitches worked.

Loop Stitch is the simplest faggoting stitch. Start by bringing the needle and thread out on the right hand side of the bottom edge, $\frac{1}{8}''$ away from the fold. The next stitch is made on the top edge $\frac{1}{4}''$ to the left of the first stitch, passing the needle over the thread. The third stitch is made on the bottom edge $\frac{1}{2}''$ away from the first, again taking the needle over the thread. Continue stitching top and bottom at $\frac{1}{2}''$ intervals until complete, as shown by the inset stitch shown on the page opposite.

Blanket Stitch can be used to link the fabric edges by working several stitches together as shown in diagram 1 and then making a similar number of blanket stitches on the opposite side. The stitches can be made close together or they can be evenly spaced.

Criss-cross faggoting stitch is shown in diagram 2. Start by bringing the needle and thread out on the left-hand bottom edge $\frac{1}{8}''$ away from the fold. The next stitch is made on the top folded edge $\frac{1}{4}''$ to the right of the first stitch, passing the needle under and over the thread. The third stitch is made on the top edge $\frac{1}{2}''$ away from the first, again taking a $\frac{1}{8}''$ stitch, passing the needle under and over the thread. Continue stitching top and bottom until complete. This

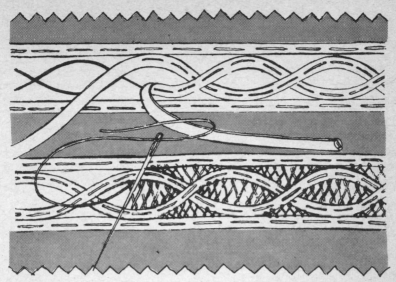

stitch can also be worked from right to left if you prefer sewing in that direction.

Knotted Stitch. Start on the top left-hand side of the prepared fabric pieces with a small stitch $\frac{1}{8}''$ away from the folded edge. Make a similar stitch on the bottom edge $\frac{1}{4}''$ towards the right. Pass the needle behind the thread as shown by diagram 3 to form a loop, with the needle sloping from left to right, making a knotted stitch over the thread. Make another stitch on the top edge $\frac{1}{2}''$ from the first and make a similar knotted stitch. Continue working top and bottom until completed. This stitch can also be worked from right to left.

Fabric Insets. Intricately-worked insets can be introduced into fag-

goting, using strips of rouleaux trimmings, cords, braids, ribbons or many other novelties. The design shown is made from $\frac{1}{2}''$ wide strips of thin crêpe which have been stitched into a thin rouleau. These strips are then tacked on to a 3'' wide paper strip into an intertwining design and loop-stitched together for inserting into a blouse front.

1. To make the rouleaux strips first cut some crossway strips of fabric, as shown on page 73, $\frac{1}{2}''$ wide for the narrowest rouleaux using crêpe or lawn, or 1'' wide for thicker fabrics such as flannel or velvet.

2. Fold the crossway strip to half its width, right side inside, and stitch $\frac{1}{8}''$ in from the raw edges, keeping the stitches an even distance from the folded edge.

3. To turn the strip right side out, insert a bodkin in one end, and with a fine sewing needle sew the material to the eye of the bodkin. Push the bodkin through the tube, turning the crossway strip into a rouleau.

4. Draw out an intertwining design on a strip of firm paper and then tack the fabric rouleaux

Simple Crochet

This method of making lacy fabrics by the use of a crochet hook and thread may seem a little complicated at first, but the stitches are surprisingly simple to work. The first requirement is to buy the right hook for the chosen thread – a Milward needlework stockist will be able to advise – which can vary

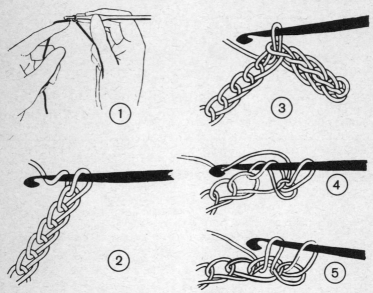

tubing – cord, braid or ribbon – over the design outline as shown on page 297.

5. Stitch the strips together as explained previously or use the stitch shown on the preceding page which is a looped stitch worked from right to left, each stitch $\frac{1}{8}''$ apart. When finished, this strip can be inset into the main fabric.

from the readily obtainable Mercer crochet threads available in a wide range of colours to dyed string, braid, raffia, ribbons, coloured wools, etc.

Abbreviations: ch., chain stitch; s.c., single crochet; d.c., double crochet; h.t., half treble; tr., treble; s.st., slip stitch.

Chain Stitch (ch.). Make a simple

298

loop at the end of the thread through which the crochet needle can be passed.

1. Hold the crochet hook between the first finger and thumb of the right hand. Loop the thread round the little finger of the left hand, across the palm and behind the forefinger, pulling the loop closed around the crochet hook as in diagram 1 opposite.

2. Pass the hook under the thread from right to left and catch the thread with the hook – this is 'threading over'. Draw the thread through the loop on the hook, making one ch. Repeat until you have as many stitches as you need – diagram 2 – remembering that one loop must remain on the hook and that your left thumb and forefinger should be kept near to the stitch on which you are working.

Slip Stitch (s.st.). Having made between 20 and 30 ch., work back along the chain with s.st., by inserting the hook from the front under the two top threads of each ch., so that the ch. already there is to the left of the hook, catching the thread with the hook, threading over, drawing through, and keeping the new loop on the hook – diagram 3. Repeat ch., as required.

Double Crochet (d.c.). Insert hook from the front under the two top threads of second ch. from hook, catch thread – diagram 4 – and draw thread through so that you have two loops on the hook – diagram 5. Thread over and draw through the two loops so that only one loop

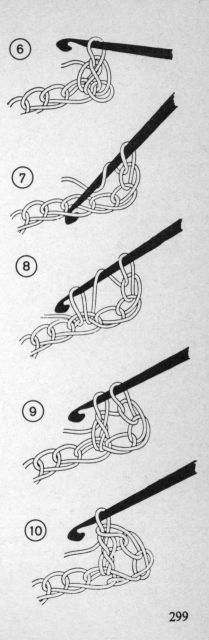

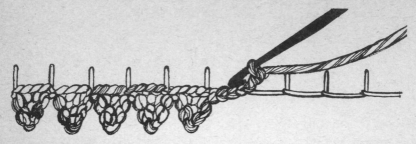

is left on hook, making one d.c. as in diagram 6.

Treble Crochet (tr.) is similar to double crochet but is worked with three loops on the hook instead of two. Pass the hook under the thread as shown in diagrams 7 and 8, thread over, and pull through so that three loops are on the hook, thread over and pull through so that two loops are on the hook as in diagram 9. Thread over again and pull through the remaining two loops, one loop remaining on hook as in diagram 10.

Crochet Edgings can be made in many different designs ranging from the finest almost lace-like edging in silk or cotton for evening wear, to the boldest chunky wool edging used on winter bedspreads.

They can be made as separate strips which are then sewn into position in much the same way as ready-made 'shop fringes' or they can be worked on to an edge as shown above. Basically the crochet edging is made up of stitches which are made through the finished edge, or through a row of blanket stitching which has been worked along the edge, picking up a loop of working thread which, when pulled through, is looped many times into a motif, and then repeating the through stitch and motif looping at regular intervals until the crochet is completed.

Crochet Scallops. First work a line of embroidery chain stitches along the finished edge of the material. The crochet scallops are then made

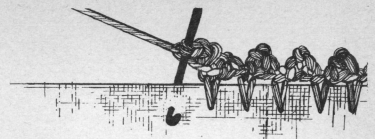

through these stitches at regular $\frac{1}{2}''$ intervals. Start by making the first crochet stitch through the first embroidery stitch, then make eight crochet stitches making the ninth through the fifth embroidery stitch. Make another eight crochet stitches and then make the ninth through the tenth embroidery stitch, continuing until the edge is completed, adding a fringe if required.

Crocheted Bobbles are made by first crocheting a simple circle. Start with five chain stitches joined end to end and then work eight stitches around the five, twelve around the eight, etc. increasing to make half the bobble and then decreasing each row to complete it. They are then filled with cotton wool, kapok or wool cuttings, to pad out into full bobbles.

These crochet bobbles or pompoms can be used singly and in groups, or they can be combined with looped rosettes or tufted pompoms, explained on pages 302–3, and used as bedspread edge decoration, on tie-belts, as scarf ends, etc.

Crochet Circles, rosettes, ovals or squares can be made using simple crochet stitches by beginning in the middle and working outwards to the edge instead of working in rows. To make a crochet circle first make a short chain of 5 stitches and join it end to end by making 1 s.st. into the first ch. Into this first circle work twice the number of stitches as in the original

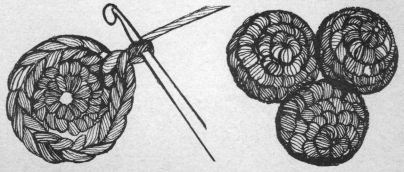

chain, continuing round again until the size required is complete. Oval or square shapes can also be made by grouping the increased stitches together instead of evenly.

Crocheted Twirls as shown by the bottom illustration on the left are made in much the same way as crochet bobbles, but instead of crocheting in ever increasing circles the stitches are worked in spiral fashion to form twirls. These twirls can be combined with the tassels described on page 304 or they can be used singly or in groups on bedspread edges, cushions, etc.

Looped Rosettes

Looped ribbon or wool rosettes can easily be made on a special multi-needle Wendy Winder or a Twilleys Multi Fleur Loom which is shown on page 59. These can be bought at most needlework shops. They are very simple to use and have the added advantage of being very quick. These looped rosettes can be made separately for incorporating with one of the other methods explained in this chapter, or for use with appliqué and embroidery, or they can be joined together to make complete garments or bedspreads in a similar way to crochet.

1. To make an open-centred round rosette wind about a yard of coloured wool around the prongs from one side to the other, progressing in a clockwise direction as shown in diagrams 1 and 2 until all the prongs have been looped twice.

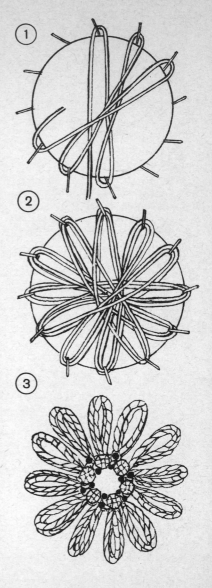

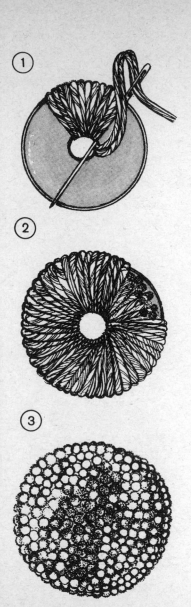

2. Cut the remaining wool to 10″ and thread it on to a wide-eyed needle. Make a stitch in the centre of the rosette and draw out between two petals. Bring the needle over and down into the centre again and draw out between the next set of petals, working clockwise until all the loops are enclosed, then finish off with a knot at the back of the rosette.

3. Many other looped rosette designs such as closed edge rosettes, beaded rosettes and rosettes with pom-pom centres can be made.

The wool used can be matching or contrasting in colour, or the colours used can be mixed or alternated to give a rainbow or graduated effect as required. Alternatively they can be made in a continuous strip using coloured string, embroidery thread, plastic or leather strips, raffia, crochet cotton or many other types of thread.

Pom-poms

To make pom-pom balls begin by cutting out two identical circles of card with a hole in the middle as in diagram 1. The size of the card can vary from that of a 10-penny piece to the size of a cocoa-tin lid.

1. Place two cards together and cover with very close stitches of coloured wool, silk or string etc., as shown in diagrams 1 and 2. When the whole of the circumference of the shape has been covered several times, slip the point of a sharp pair of scissors between the two cards on the outer edge and cut all the threads right round the outside.

2. Next draw a strong thread carefully through between the two cards and wind it several times very tightly around the middle threads fastening off with a knot, leaving the ends as a hanging cord.

3. Finally cut the cards from the outer edge to the centre, taking

oddments of coloured wool around a piece of stiff card 6″ to 8″ wide. Cut along one edge removing six or eight strands of wool. Fold the top loop over and through itself into a simple knot, making sure that the knot itself forms near the top fold. Pull the knot tight and then trim the ends level with each other. Make several more tassels, checking the tassel lengths

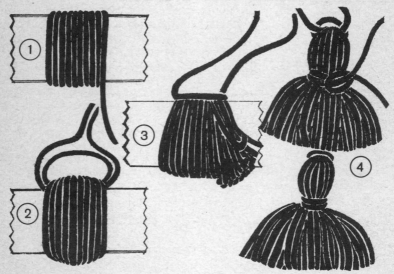

care not to cut any of the threads, and pull them out leaving the finished pom-pom as in diagram 3 on the previous page. Make several more pom-pom balls in matching or contrasting colours and fasten them into position on whatever you are making by their hanging cords.

Simple Tassels

To make a simple tassel wind some

against each other, and then stitch them into position.

1. To make a thicker tassel first cut a strip of stiff card 4″ wide and then wind ten or twelve strands of coloured wool around it as shown above, diagram 1.

2. Using a large-eyed round-ended embroidery needle pass a strong matching thread between the wool and card, looping it

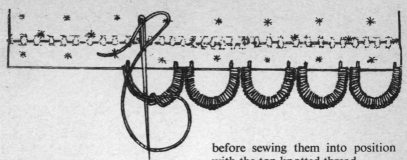

round twice as shown in diagram 2, and knotting it securely. Using a sharp pair of scissors cut the wool along the bottom edge.

3. At ½″ to 1″ down from the top fold wind a strand of wool around the tassel to form a collar, knotting the ends together securely and then slotting them through the tassel with the darning needle before cutting them neatly as in diagram 4 opposite.

Make several tassels, varying the colours and textures as needed before sewing them into position with the top knotted thread.

Looped Edges made with buttonhole stitches over thread loops can be applied to the finished edge of a garment and can be used as an edge decoration or as buttoning loops. To make each loop the same size first make four stitches along the edge over a pencil or thick knitting needle, fastening each end securely with a back stitch. Next work a blanket or buttonhole stitch over this loop, fastening the thread into the turning before

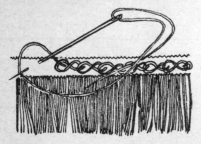

making the next loop of four threads over a pencil and so on. These loops can be decorated with tassels or left plain as required by the design.

Fringes

One of the simplest form of fringe, made from bunches of coloured wool 6″ to 8″ long which have been slotted through a blanket-stitched edge and then pulled tight through the top loop, is shown on page 305.

1. Work an even line of blanket stitches along the edge to be fringed.

2. Cut some coloured wool into 6″ to 8″ lengths by the card method of cutting explained in the previous section, using six to eight strands at a time.

3. With the aid of a large crochet hook bring the centre fold of the wool strands through a loop in the blanket stitch and then pass the cut ends through the loop.

4. Pull the tassel tight and then repeat along the edge at regular intervals, trimming the ends where necessary.

The wool used for the tassels can be matching or contrasting in colour or the colours can be mixed to give a rainbow or graduated effect as required. String, silk or raffia can be used in place of wool.

Looped Fringe, shown on the opposite page, diagram 2, can be made with strands of knitting wool, embroidery silks, strips of leather, russia braid or any novelty which is suitable. Cut several strands for each loop double the depth of the fringe plus 1″ for top loop. Insert a crochet hook into the turned back edge of material, hook on the centre fold of three cut strands. Pull the loop through the fabric and then pull the cut ends through the loop.

Shop Fringing made of twisted string, looped art silk or fluffy pom-poms can be stuck and stitched on to the hems and edges

first stick them to the edges, using Evo-Stik or a similar glue and then hand stitch as shown in the top diagram or by using an embroidery stitch as shown in the bottom diagram opposite.

Fabric Fringing. This is the easiest kind of fringing to make especially if you are using a coarse evenly woven fabric. The first thing to do is to cut the fabric edge on the

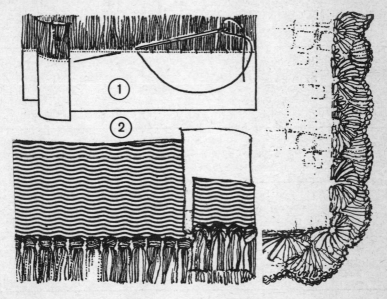

of most things from bath-mats and cushions to nursery pictures or rag dolls. Generally there is a large range of ready-made edge trimmings available at most notion counters in the larger stores or specialist sewing shops or you can make your own. To attach these made or bought fringes you should

exact grain, then measure in from the edge the exact depth of fringe required and pull a thread exactly on that mark. Just inside this pulled thread make a line of machine stitches to hold the rest of the threads in place, before pulling out the unwanted threads very carefully one by one. If the

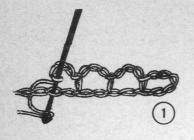

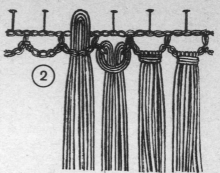

single fringe is not thick enough back it up with another piece, hand-stitching the edges together as shown in diagram 1, page 307, or machine stitching ¼″ in.

Knotted Work

To make a knotted fringed edging as shown, you will require a ball of soft string, knitting wool or something similar. Also a small amount of matching coloured crochet thread and a suitable crochet hook.

1. Make a simple crochet looped chain, as shown by diagram 1 above, and then pin this to the side of a cardboard box so that the loops are facing downwards. Alternatively make a crochet scallop as explained on page 300 or a looped edge as shown on page 305.

2. Cut some 12″ to 18″ lengths of string or wool by winding them around a 6″ or 9″ strip of firm cardboard and cutting along one of the folded edges as explained on page 304 for simple tassels. Slot five or six of the folded edges through each crochet loop and then slot the strand ends through the folded edges before pulling tight, as in diagram 2.

3. To knot the fringe, as shown in diagrams 3 and 4 below, first take a bunch of hanging threads,

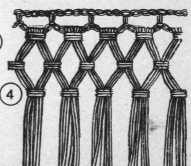

half from the left and half from the right, and knot them together, repeating with half from the left and half from the right all the way along the row to form the top row of knots.

4. To make the second row of knots, again divide the bunches of threads which hang from each knot, taking half from the left and half from the right and knotting together so that the new knots come between those of the row above.

5. To attach this fringe, or a similar ready-made one, on to the edge of a garment, first surface-pin into position and then hand stitch along the crocheted edge with matching coloured cotton.

Macramé

The simplest knotted stringwork to make is that illustrated in diagram 3 opposite. However, if you wish to be more adventurous, instead of knotting groups of threads you can knot, twist and loop single threads together as shown on this page, which when finished make the decorative macramé work shown on the right. This knotted string macramé work can also be made into long lengths for belts and insets as well as for curtain edges or bedspreads, etc. Beads can also be used, threading them into position in between the groups of knots, as also can dried seeds, small corks, pieces of plastic tubing or anything else that makes an interesting pattern and textured design. So experiment and choose the most interesting one to use.

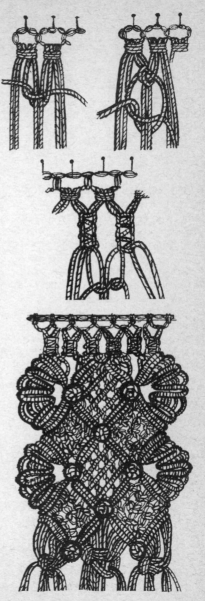

12. Embroidery Stitches

On the following twenty pages are shown some of the wide variety of embroidery stitches which can be used for decorative work. These are intended to be freely interpreted and combined with the other sewing methods explained in the other chapters of this book. As with the other decorative techniques experimentation is important.

Different designs can be worked out by experienced sewers, whilst those who are less experienced can buy extremely good transfer designs from most sewing shops. These transfers are ironed on to the fabric as a guide to the stitching details which are fully explained in the instruction leaflet sold with the

design. Also explained are the various needles to use and what embroidery threads to buy. But once you have a little experience you can try some experiments, choosing different colour combinations or different thread textures to suit your own decorative ideas.

Machine Embroidery

If you are lucky enough to have a fully automatic swing-needle sewing machine you will know how many beautiful embroidery stitches you can make. The sewing manual supplied with the machine will show you how to appliqué as shown below, how to free embroider as above, how to make scallops,

zig-zags, how to shell-edge or cord. Whether your machine is a Jones as illustrated on page 36 or a Bernina, Viking, etc. it would be well worth your time experimenting with various stitches, trying out different thread combinations, finding out how to use all the little gadgets and really learning how to make the most of your machine.

colours, but it can be great fun to supplement these with knitting wool, raffia, strands of leather and plastic, buttons, russia braid, crochet thread, rug wool, and even coloured string.

Herringbone Stitch is worked from left to right by taking small stitches as shown in diagram 1 below.

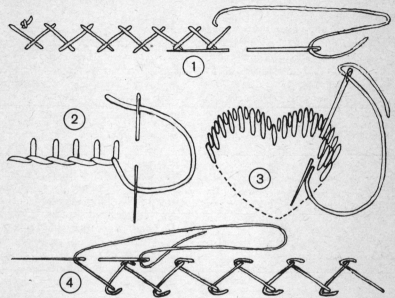

If you are really keen you could also have a lesson on embroidery stitching – this is generally offered free when purchasing a machine.

Hand Embroidery

Traditionally skeins of Anchor Stranded Cotton, Tapisserie wool, or Perlita are used for hand embroidery, as these can be bought at most shops in a wide range of

Blanket Stitch. Work from left to right, making a straight downwards stitch – as shown in diagram 2 – in such a way that the thread passes under the needle point. Pull the stitch to form a loop and repeat at regular $\frac{1}{4}''$ to $\frac{3}{8}''$ intervals.

Long and Short Stitch, as can be seen in diagram 3, is an irregular form of satin stitch. In the first row

311

the stitches should be alternately long and short, closely following the outline shape. The stitches in the following rows are worked as required to fill the shape effectively.

Feather Stitch is similar to herringbone stitch but is worked from right to left, passing the needle over the thread as shown in diagram 4, page 311. See page 319.

Buttonhole Stitch is similar to blanket stitch, shown on the previous

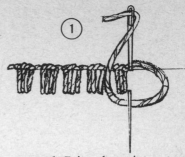

page, except that it is worked through the loop as shown above right. This stitch can be made at regular $\frac{1}{8}''$ to $\frac{1}{4}''$ intervals, or it can be grouped into an interesting pattern, working four closely together and then the next $\frac{1}{4}''$ away etc. The stitch can be used to neaten raw edges, to attach coloured patches in appliqué work, or, as its name implies, for hand-made buttonholes.

Lazy Daisy. First bring the needle through near the centre of a planned daisy. Catch a $\frac{1}{2}''$ loop down with the left thumb and then insert the needle next to where it first

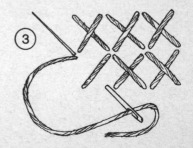

emerged. Bring the point out next to the top of the loop and then complete the stitch over the loop as shown on the left. As well as being used in groups to form a flower these stitches can be made next to each other to form an attractive border.

Cross Stitch. This stitch can be worked *en masse* by first making a line of diagonal stitches so that the bottom of one stitch is exactly below the top of the previous one, and then working a line of identical diagonal stitches in the opposite direction to complete the crosses – page 326, diagram 5 – or work the crosses separately as shown in diagram 3 below by making first a left-slanting diagonal stitch and then

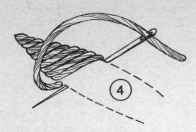

crossing it with a right-slanting one, repeating crosses as required.

Satin Stitch. Make diagonal stitches closely together across the shape to be filled as shown in diagram 4, taking care to form a neat, even edge. This stitch can also be used to outline a large shape which can then be filled with other more widely spaced stitches such as the sheaf stitches – as in diagram 6 –, cross stitch – as in diagram 3 –, bead, couching or ribbon work as described in the next chapter.

Fern Stitch. This simple stitch is just three straight stitches of equal length radiating from the same point. First bring the needle through on the outline being followed, make a $\frac{1}{2}''$ back stitch, along the outline, bring the needle back through at the first point. Next make

a similar stitch diagonally above and another one diagonally below the first stitch as shown in diagram 5, repeating stitches at regular intervals as required.

Sheaf Stitch is an attractive filling stitch consisting of three vertical stitches that are tied across the centre with two horizontal overcasting stitches. These overcasting stitches are worked round the bunch of vertical stitches with the needle only entering the fabric to pass on to the next sheaf. The

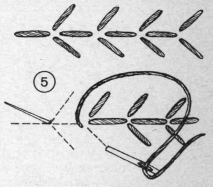

sheaves can be worked in formal rows as shown or at random spacings and differing angles as a textured filling-stitch combined with couched outlining or satin stitch.

Stem Stitch is used for outlining a design or for any thin solid line that is a main feature, such as flower stems, when it is used in combination with daisy stitch, long and short stitch, rose stitch or similar stitches. It can be made with many different kinds of thread depending on the effect required.

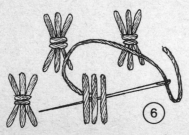

313

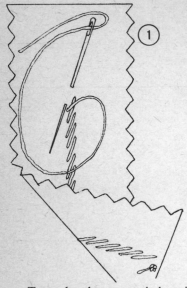

page 356. As with stem stitch many different kinds of thread can be used depending on the effect required, but generally a bold single thread is more effective than a number of loosely twisted threads.

To make the chain first bring the needle up through the fabric at the end of the line farthest from you, pull the thread towards you and slightly to the left. Hold the thread down with the left thumb and insert the needle just right of where it last emerged. Bring the point of the needle out a short distance away along the line of work. Pull the thread through, keeping the loop of thread under the needle point, and start on the next stitch.

An interesting variation of the chain stitch is the open chain

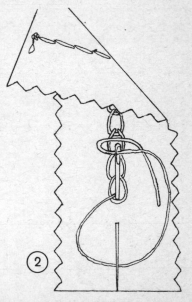

To make the stem stitch point the needle towards you and start stitching from the end of the line nearest to you. Take a stitch ½″ long bringing the needle out halfway along the previous stitch and slightly to its left. Take the next stitch ¼″ beyond the first and bring the needle out level with the end of the first stitch but slightly to its left. Proceed in this way, keeping the stitches fairly evenly spaced, as shown above.

Chain Stitch is used for outlining a design where a heavier or more decorative effect is required than can be obtained by using stem stitch. It can also be used with rows worked close together as a flower stem in combination with appliqué and ribbon work, as on

314

illustrated in diagram 4. Basically this stitch is made in the same way as the chain stitch explained opposite. The only difference is that instead of bringing the needle straight down the outline being worked the needle is taken diagonally with the point passing over the thread as shown below.

Coral Stitch is really a loosely looped side stitch and is worked as shown in diagram 3. First bring the thread up through the fabric at the end of the line nearest to you. Lay the thread along the line being worked and hold it down with the left thumb. Take a small stitch under the line and thread, bring the needle up over the loop formed on the left and pull

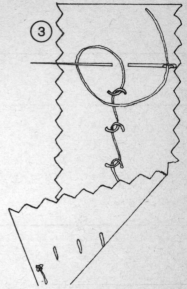

through. Take the thread and again lay it along the line of the design. Hold the thread down with the left thumb and take another small stitch from the right, under the line and thread about $\frac{1}{2}''$ from the first, bringing the needle up over the loop as shown above.

Flower Stitch is one of the simplest stitches to make. First bring the needle up through the fabric in the centre of a marked circle, drawing the thread through. Next insert the needle at the outer edge of the marked circle and bring it out again at the centre next to the first stitch as shown on the following page, diagram 1. Continue in this way until the flower is complete. This stitch can be worked in many colours and differing textures of

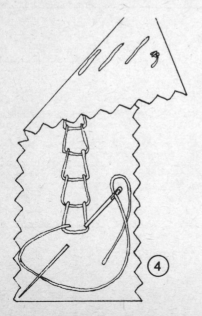

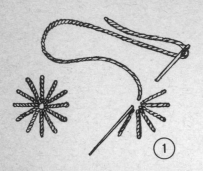

to bullion stitch or French knots, also changing the colour combinations and thread textures.

Cartwheel Stitch is another easy stitch. Again working on a marked circle about the size of a jacket button bring the needle up through the fabric on the outer edge of the circle. Next insert the needle at the centre of the circle and then bring it out on the outer edge between $\frac{1}{4}''$ to $\frac{3}{8}''$ away from the

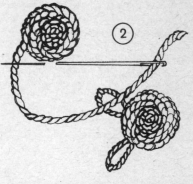

thread depending on the effect required.

Rosebud Stitch. To make the compact rambler rose stitch shown in diagram 2, first make several small satin stitches in a bright yellow thread. Next work spirally around the rose's centre with a scarlet outline stitch, working from right to left and letting the needle come out above the thread, varying the length of the stitches so that they overlap each other attractively. When making bunches of rosebuds alter the centre stitch occasionally

first stitch, with the thread under the point as shown in diagram 3, repeating the stitch until complete.

Cretan Stitch. This is another decorative stitch for making an interesting leaf shape, or it can be used as a textured filling stitch, stemming stitch, etc. First mark out the leaf or shape required. Bring the needle through centrally at the righthand side, taking a small stitch on lower line, needle pointing inwards and with the thread under the needle point as shown at A, diagram 4. Take a

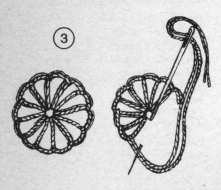

stitch on the upper line, thread under the needle as shown at B. Continue alternately towards top and bottom in this way until the shape is filled.

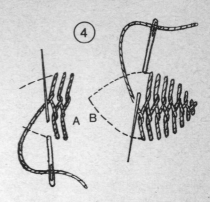

Bullion Stitch is used for embroidering small roses, daisies and tulips, or as textured centres to larger flowers. As shown by diagram 5 below, first bring the needle and thread up through the fabric and then make a simple back stitch $\frac{1}{4}''$ to $\frac{1}{2}''$ long, bringing the

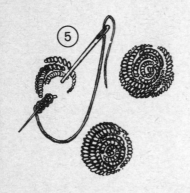

needle point out at the starting point, but do not draw the thread or the needle through. Next twist the thread around the point of the needle four or five times (as in diagram 5), and then pull the remaining thread through. Complete the stitch by inserting the needle through the fabric next to the starting thread and then pull the thread tight.

Fishbone Stitch is used for filling small shapes such as leaves or petals. Bring the needle through

at the left-hand corner of the shape and make a small straight stitch along the centre. Bring the thread through again at the point just to the right of the first one and make a sloping stitch across the base of the first stitch. Bring the thread through just below the starting point and make a similar sloping stitch to overlap the previous stitch. Continue working alternately on each side as shown in diagram 6 below until the shape is filled.

Open Cretan Stitch is worked

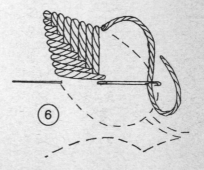

317

between two parallel lines. First
bring the thread through on the
bottom line at the left side. Insert
the needle point, towards you,
into the top line $\frac{1}{4}''$ to the right
of the first stitch with the thread
below the needle and draw through.
With the needle facing away from
you make a stitch on the bottom
line $\frac{1}{4}''$ to the right of the previous
stitch, with the thread under the
point of the needle, and draw
through. Repeat top and bottom
at regular intervals as shown in
diagram 1 on the right.

Vandyke Stitch is worked between
two upright lines $\frac{1}{2}''$ to $\frac{3}{4}''$ apart.
Bring the thread through at A,
diagram 3, which is just below
the top end of the left guide line.
Take a small horizontal stitch in
the middle of the guide lines $\frac{1}{4}''$
above A. Insert the needle at B

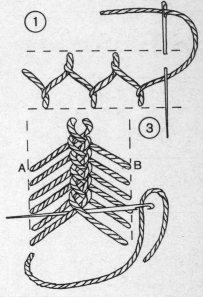

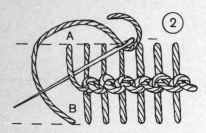

Loop Ladder Stitch. Make two
parallel lines $\frac{1}{2}''$ to $\frac{3}{4}''$ apart. Bring
the needle through in the middle
of the lines at the right-hand side
of the work. Insert the needle at
A, diagram 2, on the top line,
bringing it through at B, which is
immediately below A but on the
bottom line. With the thread to
the left and under the point of the
needle, pass the needle under the
centre of the first stitch without
piercing the fabric. Insert the
needle $\frac{1}{8}''$ to the left of A, bringing
it through $\frac{1}{8}''$ to the left of B and
again pass the needle under as
shown in the diagram.

which is opposite A, bringing the
needle through $\frac{1}{8}''$ below A. Without
piercing the fabric, pass the needle
under the centre crossed threads as
shown and insert $\frac{1}{8}''$ below B. Do
not pull the stitch too tightly as this
will make an irregular pattern.

Scroll Stitch. This stitch is worked
from left to right around a design
as an outline or border stitch. The

working thread is looped to the right and then back to the left on the fabric as shown in diagram 4. Inside this loop the needle takes a small slanting stitch to the left on the line of the design, with the thread of the loop under the point of the needle; the thread is then pulled through. Space the stitches evenly and do not pull the thread

line being followed, looping the thread as shown so that the point of the needle goes over it to form the feather stitch required. This particular stitch is very adaptable as it can be used for outlining a design, hemming, combining with cord and ribbon work, or with machine embroidery, etc.

Spiders' Web Stitch is again worked within a marked circle. First make an uneven number of straight stitches as in the flower stitch shown on page 316, diagram 1 – five, seven or nine can be used – to form the 'spokes' which are the found-

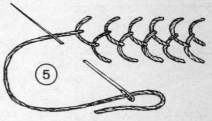

too tightly as this makes irregular scrolls.

ation of the web. Next weave under and over the spokes, not piercing the fabric (see diagram 6), until the circle is completely filled, or weave only halfway if you prefer the spiky unfinished appearance.

Feather Stitch Variations can be worked by adapting the basic feather stitch shown on page 311, diagram 4. As you can see from diagram 5, this particular variation is made by making diagonal stitches alternately above and below the

Broderie Anglaise

Broderie anglaise is usually made with white thread on white cotton lawn using blanket stitch, worked eyelets, buttonhole stitch and scalloping. *Broderie anglaise* designs are generally used in strips for borders and scalloped frills but they can

319

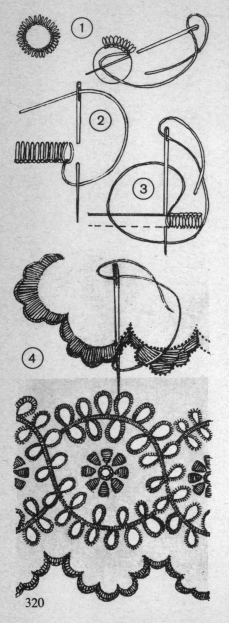

also be used with cut-work as motifs, as for the butterfly design shown opposite.

Eyelet Holes. These are small embroidered circles incorporated into a *broderie anglaise* design at regular intervals. To make the smallest eyelet holes, force open the grain into an uncut circle with a stiletto and then oversew. Larger holes are made by removing a small amount of fabric with a circular fabric punch or sharp pointed scissors. The cut edge is then oversewn, blanket-stitched or buttonholed as required, as in diagram 1 on the left.

Blanket Stitch is an integral part of *broderie anglaise* work. The stitch is made from left to right at regular $\frac{1}{8}''$ intervals. Make a straight downward stitch $\frac{1}{8}''$ long as shown in diagram 2 so that the thread passes under the needle point. Do not pull the stitch too tightly, but just enough to form the top loop before repeating around the design shape.

Buttonhole Stitch can also be used in *broderie anglaise* work. It is made in a similar way to blanket stitch except that it is worked through a double loop as shown in diagram 3 and in general is made closer together at $\frac{1}{16}''-\frac{1}{8}''$ intervals.

Scalloped Edges are another feature of *broderie anglaise*. These can be made by blanket-stitching or buttonholing around regular curves, or intricately worked in double curves with padding stitches and

a neat purl edge. The normal sort of scalloping is easy to make: simply mark out a line of curves using a jacket button as a guide. Work either buttonhole stitch or blanket stitch around these curves with the loops on the outside edges. When it is all neatly stitched, cut away the outside material, taking care not to cut any of the stitches. To make the more complex scalloped edging as shown in diagram 4 on the left, first mark out the edge to be scalloped and fill with long and short stitches which act as a padding. Work over the padding stitches with blanket stitch or with buttonhole stitches inserting the needle on the upper outline and bringing it out on the lower one with the needle over the thread, keeping the stitches evenly spaced. When all the scallops are complete, trim away the surplus fabric, taking care not to clip the stitches.

Machine Stitched broderie anglaise can also be made by those lucky enough to own an automatic swing-needle machine. Generally these machines have an attachment for making stitched eyelets whilst the scalloping and cut-out design shapes can be made with the machine set at automatic satin stitch.

Drawn Thread-Work

As its name implies, this is done by withdrawing threads from an evenly woven fabric and then decorating over the spaces left with embroidery stitches. Various decorative stitches or ribbons can be intertwined with the warp or weft threads or complete motifs such as spider's web filling can be used on open corners. Some of the French cut-work and Norwegian thread-work stitches shown on the following pages can also be used, or Faggoting, shown on page 296, or any of the other decorative methods explained in this book.

Withdrawing Threads. First cut across the required number of threads and withdraw these carefully as shown in diagram 1 leaving sufficient threads at the ends to darn away invisibly.

Darning Ends. Darn each cut thread separately into the fabric over and under each woven thread, as shown in diagram 2, pulling each stitch neatly into position.

Hem Stitch. Start by bringing the needle out two threads below open work. Next pass the needle behind two or more loose threads and then insert the needle behind the same loose threads, bringing the needle out through the fabric two threads down and two or more threads along as shown in diagram 3, in readiness for the next stitch.

Open-Lacing. Fasten a long thread at top right-hand side of open thread section. Take the needle over six threads and then pass it back under three, emerging above the thread. Make another stitch over six threads and back under three, repeating until top row is completed. Start a second row of stitches on the bottom left-hand side and reverse the stitch, over six back under three, as shown in diagram 4, until the open-lacing is finished.

Chevron Stitch is worked from left to right. Start by making a stitch over two loose threads. Next make a stitch $\frac{1}{4}''$ below and $\frac{1}{4}''$ to the right of the first stitch, passing the needle under two threads, then over the top of four threads and then under two threads as shown

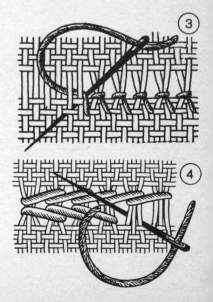

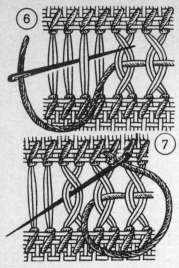

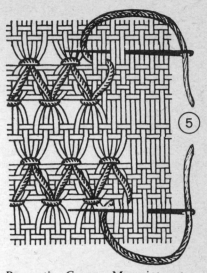

in diagram 5, repeating each subsequent stitch $\frac{1}{4}''$ above and then $\frac{1}{4}''$ below until the row is completed. When this stitch is worked over more threads, the method is the same, the number of threads or the amount of fabric being stitched to complete each chevron being regulated by your skill.

Interlacing. Interlaced hem stitch is made over groups of open threads which have been hemstitched to produce an even ladder of loose threads. Fasten a long thread at right-hand side centrally on to the first ladder. Insert the needle from left to right under the second group as in diagram 6 and twist the needle over so that it is now right to left, bringing the second group over the first one as in diagram 7. Pull thread through and repeat.

Decorative Corners. Many interesting and decorative corner and interlacing stitches can be made in openwork embroidery in addition to those already shown, including some of the stitches shown in Norwegian threadwork on page 326, etc. If you are interested in this type of work many good easy-to-follow Coats sewing pamphlets and patterns are available, either through your local needlework stockist or by post from Coats Patons Ltd., 50 Bothwell Street, Glasgow, G25 PA.

Richelieu Work

Richelieu or French cut-work, is a very distinctive form of stitched open work which is ideally suited to decorative table linen, window-blind ends, bedspread edges, dressmaking, etc. Basically it consists of cut edge interlinking motifs which have their raw edges covered by buttonhole or blanket stitches. Occasionally some surface stitchery is added to enhance this cut-work giving a distinctive decorative richness. Shown here are a few of the basic stitches used, but many others as shown elsewhere in this or our other sewing books, can be used with equal success.

Blanket Stitch is the basic stitch used in this form of cut-work. As shown in diagram 1 the stitch is made over the marking line. First bring the needle out just below the design line on the left hand edge of the motif. Insert the needle just above the line, taking a straight downwards stitch with the thread under the needle point to form a loop. Make another stitch above the line a scant $\frac{1}{8}''$ away from the previous one and repeat with the thread under the needle to form a loop again. The buttonhole stitch shown on page 320, diagram 3, can also be used but it takes a little longer to work.

Straight Stitch. This is a simple single-spaced stitch worked either in a regular or irregular manner to form an interesting pattern as can be seen in diagram 2.

Long and Short Stitch is similar to the embroidery stitch shown on

page 311, diagram 3, with the stitches being made in varying length as shown on the right in diagram 3. This stitch is generally used for filling an area requiring a textured look, and can be worked in several colours for an interesting and varied effect.

Stitched Bars are also used extensively in French cut-work. The stitch used is the same as for buttonhole stitch, the only difference being that it is worked over several looped threads as shown in diagram 4 on the right.

Satin Stitch, stem stitch, cross stitch, chain stitch and various flower stitches, together with many other decorative sewing techniques, can be used to supplement the basic cut-work design.

Automatic Stitches, which can be made on most zig-zag swing-needle machines, can also be used to great advantage to outline French cut-work instead of using the traditional buttonhole stitch, adding just a few hand finishing stitches to enrich the finished look.

Other forms of surface decoration such as slotted ribbon work, appliqué, couching, beading and faggoting, can be added, combining several different techniques into a single unified design.

Hardanger Threadwork

Hardanger or Norwegian threadwork is a form of stylized embroidery and cut-work which is at its best when made on an even-

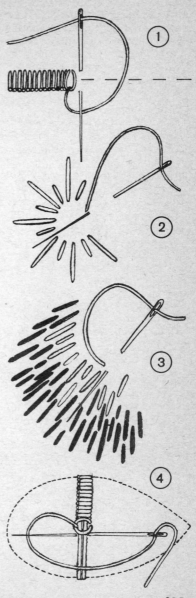

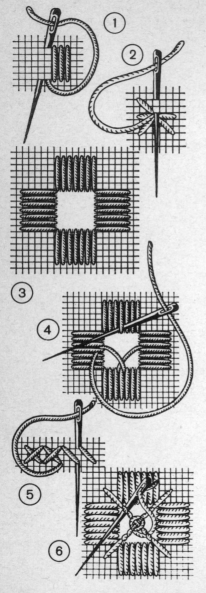

textured linen. The designs are made from blocks of satin stitch, squares of cut-work, and decorative filling stitches, which are most attractive if worked in a single colour on a different coloured ground fabric. As there are a great number of different patterns on sale at most sewing shops, only a brief outline is given below, taken from one of the many excellent Anchor Embroidery Books which can be purchased through most needlework stockists.

Satin Stitch. Work this stitch from right to left over a counted number of threads which vary in depth and length according to the design, from squares and rectangles to diamonds and triangles, or any other geometric shape – diagram 1.

Star Eyelet consists of eight stitches worked over a square of fabric, each stitch being worked from the same central hole, as shown in diagram 2 on the left.

Blocked Cutaways are satin-stitched blocks worked horizontally and vertically around a marked area. The fabric in the centre is then cut away as in diagram 3.

Dove's Eye Filling or similar looped filling stitches are worked over the cut away areas. The one shown in diagram 4 consists of stitching from the centre of each satin-stitched block, looping the thread into an attractive pattern.

Cross Stitch. Work an even line of diagonal stitches so that the bottom of one stitch is exactly below the top of the previous one, then reverse the stitch, working more diagonals to complete the crosses, as in diagram 5. Also see page 312.

Decorative Corners are made diagonally across satin-stitched cutouts. First work two twisted bars across the space as in diagram 6; the thread is then passed over and under the bars twice, and then under and over.

As can be seen from the illustration this kind of formal embroidery is ideally suited to table linen, as is the Richelieu work shown on pages 324 and 329. This type of embroidery is at its best when worked in a single colour on a different coloured ground fabric such as scarlet on holly green, or emerald on navy blue, etc.

Decorative Hems

Many of the stitches described in this chapter are very suitable for making a decorative finish on tablecloth hems, around a bedspread or for the hem of a window blind, etc. On the following two pages are just a few of the techniques which can be used – we hope you will interpret any method in any way which takes your fancy.

Ornamental Stitches such as the feather stitch shown on the following page, diagram 1, can be

used for hemming, as can a number of other stitches. As illustrated this stitch is worked from right to left through both the top fabric and turned-back hem allowance. Bring the needle up on the right, hold the thread lightly down with the left thumb, and make a short stitch $\frac{1}{2}''$ below and $\frac{1}{2}''$ to the left, keeping the thread under the needle point. Draw up the thread and then make a similar stitch $\frac{1}{4}''$ above and $\frac{1}{4}''$ to the left of the previous one with the needle passing over the loop of thread which is being held down by the left thumb. Continue working alternately above and below the previous stitch, fastening off with a back-stitch, after taking the thread through to the wrong side.

Interlacing, as in diagram 2, is worked in two separate operations. First you work an even row of herringbone stitch as shown on page 311, diagram 1, through both the top layer of fabric and turned-back hem allowance. The second row of stitches is worked in a different-coloured thread and consists of horizontal stitches interlaced with the herringbone stitch.

Machine Stitching can also be used when decorating hems especially when several lines are stitched around a scalloped hem as shown in diagram 3. The method used for making these scallops is explained on page 75 and involves facing-out

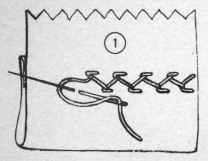

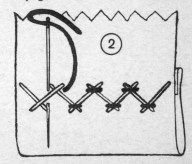

the edges with a strip of fabric or lining. The top-stitching is then made through the double thickness an even distance from the edge with a second, third and even fourth line being stitched parallel to the first. Care should be taken to ensure accuracy when stitching by using your sewing machine's stitching guide which keeps the stitching a uniform distance from the edge. Also make sure that the stitch is perfectly set for both length and tension.

A bolder effect can be achieved by using thicker top thread such as silk buttonhole twist – this requires a thicker needle and adjusted tension – or three strands of top cotton through the needle; or a contrasting colour; or by using one of the many decorative stitches which can be made automatically on a swing-needle machine.

Cut-work is another very distinctive form of stitched hem-work which is ideally suited for decorative table linen, bedspreads, window blinds, etc. Basically it consists of motifs surrounded by buttonhole or machine zig-zag stitches, the in-between areas being cut away. As explained on page 324 occasional surface stitchery is added, and an example of the effect can be seen in the illustration above.

Applied Edgings, such as the Irish crochet motifs shown above, are another form of attractive hem decoration, as is ready-made bobble fringing, macramé, tassels, etc.

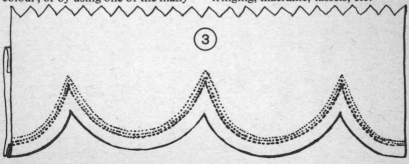

13. Bead and Ribbon Work

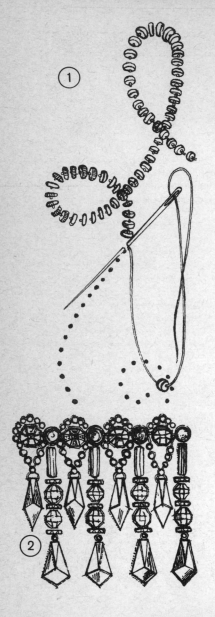

Beads and ribbons are often used as dress trimmings, on cushions or bedspreads, on belts and shoes, for lampshades or blind fringes, either by themselves or combined with embroidery stitches to add a glint and sparkle that embroidery alone does not have. Designs for beading and ribbon work are very similar to those used for embroidery and can be adapted from many of the bolder transfer designs, while many other designs can be worked out once you have had a little experience at this kind of decorative sewing.

This chapter is only intended as an introduction to bead and ribbon work: remember that there are no rules about it, and as new ideas are continually appearing on the market, it is best to keep an open mind so that you can choose the most exciting designs and trimmings now available for your sewing.

Designing Beadwork

There are almost as many ways of designing for beadwork as there are materials and workers. Some workers prefer one method, others another, and the many materials available require varying treatments. Many of the most successful designers do not work to a pre-arranged pattern, or even from a design drawn on to the fabric: they find their ideas come as the work proceeds and according to the beads selected. For most beginners however a transfer is advisable. Use an embroidery transfer, substituting a selection of beads

for some of the embroidery stitches, improvising and experimenting as your sense of design dictates.

Single Beads can be sewn on with silk or terylene thread using a thin sewing needle or a special beading needle which is very fine so that it slips through the small openings of fine beads easily. Alternatively a beading hook can be used if you are beading a large area, but this is a special technique which is best left for those who have a lot of spare time to experiment and practise.

The beading method shown in diagram 1 opposite shows how beads are sewn on one at a time along a marked-out design line, with the beads close enough together to give an interesting textured effect.

First mark the design on the right side of the material and then bring the needle up from the wrong side at the top right-hand side of the line to be followed. Insert the needle through one of the beads and take a small stitch in the material as shown, bringing the needle out far enough beyond the first bead to make room for sewing on the next one. Repeat at regular intervals until the design is complete. If the beads are to be closer together then a side or back stitch can be used.

Graduated Beads as shown on the next page are sewn on singly with a small stitch as just explained, or with a side stitch as illustrated in the diagram. Bring the needle up from

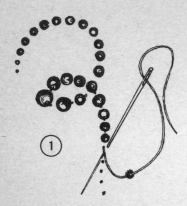

case the thread breaks during wear. First bring the needle out on the right hand side of the design. Insert it through a bead and then make a small forward stitch, allowing just enough gap between the stitches to be filled by the bead.

Grouped Beads, as shown in diagram 3 on the left, can be threaded on to the needle and held with a single stitch. To do this, first bring the needle up through the material at the end of a line and then string on enough beads to fill the space

the wrong side slightly to the left of the design line, insert it through the bead and take a small side stitch to the right of the first one, bringing the needle out far enough beyond the first bead to make room for the next one (diagram 1 above).

Large Beads can be sewn on with a normal running stitch as shown in diagram 2, but for safety a small knot or back stitch should be made after attaching several beads in

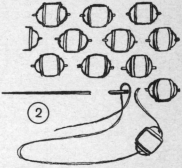

marked. Insert the needle at the other end, as shown, and make a small knot or back stitch to hold securely, adding a stitch across the centre if required. Do not cut the thread between adjacent lines unnecessarily.

Sequins. Single sequins can be sewn on with the aid of a small coloured bead as shown by diagram 5. Using a very fine needle bring it up through the fabric to the right side. Pass the needle through the centre of a sequin and a bead, and then back through the sequin

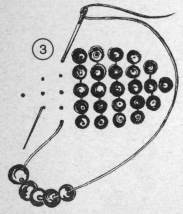

and fabric to the wrong side. Repeat to complete a pattern, making a back stitch after every tenth sequin to hold securely.

To apply sequins in rows first bring the needle up through the material and the centre hole of a sequin and then take a small stitch over the edge. Next bring the needle up again through the fabric, $\frac{1}{8}''$ away from the edge of the first and make a back stitch through the centre of another sequin which has been positioned to cover the

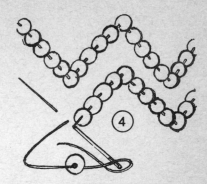

stick it down with Evo-Stik or a little nail varnish at the back.

Beaded Edges. Beads or sequins are applied to the edges of a garment in much the same way as already explained, but as it is generally better to apply them to the finished edge of a garment, take care to conceal the back of the stitches. This is done by making sure that you never bring the needle right through to the back lining but slip it in between the outside and lining layers to the next stitch.

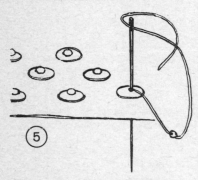

previous stitch. Repeat until all are applied. See diagram 4 on the right.

Sequin Strips. Ready-made sequin strips can be bought in many attractive patterns, as can various sequin motifs and clusters. To apply the sequin strips simply slip- or run-stitch these along the garment edge, securing the thread with a back stitch every 2″ or 3″. Sequin motifs or clusters should be stab-stitched, each cluster being secured with a knot. If the maker's thread has started to unravel it is wisest not to pull or knot it but simply

Couched Beading. A very convenient method for applying lots of beads in lines is to couch-stitch them into position. To do this first bring the needle up at the end of a line and string on as many beads as can be conveniently worked. Then using another needle and thread, couch-stitch the beaded thread on to the design lines by taking a tiny stitch over it between each four to six beads as for normal couching explained on page 292. At the end of the line pass the thread through

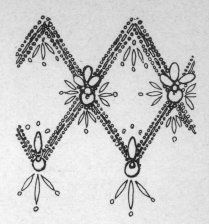

to complete the design.

Beaded Tassels can be made in an unending variety simply by threading a selection of beads on to a strong silk or terylene thread, looping, knotting and twisting them together as required. They can then be attached directly to an edge or suspended between other beads. Ready-made tassels can be bought at most large stores. They are

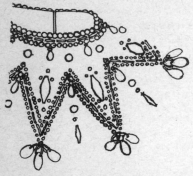

to the back and fasten securely.

Loops and Drops can be attached singly or in clusters by threading one on to your needle at a time, or a dozen. There are no rules as long as the finished effect is good and the beads do not drop off at the first wearing

Beaded Lace. Single lace motifs can be sewn on to the bodice of a net or lace dress with the aid of an assortment of beads and sequins as illustrated opposite, with a border of drops on the bottom edge

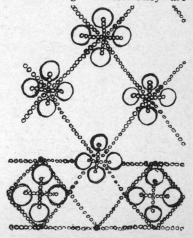

usually made on a backing tape which makes them easy to attach.

Beaded Fringes can be made by threading several small beads on to a strong silk, linen or terylene thread and then looping back through a larger bead, adding

Beaded Smocking. Another way of designing with beads is to combine them with traditional smocking as shown in the illustration at the bottom of the following page. The smocking stitch is worked as explained on pages 286–7 incorporating the beads as an integral

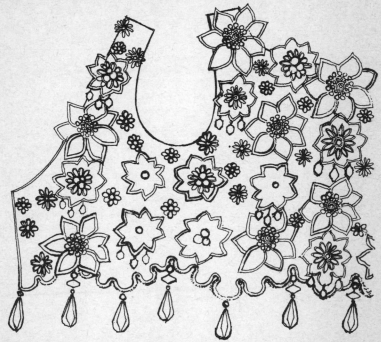

crystal drops, metal sections, coloured bugles and fluted beads as required, before once again threading several more small beads and looping back again, repeating until the decorative fringe is completed. This fringe can then be mounted on to a thin strip of tape or sewn directly around the edge.

part of the design. As in normal smocking the initial gathering is most important. Here a smocking transfer will help. These transfers consist of a series of dots in various widths which are ironed on to the wrong side of the fabric as a guide for the gathering stitches – see page 286 for details.

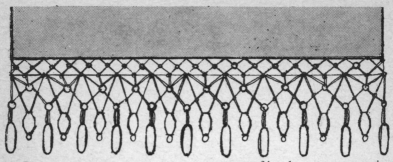

Beaded Curtains

These are usually made on a wooden strip as shown opposite so that when they are completed they can be easily hung into position. First measure the width of curtain required and buy a length of 1″ by ½″ wood cut 1″ longer. Next have a series of $\frac{1}{16}$″ holes drilled through at ½″ intervals right through the 1″ thickness from the ½″ edge. Cut a length of twine 12″ longer than the curtain drop and wax 3″ for the threading end. First thread an end-stopper bead – a chunky round antique bead as explained opposite is best – and tie the unwaxed end of the twine around it. Arrange an interesting pattern of beads on to a convenient work table as explained on page 215, paragraph 3. Slip the waxed thread through the beads one at a time and then through the first hole in the wooden strip, double knotting at the top to prevent the end slipping back through. Lay the threaded beads back on to the work table and arrange a similar or contrasting line repeating the threading as with the first line. Repeat for third, fourth and fifth rows, etc., until complete.

Antique Beads can often be bought in street markets or back-street junk-shops. The most useful sort to look out for are those used on

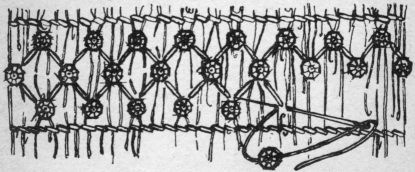

old lampshades or from beaded archways. They are usually very chunky and boldly coloured which makes them ideal for re-stringing as hems on window blinds – above – or for use as decorative blinds.

First of all clean them by washing them in mild soapy water, using a soft scrubbing brush to get into the corners and grooves, before drying them thoroughly with an ordinary hair drier and soft towel. They should be re-strung on upholstery twine using beeswax to get a point on the twine rather than using a needle. To do this cut a length of twine about 12″ longer than the beading length required and rub 3″ of the threading through a piece of beeswax several times to give it a firm end for easy threading.

Thread one end-stopper bead – a chunky round one is best – and tie the unwaxed end of the twine around it. Arrange the pattern of beads required on to a convenient work table and slip the waxed thread through the beads one at a time. The last bead is then threaded – again a chunky round one – and the thread is tied around it. Similar strings of beads can then be made and used as required. A strip of corrugated cardboard is most useful for working out difficult beaded areas as explained on page 215.

Beaded Hems for window blinds or arched valances can also be made out of old curtain beads. Again using waxed upholstery twine thread several chunky beads and

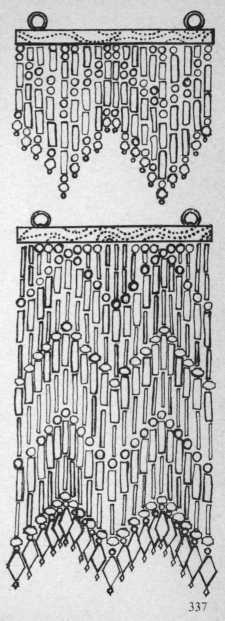

then a larger bead, loop back through a coloured drop, metal section, wooden novelty or glass bugle bead as required, and once again thread the waxed twine through several more chunky beads and a larger bead, loop back again, repeating until the hem is complete.

Beaded Presents

On these two pages are shown a few of the things which can be made with beads, from bracelets and buttons to lampshades, bags and belts. As explained earlier, a seemingly unending variety of beads and sequins can be purchased at the trimming counters of most large stores, from simple single-holed coloured discs to multi-coloured ready-made motifs, from shiny plastic to tinted crystal or fluted metal, with lots of constantly changing things in between. Just four examples of what to make are described here but many other things can easily be made by improvising on the instructions given.

Bracelets or simple beaded necklaces can be made by threading beads on to shirring elastic or beading thread. The designs can be as simple as the bracelet shown top right, or the threading can be done in a more complex way as shown bottom right. This inter-linking of groups of beads can also be used for making belts, watch straps, neckties or even bright shiny beaded bags.

Beaded Buttons. Many designs of decorative buttons can be bought

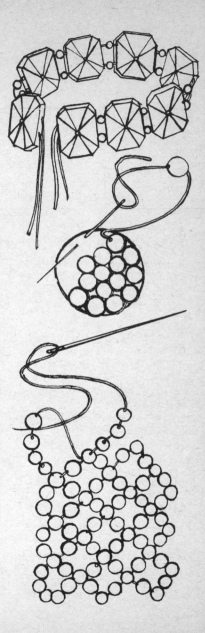

ready-made, and many more can be made by twisting, looping, twirling, plaiting or knotting cord, raffia, rouleaux, dyed string, pipe cleaners, or even electrical wire covering, and then incorporating beads, sequins, motifs, dried seeds, plastic pieces, etc. Simply try several out and if they are successful blind-stab-stitch through several times to hold firm and either work a bar across the back to act as a shank or sew on to a covered button as shown on the left.

Decorative Buckles are made by twisting, looping and knotting cord or ribbon around a simple metal buckle and then covering with beads and sequins or innumerable other ways to match buttons or cuff-links, or to use on their own.

Beaded Belts can also be made in many different ways from plaited ribbon or knotted string-work to covering a ready-made webbing belt with a pattern of beads and sequins, odd buttons, brass curtain rings, metal loops and other decorative oddments as shown on the left.

   1. Collect together as many beads, old pearl, bone or metal buttons and an assortment of small curtain rings, loops and other decorative oddments as you can find. Wash these in mild soapy water, using a soft scrubbing brush to get into the corners and grooves, and dry them thoroughly with a soft towel and hair drier.

   2. Arrange these oddments into a pleasing pattern on to a cheap

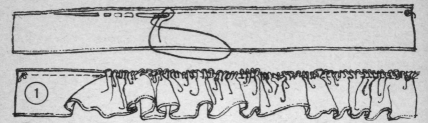

webbing or fabric belt, and using silk buttonhole twist or linen thread stitch each button, bead and loop into position, starting with the largest ones. These should be sewn on at regular intervals, with the smaller ones being attached in a decorative pattern around them and a few extra novelties scattered in between.

Ribbon Work

The simplest way of using ribbon as a trimming is to apply it flat, singly, or in bands. Frequently several colours or shades of the same colour are used with novelty types such as picot-edged, moiré and velvet ribbons interspersed with the plainer grosgrain and satin varieties. To apply flat bands of ribbon first pin the upper or inner edge of the ribbon into position and then stitch by machine or by hand on to the pinned edge leaving the other edge free.

Gathered ribbon. Ribbons can be gathered along one edge as shown above, in the middle as illustrated by diagram 2 or in a zig-zag manner as shown in diagram 3. For a ribbon frill either make a hand gathering-stitch which is pulled up to the size required, or if gathering by machine adjust the attachment to produce the fullness required. For ribbon gathered in the middle first fold the ribbon by bringing the selvedges together and crease to mark the exact centre.

Shell Gathering. A novel effect known as shell trimming is obtained by gathering the ribbon in a zig-zag from edge to edge as in

diagram 3. To ensure evenness in the gathering mark the ribbon with zig-zag creases. To do this place the ribbon right side up and fold the right-hand end so that the selvedge is lying straight across the ribbon at right angles to the rest of the ribbon, creasing the fold. Now fold the end in the opposite direction so that a second fold runs at right angles to the first crease, meeting it at the upper edge, and press. Make the third fold like the first and so on, until all the ribbon is marked. Gather along the creases as shown, adjusting the fullness evenly when you draw up the thread.

Ribbon Stitching

Slotted ribbon work is another form of bold decorative stitch-work which is very easy to do. As in normal embroidery many stitches can be made ranging from the simple ribbon bow stitch, shown by diagram 4 on the right, which is ideal for trimming a cot blanket or baby's sleeping bag, to the flower stitches shown on page 344, which would make an attractive centre-piece. The stitches are simple to carry out, but make sure you use a needle with a large eye, such as a tapestry or chenille needle, and fabric with a slightly open weave to allow the ribbon to slot in and out easily.

Ribbon Stitches. Many of the simpler decorative stitches explained at the beginning of the embroidery chapter on page 310

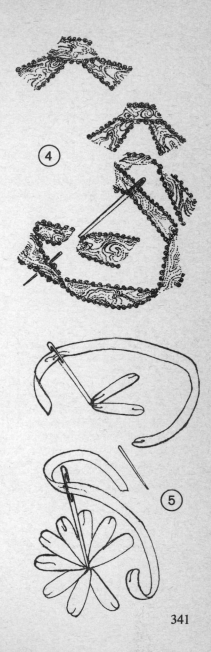

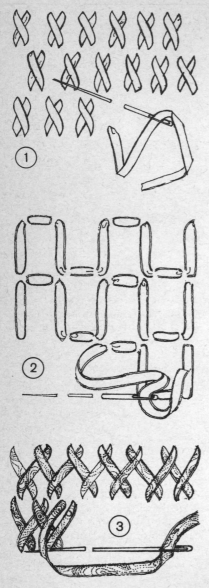

are easily adapted for stitched ribbon work. To start with ¼″ ribbon should be used with a wide-eyed blunt pointed needle on slightly open weave fabric. Apart from bringing the ribbon through from the back of the fabric when starting and taking it to the back when finishing the ribbon is never taken completely through the fabric: instead it is passed under a few top threads as described for the individual stitches.

Flower Stitch. First mark a circle using a jacket button, then with the aid of a chenille needle, or similar large oval-eyed needle, and ½ yard of ¼″ wide satin ribbon, bring the needle up through the fabric on the edge of the marked circle. Make a ¾″ long stitch at the centre of the flower, bringing the needle up on the outer edge ¼″ away from the first stitch. Make a second ¾″ stitch to the centre, bring the needle up ¼″ away from the second stitch as shown in diagram 5 on the previous page, making regular stitches at ¼″ intervals right round the flower. Take care not to draw the ribbon too tightly as this will spoil its appearance, and also be sure not to let it get twisted. Finally bring the ribbon to the back of the fabric and secure with several catch stitches.

Cross Stitch. Working from left to right bring the needle out ¼″ below the line to be worked. Make a stitch ½″ above and ¼″ to the right of the first stitch, passing the needle between the fabric weave

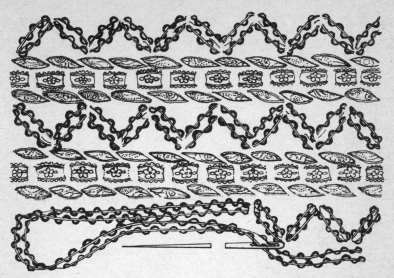

and bringing it out as shown by diagram 1. To complete the cross insert the needle $\frac{1}{2}''$ below the second stitch, left to right, bringing it out $\frac{1}{4}''$ to the right of the completed cross. Now work another complete cross by making a stitch first from right to left by inserting the needle $\frac{1}{2}''$ above and $\frac{1}{4}''$ to the left of the ribbon, etc.

Up and Down Stitch is worked from right to left as shown in diagram 2. First bring the thread out $\frac{1}{4}''$ above the line to be worked. Make a double catch stitch $\frac{1}{2}''$ below the first one by picking up just two top threads, then passing the needle over the fabric for $\frac{1}{4}''$, and then picking up another two top threads. Pull the ribbon through but not too tightly, so that it lies evenly.

Next make another double catch stitch starting $\frac{1}{2}''$ above the last one and again slotting the ribbon under two top threads, then passing over $\frac{1}{4}''$ of fabric before picking up another two top threads, and pulling the ribbon through. Repeat stitches working several lines one above the other to get an all-over effect as shown on the left.

Herringbone. As can be seen in diagram 3, ribbon herringbone stitch is worked in exactly the same way as the embroidery herringbone stitch explained on page 311. Working from left to right pass your needle under several top threads and not right through the fabric. Make a second stitch $\frac{1}{2}''$ above and $\frac{1}{4}''$ to the right of the first, again picking up only a few top threads. Repeat the stitch $\frac{1}{2}''$ below and $\frac{1}{4}''$ to the right, and then $\frac{1}{2}''$ above, etc., right along the line being worked.

Fancy ribbons can also be used as shown in the illustration on the previous page. Try out several ideas before choosing which is the nicest for a particular job – a little time spent experimenting often saves a lot of time unpicking.

Ribbon Embroidery

This is worked in softer ribbons than those used for ordinary slotted ribbon work as the ribbons are intended to crinkle slightly in the finished design, giving it a natural softness. Many ground fabrics can be used with a preference for firmer rather than softer ones, a thin lining of cotton being used as a backing for thin fabrics to give greater support to the ribbon embroidery. The design shown above is a typical specimen of the kind which can be worked with soft ribbons. The bunches of flowers and leaves are all worked in the ribbon with the exception of the stems, which are normal embroidery stem stitch, as explained on page 313. The colours of the ribbons can be as bright or as subdued as those used in other forms of embroidery, varying according to personal preference or the availability of colours. We suggest two shades of orange, one each of blue and yellow, two of pink and two of green, on a heliotrope linen fabric. Use a large-eyed tapestry, chenille or similar needle.

1. The flowers and leaves are worked as shown on the right or on page 341; the green ribbon is used for the leaves, the flowers are worked with alternate petals

of the two shades of orange for the large blooms and one shade only of pink, yellow, blue and orange, according to taste, for the tiny flowers.

The flower petals and leaves are made as shown on the right; take care not to draw the ribbon too tightly, as this spoils its appearance, and also be sure not to let it get twisted. If two colours are used in the same blossom, go all round the flower with one colour, leaving room between the petals for the next shade, which is then added using the same stitch.

2. To complete the design embroider the stems with stem stitch, or use couch-stitched cording as on page 293. The smaller leaves can either be made of single stitches of green ribbon, used in the same way as working the petals shown on page 341, or just two embroidery stitches one longer than the other, placed side by side.

3. When the flowers are finished, make several green bullion or similar embroidery stitches in the middle of each flower. Finally iron the back of the work using a slightly damp cloth and warmish iron and placing the ribbon work face downwards over a thick terry towel. Avoid ironing the front of ribbon-work as this will give it a flat lifeless appearance.

4. Combining ribbon work with couching and appliqué work is another way of using those interesting forms of surface decoration. So turn also to pages 349 and 359 to see how you can make your

ribbon work an original expression of your own ideas.

Ribbon Flowers

Simple ribbon flowers offer considerable variety by the use of different colours, textures and widths of ribbon. They can be combined with the other forms of ribbon work already explained in this chapter or they can be used with appliqué work, couching, cordwork or with many of the embroidery stitches shown in Chapter 12.

1. To make the flower shown below cut a piece of ribbon ¾″ wide and 6″ long as in diagram 1, trimming the ends diagonally. Run a gathering stitch from the point along the left-hand diagonal across the shorter side and down the right diagonal as shown.

2. Draw up the gathering thread and arrange the ribbon neatly, overlapping the ends and then sewing through the centre edges at the back as shown in diagram 2.

3. Stitch the ribbon flower into position, adding coloured bead or bold embroidery stitched centres, couched stem, cut-edge felt leaves and stem stitching as required, as in diagram 3. These flowers could be made into bunches or they could be scattered at random. Change the size and colours according to your personal preference.

Fabric Flowers

These can be made from strips of crossway fabric combined with ribbons and braid for millinery and dress trimmings. To make the fabric rose shown opposite you will

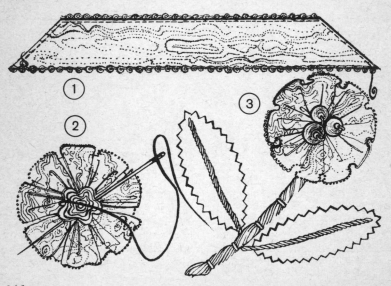

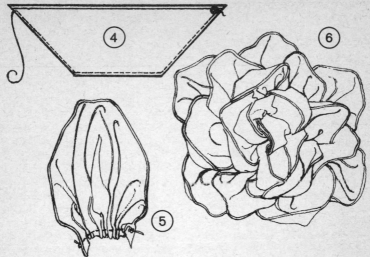

require some 1½″ strips of crossway fabric – organza, wild silk, rayon, taffeta, etc., cut as shown on page 73 – or 1½ yards of 1½″ ribbon.

1. First cut a petal pattern out of thin cardboard from a cereal box or something similar. The pattern should be the shape of the petal before it is gathered up as in diagram 4, and should measure 5″ long and 1½″ wide, with the ends cut diagonally for 1″.

2. Next cut the ribbon or fabric into petal sections using the cardboard template as a guide, so that all the petals are exactly alike, turning the template up and down so that diagonals interlock, to avoid any undue wastage.

3. Gather up each petal, starting at the extreme point, running along the diagonal to the shorter side, then straight across up the other diagonal, drawing them up to about 1½″. This may be done by hand or machine as in diagram 4.

4. Now join the individual petals, which should look like diagram 5, into one continuous strip by machine-stitching over the gathering, adding one petal at a time.

5. Mark out a 2½″ circle and arrange the petals in spiral fashion towards the centre to give the effect shown, sewing them on securely to the ground fabric, but avoiding a stiff effect. As you approach the centre arrange the petals closer together to give the look of the centre of a rose: this also helps to conceal the raw edges.

6. If you want a two-colour rose use 1 yard of 1½″ ribbon or fabric for the outside petals and ½ yard of 1″ ribbon or fabric of a different shade for the inside petals, varying

347

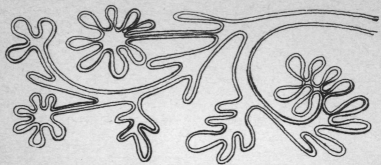

the textures or colour as required.

7. Add cordwork or couching as explained on page 293, ribbon embroidery as explained earlier in this chapter, turned-edge appliqué as on page 358, braid embroidery as on the next page, or any of the other techniques shown in this or our previous sewing books.

Braid Embroidery

This is a variation of very bold decorative embroidery which is both simple to learn and quick to do. Instead of using embroidery threads, braid of different colours, texture, and thicknesses is used in conjunction with plastic and leather couching, bead and sequin trim-

mings, appliqué centres and embroidered details.

The flower group illustrated opposite is worked by stitching a coloured braid to the required shapes, and using loops of ribbon and braid held in place by only three or four fastening stitches. The design is then decorated with beads, various embroidery stitches, and plastic insets.

Outline Braiding, as shown above, is made by sewing various coloured braids into position around the outline of the trace pattern or transfer design. Usually a simple running stitch is used as for soutache braiding explained on page 294,

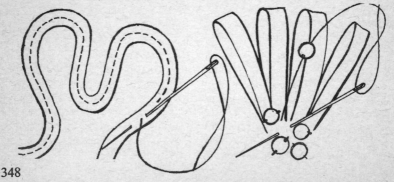

or a small back stitch ⅛″ long and worked every ⅛″ in the centre of the braid as shown below left for more intricate sections. Machine stitching can also be used provided the braid is held firmly into position.

At the curves of the design ease the braid smoothly around the outside edge so that the inside is corn are even more quickly made, a single stitch on the top fold forms the beard, whilst a smaller stitch is used at the junction of the ends. The whole design is then completed by stitching lengths of cord or braid between each looped section with some additional couching and embroidery stitches as desired.

slightly full. The curves can then be pressed into shape.

Braid Flowers are made by looping lengths of coloured braid and ribbons into various patterns, and then securing each loop with several hand stitches at both top and bottom. The looped flowers can then be decorated with beads and embroidery stitches. The ears of

Braided Appliqué. Various coloured shapes of felt and fabrics can also be used in conjunction with braid embroidery and braid flowers. These appliqué shapes are first of all roughly edge-stitched into position and then the raw edges are covered and permanently fixed by outlining the design in braid, cord and couching, before adding bead and

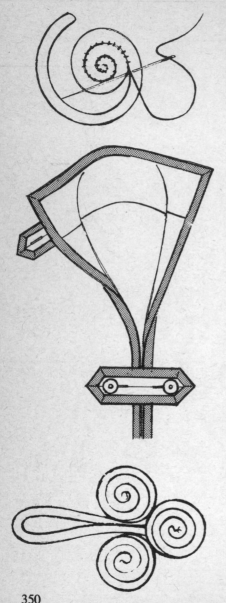

embroidery embellishments. This appliqué requires a little practice before you actually use it, but once you have mastered the technique you will find it has unending possibilities, and is fun to make and combine with one or other of the methods already described.

Dressmaker's Braiding

Braid and ribbon work can be used in dressmaking and tailoring as can be seen in the illustrations on these two pages.

Braided Edge. Tailor's braiding can be bought by the yard in many colours in silk or wool textures for use on the edges of pockets, collars and cuffs. The width of the braid should be double the finished width required. Attach over a raw edge as follows:

1. Mark the edge to be braided at the depth required – half the width of the braid – and then tack the braiding strip to this mark, right sides uppermost. Stitch into position $\frac{1}{8}''$ in from braid edge.

2. Remove tacking stitches. Turn braid to the wrong side of garment and hand-stitch on to the back of the machine-stitching as shown on page 183.

Russia Braid is another tailoring braid used to outline interesting design details such as collar and lapels, pocket flaps and cuff openings. Russia braid is a thin, twin-corded silky braid which can be bought in many colours. It can also be dyed with Dylon if an unusual colour is needed.

350

1. Tack along the centre groove of this braid into the required position – generally $\frac{1}{2}''$ to $\frac{3}{4}''$ in from the finished edge.

2. Neatly stab-stitch along the centre groove of the braid every $\frac{1}{4}''$ – as for soutache braiding, page 294 – or machine stitch into position if you are experienced.

Rick-rack Braid, like many other dressmaker's cords and ribbons, can be used singly or in groups. First tack and then top-stitch the rick-rack braid into position as shown on page 77.

Braid Piping. Prepare your braiding and edges as for a normal piped seam explained on page 74, or proceed as above, slotting a piping cord through the folded braid edge – with the aid of a bodkin – after stitching it into position.

Other Ideas. As explained in Chapter 7, froggings can be made in braid in many shapes and sizes for women's suits, children's coats or men's evening jackets, as can braid and corded buttons, braided belts and many other things, so experiment with several alternatives before deciding on the trimmings for your next garment. For instance use a cuff decoration, made by arranging an interlaced pattern of braid and cords, around the cuff of a jacket or coat, which is then slip- or stab-stitched into position. It can be teamed with novelty fastenings which can also be made in braid – or cord and fabric rouleaux – as shown on page 186 and elsewhere in this book.

351

14. Appliqué and Patchwork

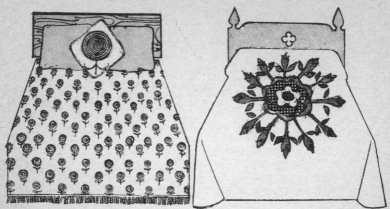

Traditionally, appliqué and patch-work were useful ways of using unwanted pieces of fabric, requiring ingenuity as well as artistry in the sorting out and the sewing together of the fabric pieces. This gave each item an individual character which is half the charm of old appliqué and patchwork. Nowadays this type of decorative sewn work is generally made from a selection of new materials bought expressly for the purpose of cutting them into small pieces and joining them together again. This, of course, defeats the original intention of both appliqué and patchwork and is liable to produce a sameness in the work, losing its traditional character.

Of course it is not always possible to collect together sufficient pieces of good material from dressmaking or furnishing left-overs to make a

large item such as a patchwork bedspread or a set of appliqué cushions, but it is a mistaken belief that lengths of new material should be cut up into several thousand pieces and then tediously sewn together again, regardless of the waste of both materials and time. Generally it is better to mix new fabric with old, bright colours with sombre ones, bold patterns with plain, giving as much thought to the fabric selection as you will to the actual sewing.

This chapter is an introduction to the many ways of making and using appliqué and patchwork. As with the other methods of decorative sewing already described, the basic idea is to add character, interest and a touch of originality to your work. So remember that your decorative sewing should be interestingly designed and well made, as ugly shapes and irregular stitching will only spoil the final look.

Appliqué

Appliqué is made by stitching various cut-out pieces of differently coloured fabrics on to a contrasting background, and then enriching and unifying the design with embroidery, braiding and linking stitches. Success depends as much on the boldness of the design as on the complementing or contrasting use of colour and texture – also, of course, on the neatness of the stitching. However, do remember to avoid over-complicated sewing

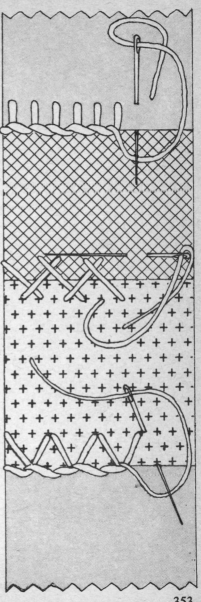

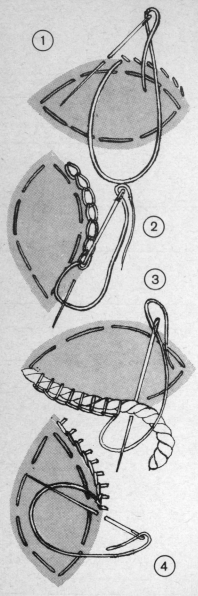

techniques; just use the simplest methods, gay colours and attractive designs. Generally insufficient forethought is given to making the best use of the materials available, so spend a little time planning and designing before putting your work in hand. Look for ideas in shops and stores, magazines and newspapers, collecting as many notes and cuttings as possible before starting on some new appliqué, so as to save yourself misdirected energy and much disappointment.

Appliqué Stitches

The three stitches shown on the left, together with those on the following two pages, are the normal stitches used for raw-edge appliqué – that is, when the appliqué shapes and motifs are cut to shape without edge turnings as in Cut and Stitched; Stitched and Cut; Inlaid Appliqué, etc. The turned-edge appliqué method is explained on page 358. Before stitching it is advisable to tack all the fabric sections and motifs into place, regardless of the method being used. Usually some of the sections will overlap one another; if this happens trim away as much of the underlapping motifs as possible to avoid too many thicknesses.

Side Stitch. The most commonly used stitch for attaching felt motifs in appliqué is the simple side stitch shown in diagram 1. Start by bringing the needle through on the right-hand corner of the appliqué motif so that it is just less than ⅛″ from the edge. Make the second stitch $\frac{1}{4}''$ above and $\frac{1}{8}''$ to the left, bring the needle out $\frac{1}{8}''$ away from the first stitch so that it is just under $\frac{1}{8}''$ in from the edge, as shown.

Chain Stitch. Make in exactly the same way as explained on page 314. Work as close to the edge of the motif as possible so that the chain stitch covers the raw edge of the motif as in diagram 2.

Blanket Stitch. Another common stitch used in appliqué. Work as

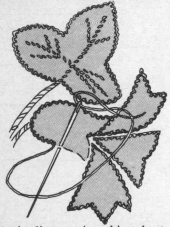

shown in diagram 4, making short stitches onto the motif, or as shown at the bottom of the previous page, using a zig-zag blanket stitch. The stitch can be made towards the motif or away from it, whichever suits the design best.

Herringbone Stitch is worked from left to right making small stitches alternately above and below the edge of the appliqué motif as shown in the middle diagram on page 353.

Couched Stitch. The couched stitches shown on page 293 can be used for attaching and neatening the edges of frayable material. The cord is arranged over the raw edge of the fabric as in diagram 3 opposite, using blanket or side stitch as preferred.

Buttonhole Stitch can be used for attaching and neatening the edges of motifs of very frayable material

with a minimum of stoppages. If you are lucky enough to have an automatic swing-needle sewing machine you will find that you will have a wide range of easy embroidery stitches which can be used on most appliqué work. Many interesting designs can be worked out even by beginners provided the appliqué is bold enough.

Appliqué Methods

Stuck and Stitched felt appliqué is

which have not been turned under. The stitch is worked as shown on page 320 with the purl edge being formed on the inside or outside of the appliqué.

Machine Stitching is made in much the same way as the various hand stitches already explained. The first essential is to tack the various motifs into position so that they can be easily machine stitched around all the interlinking edges

the easiest form of appliqué to start with. Cut out some shapes in coloured felts and stick these onto a contrasting fabric background using Copydex or Evo-stik. Secure the centres and occasionally the edges of these felt motifs with a few hand or machine stitches.

Stitched and Cut. This method is used on thin fabrics which easily fray if cut to shape before appliquéing. Cut a larger area of fabric than is needed, marking the exact shape

356

required with dressmaking chalk; then machine zig-zag or hand stitch through on to the main fabric before trimming away the surplus fabric edges.

Cut and Stitched. For cut and stitched appliqué it is best to use firmish non-frayable material which can be safely cut to shape and then either hand stitched as shown on the previous page, or machine stitched around the raw edges. The appliqué can then be decorated with couching outlines, braid or rick-rack, chain stitching and various embroidery stitches.

Cut-outs. This is a sort of reversed appliqué, with the stitched edge worked on the main body fabric. The centre fabric shape is cut away leaving a hole which is backed up with different coloured fabrics, slotted ribbons, embroidery mirrors, plastic pieces, patterned braids or anything else which takes your fancy and works.

Inlaid Appliqué is another variation – instead of overlaying the various fabric pieces to form a design, the inlaid appliqué pieces are set into the main body of fabric. Coloured felt is best for this inlaid work, but other non-frayable materials can also be used.

First cut an accurate paper shape and mark it on to the main body fabric. Next make an identically sized marking on to the contrasting fabric. Cut away the centre of the body fabric and trim the contrasting fabric to size. Now slot the contrasting inlaid section into the

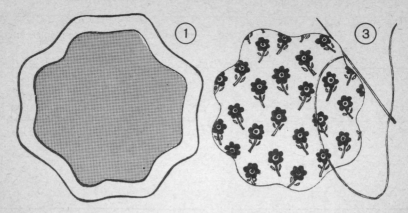

main cut-out fabric and hand-stitch together using the stitches shown on page 353. The cut-out section can now be used to set into another colour so that there is no wastage. Many lively designs can be made by this method, playing games with proportion, line, and colour, and combining it with the other appliqué or decorative methods explained in the preceding chapters of this book.

Turned-Edge Appliqué. This method is very suitable for thin frayable materials. For simple shapes or for straight edges the turnings can be creased over using a medium warm iron but for shapes a little time needs to be spent in preparation. To make an intricately shaped turned-edge motif it is best to proceed as follows:

1. First cut an accurate template the exact size and shape required –

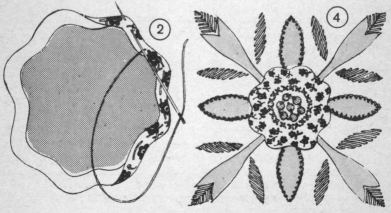

the cover of a glossy monthly magazine or card from a cereal packet is ideal – then cut a piece of fabric $\frac{1}{4}''$ to $\frac{3}{8}''$ larger than the template as shown in diagram 1.

2. Next place the card template on to the back of the fabric leaving an even turning all round. Turn the edges over the card and crease them flat with a warm iron, tacking

ribbons, russia braid, crochet thread, rug wool, and even coloured string, etc.

Appliqué Motifs can be made using any of the appliqué methods previously explained. They can be made as one-off designs for use on garments, or they can be repeated many times for decorating a bedspread or a set of cushions.

any difficult edges to hold accurately as shown in diagram 2.

3. After pressing the edge turnings flat remove the card template and any tackings, then slip-stitch into position as in diagram 3, or use side stitch or blanket stitch as explained on pages 354–5.

4. Finally boldly decorate with areas of embroidery stitches, beads, couching and braidwork, as in diagram 4, using skeins of Anchor Stranded Cotton, some Tapisserie wool, Perlita, knitting wools, raffia, strands of leather and plastic,

Appliqué Flowers

Flowers of ribbon and satin with chiffon and cording, combined with felt-work leaves and beaded centres, and decorated with an assortment of embroidery stitches and added extras, make an exciting addition to normal appliqué work. The flowers can be as simple as the one shown here or they can be grouped together as on page 349.

To make a simple ribbon rose cut six pieces of 1″ ribbon, each 2″

long, and arrange them into an overlapping circle, sewing around the circle to hold them into position. Draw the gathering thread quite tight and fasten securely by oversewing several times across the gathering. Now make another blossom using 2½″ long pieces of ribbon, but do not draw the gathering thread quite so tightly. Next slip the first flower inside the larger one and fasten the two together by stab-stitching through the centre, adding a few beads as centre stamens. Finally cut some felt leaves, pinking the edges, and add couched cord stems and embroidered veining.

Other flowers can be made by varying the ribbons or alternating the petal colours and combining them with the ribbon-work or braid-work flowers or adding small pom-poms and other extras as required – see pages 346–7, etc.

Appliqué Ideas

In order to give you a few ideas on how to design and incorporate appliqué into your sewing we have listed some suggestions on the following pages. Other ideas can also be easily adapted after a little experience, so look around in shops, books and magazines, and in other people's houses.

Fashion Appliqué. Appliqué has made a welcome come-back into fashion clothes with colourful felt motifs – as shown here – being used for both men's and women's wear. Leather fabric and fur appliqué are also widely used, as are plastic and PVC. Look at other people's clothes for ideas, see how appliqué is made and applied in your local dress shop. Experiment with designs of your own, working out a lion or tiger for the back of a boy's denim jacket, a brightly coloured flash for a man's tee-shirt, or a pretty coloured ice-cream motif for a simple crêpe dress.

Appliqué Bedspreads. Ideas for appliqué bedspreads are shown on page 352: small flower motifs sewn onto a plain fabric, made with a companion pillow cover; or a formal turned-edge appliqué of coloured and patterned flowers slip-stitched onto the centre of a white marcella bedspread. The flower arrangement was then embroidered with various stitches and traditional couching. Also shown are children's bedspreads made with matching cushions and bed-heads. Several methods for making bedspreads, bed-heads and pillow covers are shown in Chapter 10.

Appliqué Cushions, like appliqué bedspreads, can be designed and made in many different ways for they can be all shapes and sizes, covered in all sorts of fabrics, decorated with all kinds of surface treatments and made with a variety

361

of technical methods. The only guiding principle is that the finished cushion must be useful and decorative.

1. To make a simple appliqué cushion first cut two identical rectangles of fabric and appliqué the chosen design on to the right side of one of these pieces. Next lay the rectangles of fabric together face to face with edges exactly matching. Stitch all round $\frac{1}{2}"$ in, leaving a turning-through opening 6" long in the middle of one side.

2. Turn cushion through this gap so that the fabric and appliqué is right side out, and then fill with kapok, polythene cuttings, or similar inexpensive filling before slipstitching the gap edges together.

3. If the cushion is like one of the garden cushions illustrated on the previous page it is best to make a paper pattern for the basic rectangular shape so that each cushion is the correct size and shape.

Toy Cushions. To make a nursery cushion follow the general making and designing techniques explained in Chapter 9. Avoid using any easily detachable trimmings, concentrate on large areas in striking colour combinations rather than intricately sewn details. For instance the cow-shaped toy cushion made in cream-coloured corduroy with contrasting patches of soft leather or felt appliquéd on, an embroidered fabric-and-felt head filled with kapok, stuffed fabric legs and a rug-wool tail.

A lot of other interesting and

unusually shaped designs – a pig, snail, or owl-shaped cushion – can be made by first roughing out the shape on a sheet of wrapping paper, experimenting with coloured felt-tipped pens, and adding an assortment of felt and fabric cut-outs and other extras, in much the same way as explained for appliqué

forgetting as much as possible the intricate details and subtleties of fine sewing. The designs shown on the right and those in Chapter 4 are only intended to illustrate the range of designs which can be made for both boys and girls. Many more can easily be made by those who like to experiment; ideas

pictures on page 364. Instead of filling the cushion with kapok you could sew a 6″ zip fastener on to the turning-through gap so that it can be used for a nightie case as on page 15, etc.

Appliqué Toys, party bibs, fancy dress or beach clothes and children's presents should be bold and colourful, using big details, unusual trimmings and interesting extras,

range from traditional Christmas stockings to a space-age cosmonaut's outfit.

Party Bib. To make the bib shown on the left you will need a 9″ × 12″ rectangle of cotton fabric, 1 yard of edging lace, some coloured bias binding for the neck, some ribbon for the bow, and some odd scraps of coloured felt, patterned fabric and other trimmings for the appli-

qué work. Mark out the neck shape with the aid of a cocoa tin and round off the corners with a saucer, trimming the raw edges with the lace and binding the neck with bias strip. Boldly design and stitch the appliqué pattern and finally add a pretty ribbon each side of the neck for tying into a bow.

Appliqué pictures or wall-hangings can be made in many ways, from the simple felt stuck-and-stitched nursery picture shown previously, to the companion picture cushions shown on page 373, to the intricately worked portrait on page 375.

The materials which can be used include a mixture of coloured and textured fabrics and felts, braids and beads, raffia, coloured wools, and strands of leather and plastics, in fact anything which is fun to experiment with.

Start by roughing out your design with coloured felt-tipped pens on to a sheet of wrapping paper, adding an assortment of

felt and fabric cut-outs and other extras as required. Spend a little time looking through some illustrated books. If you are making a nursery picture look through Kate Greenaway's illustrations for Mother Goose, one of Dick Bruna's Christmas Books, or some of Gallery Five's party cards. If you

feel of the design, shifting the cut-outs around to obtain the best balance before sewing into place.

The design should be your own personal creation, and not simply sewn copies of other people's work – it is the personal touch and variation on an idea which makes appliqué pictures interesting, rather

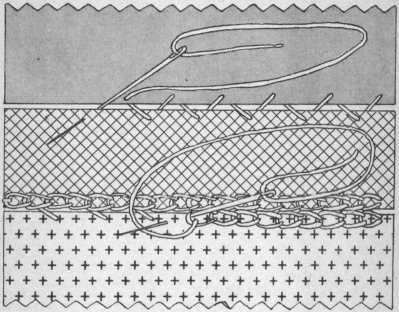

wish to make something more sophisticated then look at one of Edmund Dulac's picture books, or if you would like to make an 'op-pop' art or space-age-inspired design you could work from a Dr Who's Weekly. After looking at these illustrations, try putting different pleasing shapes and interesting textures together to get a

than a line-for-line copy of a Rubens, Van Gogh or Constable. Also try experimenting with different techniques, combining braid and ribbon work with stuck-and-stitched appliqué work, or embroidery stitches, adding some beading, tufting and a knotted fringe. In fact try anything which encourages you to sew, but remember that whatever your final choice, your appliqué work must be interesting to look at, and have bold colours and exciting textures, and that it should have been fun to put together.

Patchwork

Like appliqué, this is a traditional method for using oddments of fabric in an interesting and decorative way. As explained on page 352 the using up of dressmaking and furnishing fabric left-overs, mixed with some new fabrics, is half the charm of patchwork, giving each item a distinctive character. Of course it is not always possible to collect together enough oddments of suitable material, but it is not a good idea to cut up lengths of new materials in order to sew them together again. Generally it is better to mix old fabrics with new ones, contrast bright and sombre colours and plain and patterned fabrics. Make the best use of the remnants you have available by giving some forethought to the design, and allow sufficient time for sorting out and planning your patchwork before starting to sew, as this will avoid much frustration and wasted time and energy.

Felt Patchwork

This is the simplest patchwork to sew as no turning under of raw edges is required. The felt pieces should be cut and arranged in an interlocking design, using accurate

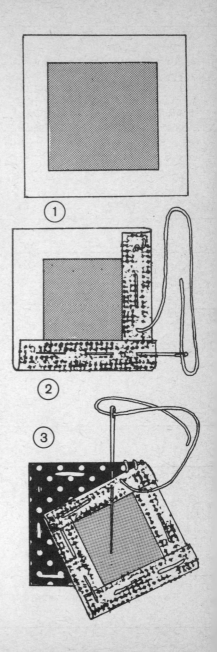

templates to cut squares, triangles or diamonds – as in the traditional patchwork explained on the next page – or the fabrics can be cut into individual interlocking sections, as in crazy patchwork explained on page 371. These interlocking shapes are then sewn together using the simple over-and-under stitch shown on page 365, giving a fish-bone effect, printed chintz to op-art irregularity using psychedelic colouring. Some thought therefore must be given to the choice of fabrics, as a mixing of colour and texture is necessary to achieve the character required. The juxtaposition of plain and patterned fabric will give an entirely different effect to that of all-patterned or all-plain fabrics.

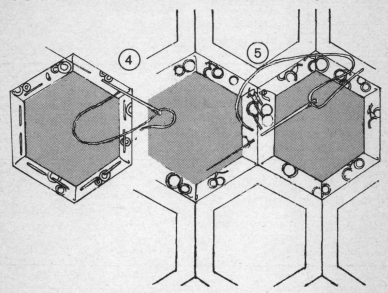

which can then be decorated with chain-stitch, as shown, or with one of the many other embroidery stitches shown in Chapter 12. Alternatively, one of the more decorative insertion stitches can be used, as shown on page 369.

Traditional Patchwork

This has many variations, ranging from very formal arrangements of

However, the most suitable materials for most traditional work are plain and printed cotton fabrics, although some medium-weight silks, velvets, needlecords and even thin woollen fabrics can be used. However, on one piece of work it is best to keep to one type of material; otherwise the patches are inclined to pull each other out of shape.

You will need to buy or make

① Brick Patchwork

② Fish-scale Patchwork

③ Lapped Patchwork

④ Crazy Patchwork

some accurately shaped templates for cutting out the fabric pieces, the most popular shapes being squares, rectangles, triangles, diamonds, hexagons and octagons, with shell or fish-scale shapes as interesting alternatives. Bought templates are usually in metal or plastic; you can make your own in stiff card if you can cut them perfectly accurately. You should also buy or make some paper shapes $\frac{1}{4}''$ smaller than the fabric templates. These are used as a guide for turning in the fabric edges accurately.

1. Using the templates as a cutting guide, cut several dozen pieces of differently coloured or patterned cotton fabrics.

2. Place a paper shape on the wrong side of a cut shape of fabric, leaving an even $\frac{1}{4}''$ turning all round as in diagram 1 on page 366. Turn in the edges and tack flat.

3. Lay out the tacked sections, and arrange them into a pattern, cutting and tacking some more sections to add variety or to give the design effect required.

4. When you have decided on an arrangement, join the pieces together. This can be done as shown on page 366 by placing two fabric pieces together, edge to edge with right sides face to face, and hand-stitching together with small stitches. Or use the stitch shown on page 367: the pieces to be joined are placed edge to edge, wrong side up so that the hand stitch goes through the edges as shown. Care should be taken when sewing to match the edges carefully, leaving no gaps in the stitching. Lay another fabric shape next to the second and stitch together, adding a third and fourth and so on.

5. Next place one patch below the first, then another patch below the second, and so on, until you have sewn all the pieces into a 'block'. Make several blocks in this way before joining them all together into the finished shape. Finally, remove the tacking stitches and inner paper shapes before pressing.

6. The patchwork should now be lined, so that the raw edges on the back of the work are covered and protected. A thin cotton fabric is best, even for silk work. An inter-lining can also be introduced between the patches and the lining – terylene wadding, domette, flannelette or a thin blanket – as in quilting, page 288. The layers must be carefully tacked together from side to side and end to end while they are lying flat on a table.

7. The next process is to join the edges together. They can be turned in and slip-stitched together, or bound in a matching or contrasting colour, or a covered piping cord can be introduced. A fringe can also be used as can a lace edging, crochet loops, pom-poms or many other methods explained earlier in the book.

Lapped Patchwork. This variation on traditional patchwork is most suited to the fish-scale design shown in diagram 2. Prepare the fabric sections and paper shapes as explained before, but instead of

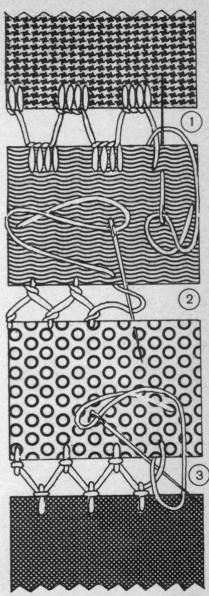

creasing over all the turnings just fold over and tack around the top curve, leaving the rest of the turnings free. Lay four scales face up with the creased-over top curves facing away from you, and their corners overlapping ¼″. Lay four more patchwork scales below these so that the top of the curve just laps ¼″ over the lower turnings of the first row of scales.

Pin the intersections together and tack through the second row top curves through the underlap allowances. Either turn to the back and hand-stitch the lapped edges together, taking care that no stitches show on the right side, or machine top-stitch neatly into blocks before joining more scale sections together.

Applied Patchwork. In applied patchwork, as explained on the previous few pages, the patchwork shapes are arranged in an interesting design on to a contrasting background material in a similar way to appliqué. Cut, tack and stitch the patchwork sections together, arranging them in a geometric or irregular pattern. The outside edge of the motif is then turned under all round, arranged into position on the background fabric and machine or hand stitched all round.

If a number of the patches overlap each other the under sections can be cut away to within ½″ of the top section in order to reduce the thicknesses.

Finally remove all tacking before pressing with a damp cloth and medium warm iron.

Crazy Patchwork. Either the traditional or the lapped method of patchwork can be used to join the pieces together, provided accurately cut pieces of interlocking paper shapes are first prepared. An easy way of doing this is to draw out the irregular design you want on a sheet of cheap cartridge paper, cut along each line, having numbered the pieces, and then cut the fabric pieces $\frac{1}{4}''$ larger all round than the paper pieces. Next place each paper shape on to the wrong side of a fabric section and turn the edges over all round, tacking the turnings flat. Take the next patchwork shape and turn under all edges except the edge adjacent to the first section, which should be slip-stitched into position. The third shape is also tacked into shape except where the first and second sections overlap, which are then stitched into position. Proceed with tacking and lapping until the crazy patchwork is complete as shown on the left and on page 368.

Border Patchwork differs from the other methods of patchwork in that it can be designed and made in a way which combines other decorative methods. For instance it can consist of a series of differently shaped interlocking sections of fabric, top-stitched together by machine onto a plain background strip. Some of the larger sections are then padded with a little wadding and decorated with machine embroidery combined with French cut-work and faggoting.

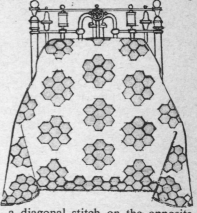

Open Patchwork. This type of patchwork is made by using the open-work stitches illustrated on page 369. These stitches are made between patchwork shapes or sections which have been stitched together in the traditional way.

1. This shows a group of blanket stitches which are made on alternate sides of the fabrics being joined. First make four $\frac{1}{4}''$ deep blanket stitches on the left side, each stitch being $\frac{1}{8}''$ from the previous one, then four on the right side – see page 369.

2. The criss-cross stitch is made alternately top and bottom as shown in diagram 2. Each stitch is made $\frac{1}{8}''$ in from the edge, $\frac{1}{4}''$ away from the previous one, with the needle passing through the looped thread as shown on page 369.

3. The zig-zag knotted stitch is made by passing the needle under and through the looped thread as shown in diagram 3, before making a diagonal stitch on the opposite side $\frac{1}{4}''$ away from the previous one.

Knitted and Crochet Patchwork is an ideal way of using knitted samples and crochet squares by joining them together in an even or irregular manner as a bedspread, cushion cover, or travelling rug. Knit or crochet a number of rectangles and squares, using different stitches in a variety of colours, and join them together with wool, using the insertion stitches shown on page 369. Circular and oval

samplers can also be used, joining these together with faggoting stitches and crochet criss-cross chains, giving an open-work design. This type of open patchwork can be left unlined, or a colourful effect can be achieved by using a contrasting fabric behind the sections of open-work as a lining.

Patchwork Ideas

Traditionally the main use for patchwork has been for bedspreads and cushion covers. Many beautiful designs have been worked out by different nationalities who have developed their own characteristic patchwork styles – the American use of fruit and flowers, the Canadian designs based on birds and animals, and the English geometric style. For those who wish to design and make a bedspread using a kaleidoscope of rich coloured fabric, put together with ingenuity and artistry, a few ideas are listed below.

Patchwork Cushion Covers can be made in many exciting ways using patchwork sections combined with appliqué cushion methods. The designs can range from the fun cushion designs shown on this page to others shown throughout this book, using combined methods of crochet, patchwork, ribbon work, appliqué, couching, beading and many other decorative techniques.

Patchwork Bedspreads. There are many different ways of making decorative bedspreads and covers. Most are extremely simple and can easily be made by the most inexperienced needlewoman. Just a few methods are explained below, but many other methods described in this book can also be easily

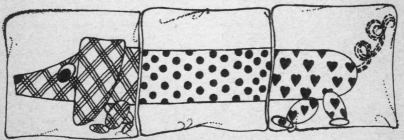

adapted to make your covers visually interesting.

Motifs of Patchwork in a geometric design are made from a selection of brightly coloured and patterned cotton fabrics joined together in the traditional way and then either machine- or hand-appliquéd into a formal arrangement. Random or crazy patchwork can also be used.

Crochet Patchwork bedspreads can be made from circular motifs of crochet stitched to a backing of coloured lawn and then linked together with open-work and crochet criss-cross chains. The circular motifs can be made in many varying patterns and sizes provided they form a unified design when stitched to the background fabric.

Knitted Patchwork bedspreads can be made out of a number of 8" or 9" rectangles and squares made out of brightly coloured wool samplers using a variety of stitches. Simply sew the knitted samplers together forming a pleasing pattern. Squares of crochet can also be used, and coloured pieces of fabric sewn together with the knitting into a formal or crazy pattern.

Embroidered Patchwork bedspreads can be made using the instructions given on the previous pages together with those on making a quilted bedspread, page 282. Other designs – apart from those already mentioned earlier in the book – incorporating unusual colourings and bold patterns combining appliqué and patchwork with other decorative techniques can be made by those who like experimenting.

Fashion Patchwork. Patchwork, like appliqué, has made a welcome come-back into fashion clothes. Look for ideas in shops and stores, books and magazines, seeing how the patchwork is made and used, so that your designs make use of these techniques in an up-to-date way.

Patchwork Toys, children's party things and presents using bold designs and colourful fabrics combined with unusual trimmings and interesting extras can be made by using and adapting the designs in this and other sewing books.

We hope the foregoing pages will have given you an introduction to sewing, taught you how to look for new ideas and how to experiment. As we have stressed throughout this book, you don't have to be an expert to make things successfully, but you do have to enjoy sewing and be open to new ideas. Fabric colours and textures should mean something to you, so that you acquire an instinctive feeling about what to use for a design, and you should be willing to experiment so that your sewing has a touch of magic. Have the courage of your convictions, developing a sixth sense about your work, and your ideas will acquire that touch of alchemy which turns ordinary sewing into original, interesting and exciting decorative items, whether they are for your family, your home, your friends or yourself.

Index

More about Penguins and Pelicans

Penguinews, which appears every month, contains details of all the new books issued by Penguins as they are published. From time to time it is supplemented by *Penguins in Print*, which is a complete list of all available books published by Penguins. (There are well over four thousand of these.)

A specimen copy of *Penguinews* will be sent to you free on request. For a year's issues (including the complete lists) please send 30p if you live in the United Kingdom, or 60p if you live elsewhere. Just write to Dept EP, Penguin Books Ltd, Harmondsworth, Middlesex, enclosing a cheque or postal order, and your name will be added to the mailing list.

Note: *Penguinews* and *Penguins in Print* are not available in the U.S.A. or Canada